Metaheuristic Computation with MATLAB®

Metaheuristic Computation with MATLAB®

Erik Cuevas
Alma Rodríguez

CRC Press
Taylor & Francis Group
Boca Raton London New York

CRC Press is an imprint of the
Taylor & Francis Group, an **informa** business

A CHAPMAN & HALL BOOK

First edition published 2021
by CRC Press
6000 Broken Sound Parkway NW, Suite 300, Boca Raton, FL 33487-2742
and by CRC Press

2 Park Square, Milton Park, Abingdon, Oxon, OX14 4RN

First issued in paperback 2022

© 2021 Taylor & Francis Group, LLC

CRC Press is an imprint of Taylor & Francis Group, an Informa business

No claim to original U.S. Government works

Visit the Taylor & Francis Web site at
http://www.taylorandfrancis.com

and the CRC Press Web site at
http://www.crcpress.com

Library of Congress Cataloging-in-Publication Data
Names: Cuevas, Erik, author. | Rodríguez, Alma (Computer science scholar), author.
Title: Metaheuristic computation with MATLAB® / Erik Cuevas,
Alma Rodríguez.
Description: First edition. | Boca Raton : CRC Press, 2020. | Includes
bibliographical references and index.
Identifiers: LCCN 2020014306 | ISBN 9780367438869 (hardback) |
ISBN 9781003006312 (ebook)
Subjects: LCSH: MATLAB. | Metaheuristics. | Mathematical optimization.
Classification: LCC QA76.9.A43 C84 2020 | DDC 519.6--dc23
LC record available at https://lccn.loc.gov/2020014306

ISBN: 978-0-367-52380-0 (pbk)
ISBN: 978-0-367-43886-9 (hbk)
ISBN: 978-1-003-00631-2 (ebk)

DOI: 10.1201/9781003006312

Typeset in Minion
by codeMantra

Contents

Preface

Optimization applications are countless. Almost all processes of practical interest can be optimized to improve their performance. Currently, there is no company that considers the solution of optimization problems within its activities. In general terms, many processes in science and industry can be formulated as optimization formulations. Optimization occurs in the minimization of the time spent for the execution of a task, the cost of a product, and the risk in an investment or the maximization of profits, the quality of a product, and the efficiency of a device.

The vast majority of the optimization problems with practical implications in science, engineering, economics, and business are very complex and difficult to resolve. Such problems cannot be solved accurately by using classical optimization methods. Under these circumstances, metaheuristic computation methods have emerged as an alternative solution.

Metaheuristic algorithms are considered generic optimization tools that can solve very complex problems characterized by having very large search spaces. Metaheuristic methods reduce the effective size of the search space through the use of effective search strategies. In general, these methods allow solving problems faster and more robust than classical schemes. In comparison to other heuristic algorithms, metaheuristic techniques are simpler to design and implement.

Metaheuristic methods represent an important area in artificial intelligence and applied mathematics. During the last 10 years, a set of several metaheuristic approaches have appeared, which allow the intersection of different disciplines including artificial intelligence, biology, social studies, and mathematics. Most of the metaheuristic methods use as inspiration existing biological or social phenomena which at a certain level of abstraction can be regarded as models of optimization.

Recently, metaheuristic algorithms have become popular in science and industry. An indicator of this situation is the large number of specialized journals, sessions, and conferences in this area. In practice, metaheuristic schemes have attracted great interest, since they have proved to be efficient tools for the solution of a wide range of problems in domains such as logistics, bio-informatics, structural design, data mining, and finance.

The main purpose of this book is to provide a unified view of the most popular metaheuristic methods. Under this perspective, the fundamental design principles as well as the operators of metaheuristic approaches which are considered essential are presented. In the explanation, not only the design aspects but also their implementation have been considered using the popular software MATLAB®. The idea with this combination is to motivate the reader with the acquired knowledge of each method to reuse the existing code, configuring it to his/her specific problems. All the MATLAB codes contained in the book, as well as additional material, can be downloaded from www.crcpress.com/9780367438869.

This book provides the necessary concepts that enable the reader to implement and modify the already known metaheuristic methods to obtain the desired performance for the specific needs of each problem. For this reason, the book contains numerous examples of problems and solutions that demonstrate the power of these methods of optimization.

The material has been written from a teaching perspective. For this reason, the book is primarily intended for undergraduate and postgraduate students of Artificial Intelligence, Metaheuristic Methods, and/or Evolutionary Computation. It can also be appropriate for courses such as Optimization and Computational Mathematics. Likewise, the material can be useful for researchers from metaheuristic and engineering communities. The objective is to bridge the gap between metaheuristic techniques and complex optimization problems that profit on the convenient properties of metaheuristic approaches. Therefore, students and practitioners, who are not metaheuristic computation researchers, will appreciate that the techniques discussed are beyond simple theoretical tools since they have been adapted to solve significant problems that commonly arise in such areas.

Due to its content and structure, the book is suitable to fulfill the requirements of several university subjects in the area of computing sciences, artificial intelligence, operations research, applied mathematics, and some other disciplines. Similarly, many engineers and professionals that work in the industry may find the content of this book interesting. In this case, the simple explanations and the provided code can assist practitioners in finding the solution of optimization problems which normally arise in various industrial areas.

Our original premise has been that metaheuristic methods can be easily exposed to readers with limited mathematical skills. Consequently, we try to write a book in which the contents are not only applicable but also understandable for any undergraduate student. Although some concepts can be complex themselves, we try to expose them clearly without trying to hide their implicit difficulty.

The book is structured so that the reader can clearly identify from the beginning the objectives of each chapter and finally strengthen the knowledge acquired through the implementation of several MATLAB programs. The book has been conceived for an introductory course. The material can be covered in a semester. The book consists of nine chapters, and the details in the contents of each chapter are described below.

Chapter 1 introduces the main concepts that are involved in an optimization process. In this way, once the optimization problem is generically formulated, the methods used for its solution are then classified. Considering that the book focuses on the study of metaheuristic techniques, traditional gradient-based algorithms will be only marginally treated. Another important objective in this chapter is to explain the main characteristics of the evolutionary algorithms introducing the dilemma of exploration and exploitation. Furthermore, the acceptance and probabilistic selection are also analyzed. They are two main operations used in most metaheuristic methods. Finally, three of the first evolutionary methods are exposed, which have been considered as the basis for creation of new algorithms. The idea with this treatment is to introduce the concepts of metaheuristic methods through implementing techniques that are easy to understand.

In **Chapter 2**, the metaheuristic techniques known as Genetic Algorithms (GAs) are introduced. They implement optimization schemes that emulate evolutionary principles found in nature. GAs represent one of the most important search approaches in several problem domains, such as the sciences, industry, and engineering. The main reasons for their extensive use are their flexibility, ease of implementation, and global context. Among different GAs, we will examine in detail binary-coded and real-parameter GAs. In this chapter, several MATLAB implementations will be discussed and explained.

Chapter 3 describes the operation of Evolutionary Strategies (ES). The evolution process that the ES method implements to solve optimization problems is also discussed. Throughout this chapter, the operators used by the ES are defined along with their different variants and computational implementation in the MATLAB environment.

Chapter 4 describes the inspiration of the Moth–Flame Optimization (MFO) algorithm as well as the search strategy it implements to solve optimization problems. Throughout this chapter, the operators used by the MFO are defined with the objective of analyzing the theoretical concepts involved that allow the computational implementation of the algorithm in the MATLAB environment. Then, the algorithm is used to solve optimization problems. The examples illustrate the use of MFO for solving problems with and without constraints.

Chapter 5 analyzes the Differential Evolution (DE) scheme. This approach is a population algorithm that implements a direct and simple search strategy. Under its operation, DE considers the generation of parameter vectors based on the addition of the weighted difference between two members of the population. In this chapter, the operative details of the DE algorithm are discussed. The implementation of DE in MATLAB is also described. The objective of this chapter is to provide to the reader the mathematical description of the DE operators and the capacity to apply this algorithm in the solution of optimization problems. To do this, in the subsequent sections, the use of the DE algorithm is considered in two aspects: the first is the resolution of an optimization problem minimizing a mathematical benchmark function, and the second, the solution of engineering problems that require an optimal design in their parameters considering some design restrictions.

Chapter 6 presents the Particle Swarm Optimization (PSO) method. This scheme is based on the collective behavior that some animals present when they interact in groups. Such behaviors are found in several animal groups such as a school of fish or a flock of birds. With these interactions, individuals reach a higher level of survival by collaborating together, generating a kind of collective intelligence. This chapter describes the main characteristics of the PSO algorithm, as well as its search strategy, considering also the solution of optimization problems. In the chapter, the operators used by the PSO are defined with the objective of analyzing their theoretical concepts involved that allow the computational implementation of the algorithm in the MATLAB environment. Then, the algorithm is used to solve real-world applications. The examples illustrate the use of PSO for solving problems with and without restrictions.

In **Chapter 7**, the Artificial Bee Colony (ABC) algorithm is analyzed. In this chapter, the parameters of the ABC algorithm, as well as the information necessary to implement it, will be discussed in detail. In Section 7.1, a semblance of the ABC algorithm, as well as its most relevant characteristics, will be discussed. In Section 7.2, the complete algorithm is presented, reserving a sub-section for each component of the algorithm. However, a special emphasis is placed on Section 7.2.6, where an optimization example of a two-dimensional function using MATLAB is presented. Then, the results obtained will be discussed. Finally, in Section 7.3, a summary of recent applications of the ABC algorithm in the area of image processing is presented.

In **Chapter 8**, the main characteristics of the Cuckoo Search (CS) scheme are discussed. Due to its importance, a multimodal version of the CS method is also reviewed. CS is a simple and effective global optimization algorithm that is inspired by the breeding behavior of some cuckoo species. One of the most powerful features of CS is the use of Lévy flights to generate new candidate solutions. Under this approach, candidate solutions are modified by employing many small changes and occasionally large jumps. As a result, CS can substantially improve the relationship between exploration–exploitation, still enhancing its search capabilities. Despite such characteristics, the CS method still fails in providing multiple solutions in a single execution. In order to overcome such inconvenience, a multimodal optimization algorithm called the multimodal CS (MCS) is also presented. Under MCS, the original CS is enhanced with multimodal capacities by means of (1) the incorporation of a memory mechanism to efficiently register potential local optima according to their fitness value and the distance to other potential solutions, (2) the modification of the original CS individual selection strategy to accelerate the detection process of new local minima, and (3) the inclusion of a depuration procedure to cyclically eliminate duplicated memory elements.

In **Chapter 9**, the most common techniques used by metaheuristic methods to optimize multimodal problems are analyzed. Since the shared function scheme is the most popular, this procedure will be treated in detail in this chapter. Additionally, in the end, we will discuss the algorithm of fireflies. Such a method inspired by the attraction behavior of these insects incorporates special operators that maintain interesting multimodal capabilities.

Considering that writing this book has been a very enjoyable experience for the authors and that the overall topic of metaheuristic computation has become a fruitful subject, it has been tempting to introduce a large amount of new material and novel evolutionary methods. However, the usefulness and potential adoption of the book seems to be founded over a compact and appropriate presentation of successful algorithms, which in turn has driven the overall organization of the book that we hope may provide the clearest picture to the reader's eyes.

Acknowledgments

There are many people who are somehow involved in the writing process of this book. We thank the complete metaheuristic group at the Universidad de Guadalajara in Mexico for supporting us in this project. We express our gratitude to Randi Cohen, who warmly sustained this project. Acknowledgments also go to Talitha Duncan-Todd, who kindly helped in the edition process.

Erik Cuevas
Alma Rodríguez
Guadalajara, Mexico

Authors

Erik Cuevas is currently working as a Professor in the Department of Electronics at the University of Guadalajara, Mexico. He completed his B.E in Electronics and Communication Engineering from the University of Guadalajara in 1996, and his postgraduate degree M.E in Applied Electronics from ITESO, Guadalajara, Mexico, in 1998. He received his PhD in Artificial Intelligence from Freie Universität Berlin, Germany, in 2007. Dr. Cuevas currently serves as an editorial board member or associate editor in *Applied Soft Computing, Applied Mathematical Modelling, Artificial Intelligence Review, International Journal of Machine Learning and Cybernetics, ISA Transactions, Neural Processing Letters and Mathematics and Computers in Simulation*. His research interests include metaheuristics and evolutionary computation in a wide range of applications such as image processing and machine learning.

Alma Rodríguez is a PhD candidate currently working as a Professor in the Department of Computer Science at the University of Guadalajara, Mexico. She is also working as Professor at the Guadalajara campus of Universidad Panamericana, Mexico. In 2011, she graduated with a degree in mechatronics engineering from Centro de Enseñanza Técnica Industrial. In 2017, she completed her postgraduate degree M.E in Computer Science and Electronics from Universidad de Guadalajara. Her research interests include metaheuristic and evolutionary computation in a wide range of applications such as image processing and machine learning.

CHAPTER 1

Introduction and Main Concepts

OBJECTIVE

The objective of this chapter is to introduce the main concepts that involve an optimization process. In this way, once the optimization problem is generically formulated, the methods used for its solution are then classified. Considering that the book focuses on the study of metaheuristic techniques, traditional gradient-based algorithms will be only marginally treated. Another important objective of this chapter is to explain the main characteristics of evolutionary algorithms, introducing the dilemma of exploration and exploitation. Furthermore, acceptance and probabilistic selection are also analyzed. These are the two main operations used in most metaheuristic methods. Finally, three of the first evolutionary methods which have been considered as the basis for the creation of new algorithms have been exposed. The idea with this treatment is to introduce the concepts of metaheuristic methods, through implementing techniques that are easy to understand.

1.1 INTRODUCTION

Optimization has become an essential part of all disciplines. One reason for this consideration is the motivation to produce products or quality services at competitive prices. In general, optimization is the process of finding the "best solution" to a problem among a big set of possible solutions (Baldick, 2006).

An optimization problem can be formulated as a process in which it is desired to find the optimum value $x*$ that minimizes or maximizes an objective function $f(\mathbf{x})$. Such that

$$\text{Minimize/Maximize} \quad f(\mathbf{x}), \quad \mathbf{x} = (x_1,\dots,x_d) \in \mathbb{R}^d \tag{1.1}$$
$$\text{Subject to:} \quad \mathbf{x} \in \mathbf{X},$$

where **x** represents the vector of decision variables, while d specifies its dimension. **X** symbolizes the set of candidate solutions, also known as the solution search space. In many occasions, the bounds of the search space are located by the lower (l_i) or upper (u_i) limits of each decision variables such that $\mathbf{X} = \left\{ \mathbf{x} \in \mathbb{R}^d \mid l_i \leq x_i \leq u_i,\ i = 1, \ldots, d \right\}$.

Sometimes it is necessary to minimize $f(\mathbf{x})$, but in other scenarios it is necessary to maximize. These two types of problems are easily converted from one to another through the following relationship:

$$\min_{\mathbf{x}^*} f(\mathbf{x}) \Leftrightarrow \max_{\mathbf{x}^*} \left[-1 \cdot f(\mathbf{x}) \right]$$

$$\max_{\mathbf{x}^*} f(\mathbf{x}) \Leftrightarrow \min_{\mathbf{x}^*} \left[-1 \cdot f(\mathbf{x}) \right] \tag{1.2}$$

To clarify these concepts, the following minimization problem is presented as an example:

$$\text{Minimize} \quad f(x) = x^4 + 5x^3 + 4x^2 - 4x + 1$$

$$\text{Subject to:} \quad x \in [-4, 1] \tag{1.3}$$

In this formulation, the minimization of a function with a single decision variable $(d = 1)$ is presented. The search space **X** for this problem is integrated by the interval from -4 to 1. Under these circumstances, the idea is to find the value of x for which $f(x)$ presents its minimum value, considering all the set of possible solutions defined within the range $[-4,1]$. The x element that solves this formulation is called the optimum value and is represented by $x*$. Figure 1.1 shows a graphical representation of the function to minimize.

Figure 1.1 shows the solutions A and B which correspond to two different minima obtained from $f(x)$. This type of function is known as multimodal since it contains several prominent minima. The minimum represented by point A represents the optimal solution to $f(x)$, while B is only a local minimum of $f(x)$.

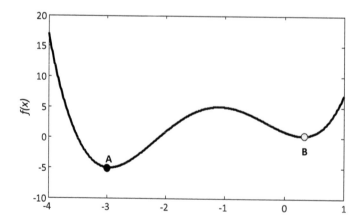

FIGURE 1.1   Graphical representation of the optimization problem formulated in Eq. 1.3.

1.2 CLASSICAL OPTIMIZATION METHODS

In general, the function $f(\mathbf{x})$ could be nonlinear with regard to its decision variables $\mathbf{x}$. Due to this complexity, optimization methods implement iterative processes for the efficient exploration of the search space.

There are two kinds of algorithms used to solve these problems (Yang, 2010): classical techniques and metaheuristic methods. Traditional schemes are based on the use of the gradient of $f(\mathbf{x})$ for the generation of new candidate solutions. In the case of metaheuristic methods, they do not require functional information of the derivative in $f(\mathbf{x})$ to perform a search strategy that minimizes (or maximizes) a specific objective function. Instead of this, a set of heuristic rules are implemented to conduct the search process. Some of these rules are based on the reproduction of phenomena present in nature or society.

For the operation of classical optimization algorithms, they require that the objective function presents two fundamental requirements for their use: $f(\mathbf{x})$ must be twice differentiable, and $f(\mathbf{x})$ must have only a single optimum (Venkataraman, 2009).

This section considers a basic review of gradient-based optimization techniques. Since the book discusses in-depth metaheuristic methods, the analysis of classical techniques is only marginally treated. For detailed information, it is recommended to the reader referring to other books.

1.2.1 The Gradient Descent Method

The gradient descent technique is one of the first techniques for the minimization of multidimensional objective functions (Dennis, 1978). This method represents the basis on which are founded several other more sophisticated optimization algorithms. Despite its slow convergence, the gradient descent method is more frequently used for the optimization of nonlinear functions. Such fact is due to its simplicity and easy implementation.

Under this method, starting from an initial point $\mathbf{x}^0$, the candidate solution is modified iteratively during a number of $Niter$ iterations so that may tentatively find the optimal solution $\mathbf{x}*$. Such iterative modification is determined by the following expression (Hocking, 1991):

$$\mathbf{x}^{k+1} = \mathbf{x}^k - \alpha \cdot \mathbf{g}(f(\mathbf{x})), \tag{1.4}$$

where k represents the current iteration and α symbolizes the size of the search step.

In Eq. 1.4, the term $\mathbf{g}(f(\mathbf{x}))$ represents the gradient of the function $f(\mathbf{x})$. The gradient $\mathbf{g}$ of a function $f(\mathbf{x})$ at the point g $\mathbf{x}$ expresses the direction in which the function presents its maximum growth. Thus, in the case of a minimization problem, the descent direction can be obtained (multiplying by −1) considering the opposite direction to $\mathbf{g}$. Under this rule, it guarantees that $f\left(\mathbf{x}^{k+1}\right) < f\left(\mathbf{x}^k\right)$, which means that the newly generated solution is better than the previous one.

In general, although the formulation of an optimization problem involves the definition of an objective function $f(\mathbf{x})$, this is only for educational purposes and demonstration. In practice, its definition is not known deterministically. Their values are known only at the points sampled by the optimization algorithm. Under these circumstances, the gradient $\mathbf{g}$ is calculated using numerical methods.

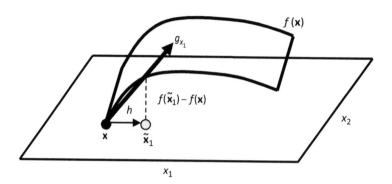

FIGURE 1.2   Graphical representation of the numerical calculation process of the gradient.

1.2.2 Gradient Computation

The gradient of a multidimensional function $f(\mathbf{x})$ $\left(\mathbf{x}=(x_1,\ldots,x_d)\in\mathbb{R}^d\right)$ represents the way in which the function changes with respect to one of their d dimensions. Therefore, the gradient g_{x_1} expresses the magnitude in which $f(\mathbf{x})$ varies with respect to x_1. This gradient g_{x_1} is defined as

$$g_{x_1} = \frac{\partial f(\mathbf{x})}{\partial x_1} \tag{1.5}$$

To numerically calculate the gradient g_{x_i}, the following procedure (Mathews & Fink, 2000) is conducted:

1. A new solution $\tilde{\mathbf{x}}_i$ is generated. This solution $\tilde{\mathbf{x}}_i$ is the same as $\mathbf{x}$ in all the decision variables except in x_i. This value will be replaced by $x_i + h$, where h is a very small value. Under these conditions, the new vector $\tilde{\mathbf{x}}_i$ is defined as

$$\tilde{\mathbf{x}}_i = (x_1, x_2, \ldots, x_i + h, \ldots, x_d) \tag{1.6}$$

2. Then, the gradient g_{x_i} is computed through the following model:

$$g_{x_i} \approx \frac{f(\tilde{\mathbf{x}}_i) - f(\mathbf{x})}{h} \tag{1.7}$$

Figure 1.2 shows a graphical representation of the numerical calculation process of the gradient, considering a simple example, where two dimensions (x_1, x_2) of $f(\mathbf{x})$ are contemplated.

1.2.3 Computational Example in MATLAB

To illustrate the operation of the gradient descent algorithm and its practical implementation in MATLAB®, it is considered to solve the following minimization problem:

$$\text{Minimize} \quad f(x_1, x_2) = 10 - e^{-\left(x_1^2 + 3x_2^2\right)}$$

$$-1 \le x_1 \le 1 \tag{1.8}$$

Subject to:

$$-1 \le x_2 \le 1$$

Under this formulation, a two-dimensional function $f(x_1, x_2)$ is considered within a search space defined on the interval $[-1,1]$ for each of the decision variable x_1 and x_2. Figure 1.3 shows a representation of the objective function $f(x_1, x_2)$.

From Eq. 1.8, it is clear that the function $f(x_1, x_2)$ can be derived twice and is also unimodal (it has only a minimum). For such reasons, it fulfills the requirements to apply the gradient descent method in order to obtain the optimal value.

The minimization process of $f(x_1, x_2)$ through the gradient descent method is presented in the form of pseudocode in Algorithm 1.1. The procedure starts selecting randomly a candidate solution $\mathbf{x}^k$ ($k = 0$), within the search space defined on the interval $[-1,1]$ for each of the variables x_1 and x_2. Then, gradients g_{x_1} and g_{x_2} are calculated at the point $\mathbf{x}^k$. With this information, a new solution $\mathbf{x}^{k+1}$ is obtained as a result of applying Eq. 1.4. Since $f(x_1, x_2)$ involves two decision variables, the new solution can be built by Eq. 1.4 considering each variable separately. Therefore, the new solution is updated as follows:

$$x_1^{k+1} = x_1^k - \alpha \cdot g_{x_1}$$
$$x_2^{k+1} = x_2^k - \alpha \cdot g_{x_1} \tag{1.9}$$

This process is repeated iteratively until a maximum number of iterations *Niter* has been reached.

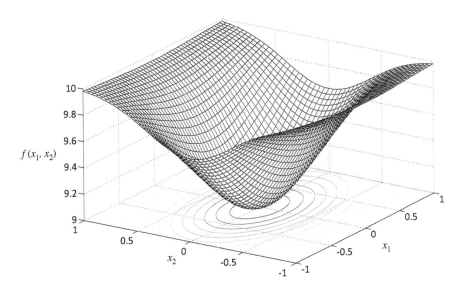

FIGURE 1.3 Graphical representation of the function $f(x_1, x_2) = 10 - e^{-\left(x_1^2 + 3x_2^2\right)}$.

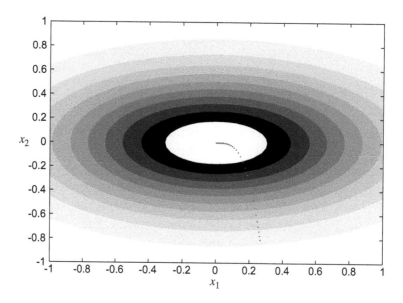

FIGURE 1.4 Solution trajectory produced during the execution of Program 1.1.

The program shows the implementation of Algorithm 1.1 in MATLAB. In the operation of the program, first the function $f(x_1, x_2)$ is plotted in order to appreciate their main characteristics. Then, in an iterative process, a set of solutions are produced from the initial point $\mathbf{x}^0$ to the optimal value. The trajectory experimented by the solutions during the optimization process is also illustrated in Figure 1.4.

Algorithm 1.1 Gradient Descent Method to Solve the Formulation of Eq. 1

1. $k \leftarrow 0$
2. $x_1^k \leftarrow$ Random $[-1,1]$, $x_2^k \leftarrow$ Random $[-1,1]$
3. **while** $(k < Niter)$ {
4. $g_{x_1} \leftarrow \dfrac{f(x_1^k + h, x_2^k) - f(x_1^k, x_2^k)}{h}$, $g_{x_2} \leftarrow \dfrac{f(x_1^k, x_2^k + h) - f(x_1^k, x_2^k)}{h}$
5. $x_1^{k+1} \leftarrow x_1^k - \alpha \cdot g_{x_1}$, $x_2^{k+1} \leftarrow x_2^k - \alpha \cdot g_{x_2}$
6. $k \leftarrow k+1$}

Program 1.1 Implementation of the Gradient Descent Method in MATLAB®

```
%%%%%%%%%%%%%%%%%%%%%%%%%%%%%%%%%%%%%%%%%%%%%%%%%%%%%%%%%%%%%%%%%%
% Gradient descent example
% Erik Cuevas, Alma Rodríguez
%%%%%%%%%%%%%%%%%%%%%%%%%%%%%%%%%%%%%%%%%%%%%%%%%%%%%%%%%%%%%%%%%%
% Clean memory
clear all
% Formulation of the optimization problem Eq. 1.8
```

```
funstr='10-(exp(-1*(x^2+3*y^2)))';
f=vectorize(inline(funstr));
range=[-1 1 -1 1];
% Draw the function
Ndiv=50;
dx=(range(2)-range(1))/Ndiv; dy=(range(4)-range(3))/Ndiv;
[x,y] =meshgrid(range(1):dx:range(2),range(3):dy:range(4));
z=(f(x,y));
figure(1);  surfc(x,y,z);
% Define the number of iterations
k=0;
niter=200;
% Gradient step size h definition
hstep = 0.001;
% Step size of the Gradient descent method
alfa=0.05;
%Initial point selection
xrange=range(2)-range(1);
yrange=range(4)-range(3);
x1=rand*xrange+range(1);
x2=rand*yrange+range(3);
% Optimization process
while (k<niter)
        % Function evaluation
        zn=f(x1,x2);
        % Computation of gradients gx1 y gx2
        vx1=x1+hstep;
        vx2=x2+hstep;
        gx1=(f(vx1,x2)-zn)/hstep;
        gx2=(f(x1,vx2)-zn)/hstep;
        % Draw the current position
        figure(2)
        contour(x,y,z,15); hold on;
        plot(x1,x2,'.','markersize',10,'markerfacecolor','g');
        hold on;
        % Computation of the new solution
        x1=x1-alfa*gx1;
        x2=x2-alfa*gx2;
        k=k+1;
end
```

1.3 METAHEURISTIC METHODS

Classical gradient-based methods represent the fastest algorithms for nonlinear optimization (Reinhardt, Hoffmann, & Gerlach, 2013). An advantage of these techniques is that they guarantee to obtain the optimal solution to the optimization problem. However, its application is clearly restricted, since it is required that the objective function maintains the conditions of two times differentiable and unimodality (Bartholomew-Biggs, 2008). Real optimization problems usually produce objective functions that do not meet any of these conditions. Many of these functions present a multimodal behavior (several minima). Under these conditions, the use of gradient-based methods would converge to a local minimum, without the possibility to explore the search space. Figure 1.5a shows an example of a multimodal function. There exist many scenarios in which an objective function could not be differentiable. One simple example is to consider the application of a rounding operation over the original function. As a result, a differentiable function can turn into a non-differentiable one. Figure 1.5b shows the rounded version of the function $f(x_1,x_2)=10-e^{-\left(x_1^2+3x_2^2\right)}$ presented in Figure 1.3.

Metaheuristic schemes (Simon, 2013) do not use the gradient information of an objective function. This fact makes possible that metaheuristic methods can optimize objective functions as complex as required by the application. In some cases, the objective function may even contain simulations or experimental models.

Metaheuristic algorithms do not need functional information of the derivative to generate its search strategy that minimizes (or maximizes) a particular objective function. Instead, such methods use heuristic rules for the construction of search patterns. These rules, in many cases, are based on the simulation of different natural and social processes. Since metaheuristic methods do not consider the use of derivatives, they do not possess relevant information about the objective function. Under these conditions, these techniques result in slower approaches in comparison to the gradient-based methods.

Metaheuristic methods are stochastic, which means that they use random processes to determine the directions of the search strategy. Because of this, it is difficult to conduct analytical techniques for the analysis of such methods. Therefore, most of their properties have been discovered experimentally.

Although some metaheuristic algorithms have been designed to simulate the behavior of biological phenomena, like the natural selection process in the case of genetic algorithms, in its overall conception, such methods are considered as optimization schemes.

Some authors use the term population-based optimization algorithms to refer to metaheuristic techniques. Such nomination emphasizes the concept that metaheuristic schemes usually consist of a population of candidate solutions to optimize a particular problem.

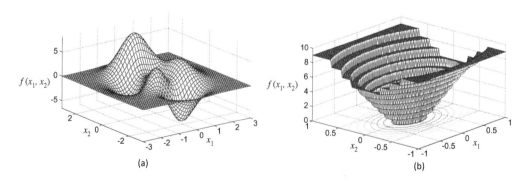

FIGURE 1.5 Objective function types (a) multimodal or (b) not differentiable.

Each of these candidate solutions behaves as a search agent that leads the search strategy. The idea is that as time passes, the population evolves until it eventually reaches the optimal solution. However, this concept is not completely appropriate, since there are many metaheuristic approaches which consist of a single candidate solution (simulated annealing or evolutionary strategies) so that on each iteration, only this solution is updated. This reasoning considers that metaheuristic methods are more general than simple population techniques.

Sometimes the term computational intelligence is used to refer to metaheuristic techniques. Under this concept, the idea is to differentiate metaheuristic methods of expert systems which are considered a traditional discipline of artificial intelligence. Expert systems model deductive reasoning, while metaheuristic algorithms model inductive reasoning. Computational intelligence is a more general area than metaheuristic methods and includes other approaches such as neural networks and fuzzy systems. Thus, the use of such approaches is not restricted to the field of optimization.

Several academics use the term bio-inspired algorithms to refer to metaheuristic methods. However, this conception is not correct, since various metaheuristic techniques such as differential evolution and the imperialist algorithm are not inspired by nature. There are some other approaches such as evolutionary strategies and learning by an opposition that have a very weak connection with biological processes. Under these conditions, it is clear that the metaheuristic methods constitute a concept that is more general than the bio-inspired algorithms.

Some authors often replace the term metaheuristic computation by heuristic algorithms. Heuristic, which comes from the Greek, means find or discover. Heuristic algorithms are methods that use intuitive rules based on common sense to solve problems. Such algorithms do not expect to find the best solution, but any sufficiently acceptable solution. The term metaheuristic is used to describe a generic family of heuristic algorithms. Therefore, most, if not all, of the algorithms discussed in this book can be considered as metaheuristics.

Many researchers separate metaheuristic methods from techniques based on swarm principles. Swarm algorithms consider the collective intelligence shown by the behavior of groups of animals or insects. Two prominent algorithms in this category are Ant Colony Optimization and Particle Swarm Optimization. Since the mechanism for implementing swarm algorithms is similar to metaheuristic methods, in this book, the swarm algorithms are considered as methods of metaheuristic computation.

From the previous discussions, it can be concluded that the terminology with which metaheuristic methods have been defined is vague and dependent on a particular context. In this book, and in order to amalgamate all points of view, metaheuristic algorithms are defined as algorithms that do not consider gradient information to modify one or more candidate solutions during the optimization process. In these methods, the search strategy is determined by the combination of stochastic processes and deterministic models.

Metaheuristics are currently one of the most prolific areas in sciences and engineering. A reflex of its popularity is the large number of specialized journals and conferences available in the subject. The number of proposed algorithms in the literature that fall into the category of metaheuristics is very large so that a review of all the algorithms in a single document is virtually impossible. Due to restrictions of space and coverage, this book describes in detail those metaheuristic methods that, according to the literature, are the most popular. With this in mind, it has been decided to divide the methods into two classes. The first class corresponds to those techniques that are considered the first approaches in using the concepts of metaheuristic computation. These techniques have been the basis of many other algorithms. For this reason, such methods have been included in the book. However, according to recent literature, they are not considered popular anymore. Since these techniques are treated as a reference, its discussion is not very detailed in this book. Therefore, they are addressed in this chapter. The second class of algorithms involves metaheuristic methods that, according to the literature, are the most popular. Such popularity means that they are the most applied, modified, combined, and analyzed between the entire set of methods of metaheuristic computation. As these algorithms in the opinion of the author are the most important, its description is deeper so that they are treated throughout the book in separate chapters. Table 1.1 describes the methods and the chapter in which they will be discussed.

This book has been written from a teaching perspective, in such a way that the reader can implement and use the algorithms for the solution of his/her optimization problems. The presented material, the discussed methods, and implemented programs are not available in any other book that considers metaheuristic methods as subject.

The book has two unique features. The first characteristic is that each method is explained considering a detailed level. Therefore, it is possible to calibrate and change the parameters of the methods in question. Under the perspective of this book, each metaheuristic technique is addressed through the use of simple and intuitive examples so that the reader gradually gets a clear idea of the functioning of each method.

The second characteristic is the implementation of each metaheuristic method in MATLAB. Most of the texts of metaheuristic computation explain the algorithms, differing in degree of detail and coverage of each method. However, many texts fail to provide implementation information. This problem from the point of view of the authors of this book is no less since most readers understand the methods completely when the theoretical concepts are compared with the provided lines of code in its implementation.

TABLE 1.1   Metaheuristic Methods and Their Distribution through the Book

Class 1		Class 2	
Chapter	**Algorithm**	**Chapter**	**Algorithm**
1	Random Search	2	Genetic Algorithms (GA)
1	Simulated Annealing	3	Evolutionary Strategies (ES)
		4	Moth–Flame Optimization (MFO)
		5	Differential Evolution (DE)
		6	Particle Swarm Optimization (PSO)
		7	Artificial Bee Colony (ABC)
		8	Cuckoo Search (CS)
		9	Metaheuristic Multimodal Optimization

1.3.1 The Generic Procedure of a Metaheuristic Algorithm

In this section, the optimization process and its main concepts are discussed from the point of view of the metaheuristic computation paradigm. The idea is to clearly define the nomenclature used by these methods.

Most of the metaheuristic methods have been designed to find the optimal solution to an optimization problem formulated in the following way:

$$\text{Minimize/Maximize} \quad f(\mathbf{x}), \quad \mathbf{x} = (x_1, \dots, x_d) \in \mathbb{R}^d$$
$$\text{Subject to:} \quad \mathbf{x} \in \mathbf{X}, \tag{1.10}$$

where $\mathbf{x}$ represents the vector of decision variables (candidate solution), while d specifies the number of dimensions. $\mathbf{X}$ symbolizes the set of possible candidate solutions, also known as the search space. On many scenarios, the search space is bounded by the lower (l_i) or upper (u_i) limits of each decision variable d so that $\mathbf{X} = \left\{ \mathbf{x} \in \mathbb{R}^d \mid l_i \leq x_i \leq u_i, \ i = 1, \dots, d \right\}$.

To solve the problem formulated in Eq. 1.10, a metaheuristic algorithm maintains a single solution $\left(\mathbf{x}^k \right)$ or a population of N candidate solutions $\mathbf{P}^k \left(\mathbf{x}_1^k, \mathbf{x}_2^k, \dots, \mathbf{x}_N^k \right)$, which evolve (change their values) during a determined number of iterations $(Niter)$, from an initial state to the end. In the initial state, the algorithm initializes the set of candidate solutions with a random value within the limits of the search space $\mathbf{X}$. In every generation, a set of metaheuristic operators is applied to candidate solutions $\mathbf{P}^k$ to build a new population $\mathbf{P}^{k+1}$. The quality of each candidate solution x_i^k is then evaluated through an objective function $f(\mathbf{x}_i^k) \ (i \in [1, 2, \dots, N])$ that describes the optimization problem. Usually, during the evolution process, the best solution $\mathbf{m}$ from all candidate solutions maintains a special consideration. The idea is that at the end of the evolution process, this solution represents the best possible solution. Figure 1.6 shows a graphical representation of the optimization process from the point of view of the metaheuristic computation paradigm. In the nomenclature of metaheuristic algorithms, a generation is known as an iteration, while the objective function value $f\left(\mathbf{x}_i^k \right)$ produced by the candidate solution $\mathbf{x}_i^k$ is known as the "fitness" value of $\mathbf{x}_i^k$.

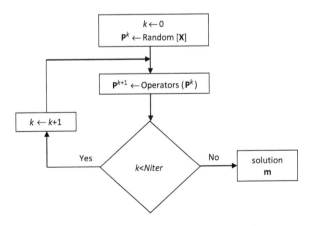

FIGURE 1.6   Optimization process from the point of view of metaheuristic computation paradigm.

1.4 EXPLOITATION AND EXPLORATION

Exploration is defined as the process of searching for new solutions. On the other hand, exploitation refers to the refinement of existing solutions, which in the past have proven to be successful in similar conditions. Exploration is risky since the quality of the solution is uncertain. However, exploration can be very profitable, since incidentally, it is possible to find the best solution. Exploitation is a more conservative process since the effects of the candidate solution are already known. Both concepts, exploration and exploitation, are conflicting. Promoting one means to decrease the other. Under such conditions, an agent or search strategy must combine both features to find competitively the optimal solution for a specific problem. In its operation, a metaheuristic approach should conduct the exploration and exploitation of the search space. In the context of metaheuristic methods, exploration refers to the process of searching for new solutions in the search space. Exploitation is the mechanism to refine locally the best solutions previously found in the search process, with the aim of improving them. Pure exploration degrades the accuracy of the produced solutions during the optimization process. On the other hand, pure exploitation allows to improve already existing solutions, but adversely it limits the search strategy so that solutions are easily trapped in local optima. Under these conditions, the ability of a metaheuristic method to find the optimal solution depends on its capacity to balance the exploration and exploitation processes in the search space. So far, the problem of balancing exploration–exploitation has not been solved convincingly. Therefore, each metaheuristic scheme implements a particular solution for its handling (Deb, 2001).

1.5 PROBABILISTIC DECISION AND SELECTION

The probabilistic decision and selection are two operations recurrently used for many metaheuristic methods. The operation of decision probability refers to the case of executing an action conditioned to a certain probability. On the other hand, the selection probability considers the process of selecting an element of a set, so that the items with the best quality have a greater chance of being selected, compared with those that have lesser quality.

1.5.1 Probabilistic Decision

The probabilistic decision is an operation used frequently by metaheuristic methods to condition the execution of different operators for searching for new solutions. The operation of the probabilistic decision can be formulated as how to execute an action **A** conditioned to a probability P_A. Since the probability dictates the frequency in which an action will be executed, its value must be a valid probability $(P_A \in [0,1])$. Under these conditions, the process of acceptance or rejection of the action **A** is as follows: first, generates a random number r_A under a uniform distribution **U** $[0,1]$. If the value r_A is less than or equal to P_A, the action **A** is performed; otherwise, action **A** will have no effect.

Program 1.2 Probabilistic Decision Implementation

```
%%%%%%%%%%%%%%%%%%%%%%%%%%%%%%%%%%%%%%%%%%%%%%%%%%%%%%%%%%%%%%%%%
% Probabilistic decision example
%%%%%%%%%%%%%%%%%%%%%%%%%%%%%%%%%%%%%%%%%%%%%%%%%%%%%%%%%%%%%%%%%
```

```
% Erik Cuevas, Alma Rodríguez
%%%%%%%%%%%%%%%%%%%%%%%%%%%%%%%%%%%%%%%%%%%%%%%%%%%%%%%%%%%%%
% Clear memory
clear all
% Variable initialization
ActionA=0;
NoActionA=0;
% Begin the iterative process
for i=1:10000
        % Random number generation U [0,1]
        rA=rand;
        % Probabilistic decision
        if (rA<=0.7)
                ActionA=ActionA+1;
        else
                NoActionA=NoActionA+1;
        end
end
```

As metaheuristic algorithms are iterative, the probability P_A expresses the frequency with which an action **A** is executed. Therefore, if the value P_A is near to zero, the action **A** will be poorly executed. While if the value of P_A is close to one, action **A** will be executed practically on all occasions. From the point of view of implementation, a random number uniformly distributed (**U** [0,1]) is generated by the **rand** function.

To show the implementation of a probabilistic decision operation, the program illustrated in Program 1.2 has been developed. The program considers 10,000 iterations, of which 70% $(P_A = 0.7)$ will perform the action to **A**, while the remaining 30% do not. Under these conditions, after running the program, the action ActionA will be executed approximately 7,000 times, while NoActionA will be executed around 3,000 times.

1.5.2 Probabilistic Selection

The probabilistic selection considers the process of selecting an element of a set, so that the items with the best quality (according to a certain objective function) have a greater chance of being chosen, compared with those that have lesser quality.

Methods of metaheuristic computation frequently have to choose a solution $\mathbf{x}_e^k$ from a population of elements $\mathbf{P}^k\left(\mathbf{x}_1^k, \mathbf{x}_2^k, \ldots, \mathbf{x}_N^k\right)$, where $e \in [1, 2, \ldots, N]$. In the selection, it must consider the fitness quality of the solutions $\left(f\left(\mathbf{x}_1^k\right), f\left(\mathbf{x}_2^k\right), \ldots, f\left(\mathbf{x}_N^k\right)\right)$, so that better solutions are more likely to be chosen. Under this selection process, the probability of selecting the solution $\mathbf{x}_e^k$ among the other $N-1$ solutions is defined as

$$P_e = \frac{f\left(\mathbf{x}_e^k\right)}{\sum_{i=1}^{N} f\left(\mathbf{x}_i^k\right)} \tag{1.11}$$

TABLE 1.2 Characteristics of Each Solution from the Numerical Example of Probabilistic Selection

Solution	$f(\cdot)$	P_e	P_e^A
$\mathbf{x}_1^k$	$f\left(\mathbf{x}_1^k\right) = 25$	$P_1 = 0.25$	$P_1^A = 0.25$
$\mathbf{x}_2^k$	$f\left(x_2^k\right) = 5$	$P_2 = 0.05$	$P_2^A = 0.30$
$\mathbf{x}_3^k$	$f\left(\mathbf{x}_3^k\right) = 40$	$P_3 = 0.40$	$P_3^A = 0.70$
$\mathbf{x}_4^k$	$f\left(\mathbf{x}_4^k\right) = 10$	$P_4 = 0.10$	$P_4^A = 0.80$
$\mathbf{x}_5^k$	$f\left(\mathbf{x}_5^k\right) = 20$	$P_5 = 0.20$	$P_5^A = 1.00$

Another important concept associated with the solution $\mathbf{x}_e^k$ is the cumulative probability P_e^A. This cumulative probability is defined as

$$P_e^A = \sum_{i=1}^{e} P_i \tag{1.12}$$

Under these conditions, the cumulative probability P_N^A of the last solution of the population $\mathbf{P}^k$ is equal to one.

Once calculated, the probabilities $\{P_1, P_2, \ldots, P_N\}$ and the cumulative probabilities $\{P_1^A, P_2^A, \ldots, P_N^A\}$ of all the solutions contained in the population $\mathbf{P}^k$. The selection process can be explained as follows: first, a random number r_S is generated considering a uniform distribution U [0,1]. Then, iteratively, a test process is conducted. Therefore, starting with the first solution, it is checked if $P_1^A > r_S$. If this condition is not met, the second solution is considered. This process continues testing each solution e until the condition $P_e^A > r_S$ has been reached. As a result of this procedure, the solution $\mathbf{x}_e^k$ would be selected.

In order to clarify this process, a numerical example is developed. Assume a population $\mathbf{P}^k$ with five elements $\left(\mathbf{x}_1^k, \mathbf{x}_2^k, \mathbf{x}_3^k, \mathbf{x}_4^k, \mathbf{x}_5^k\right)$, whose qualities (fitness values), probabilities, and cumulative probabilities are shown in Table 1.2. Given these values, the selection process is the following: a uniformly distributed random value r_S (U [0,1]) is generated. Considering that the produced value was $r_S = 0.51$, it is tested by using the first element if $P_1^A > r_S$. As this does not happen, it is proven with the second solution in the same condition $P_2^A > r_S$. As the condition is still not satisfied, the third solution is tested $P_3^A > r_S$. As the condition is fulfilled, the selected element is $\mathbf{x}_3^k$.

1.6 RANDOM SEARCH

The random search method (Matyas, 1965) is the first method which based its optimization strategy on a full stochastic process. Under this method, only a candidate solution $\mathbf{x}^k$ is maintained during the process of evolution. In each iteration, the candidate solution $\mathbf{x}^k$ is modified by adding a random vector $\Delta\mathbf{x}$. Therefore, the new candidate solution is modeled using the following expression:

$$\mathbf{x}^{k+1} = \mathbf{x}^k + \Delta\mathbf{x} \tag{1.13}$$

Assuming that the candidate solution $\mathbf{x}^k$ has d dimensions $\left(x_1^k, x_2^k, \ldots, x_d^k\right)$, each coordinate is modified $\left(\Delta \mathbf{x} = \{\Delta x_1, \Delta x_2, \ldots, \Delta x_d\}\right)$ through a random disturbance Δx_i $\left(i \in [1, 2, \ldots, d]\right)$ modeled for a Gaussian probability distribution defined as

$$p(\Delta x_i) = \frac{1}{\sigma_i \cdot \sqrt{2\pi}} \exp\left(-0.5 \cdot \frac{(\Delta x_i - \mu_i)}{\sigma_i^2}\right) = N(\mu_i, \sigma_i), \tag{1.14}$$

where σ_i and μ_i symbolize the standard deviation and the mean value, respectively, for the dimension i. As the value Δx_i represents a local modification around x_i^k, the average value is assumed zero $\left(\mu_i = 0\right)$.

Once computed $\mathbf{x}^{k+1}$, it is tested if the new position improves the quality of the previous candidate solution $\mathbf{x}^k$. Therefore, if the quality of $\mathbf{x}^{k+1}$ is better than $\mathbf{x}^k$, the value of $\mathbf{x}^{k+1}$ is accepted as the new candidate solution; otherwise, the solution $\mathbf{x}^k$ remains unchanged. This process can be defined for the case of minimization problem as

$$\mathbf{x}^{k+1} = \begin{cases} \mathbf{x}^{k+1} & si \ f\left(\mathbf{x}^{k+1}\right) < f\left(\mathbf{x}^k\right) \\ \mathbf{x}^k & si \ f\left(\mathbf{x}^{k+1}\right) \geq f\left(\mathbf{x}^k\right) \end{cases} \tag{1.15}$$

This replacement criterion of accepting only changes that improve the quality of candidate solutions is known as "greedy." In random search, the perturbation $\Delta \mathbf{x}$ imposed to $\mathbf{x}^k$ could provoke that the new value $\mathbf{x}^{k+1}$ may not be located within the search space $\mathbf{X}$. Outside the search space $\mathbf{X}$, there is no definition of the objective function $f(\mathbf{x})$. To avoid this problem, the algorithm must protect the evolution of the candidate solution $\mathbf{x}^k$, so that if $\mathbf{x}^{k+1}$ falls out of the search space $\mathbf{X}$, it should be assigned a very poor quality (represented by a very large value). This is, $f\left(\mathbf{x}^{k+1}\right) = \infty$ for the case of minimization or $f\left(\mathbf{x}^{k+1}\right) = -\infty$ for the maximization case.

1.6.1 Computational Implementation in MATLAB

To illustrate the operation of the random search algorithm and its practical implementation in MATLAB, in this section, the random search method is used to solve the following maximization problem:

$$\text{Maximize} \quad f(x_1, x_2) = 3 \cdot (1 - x_1)^2 \cdot e^{\left(-\left(x_1^2\right)-(x_2+1)^2\right)} + 10 \cdot \left(\frac{x_1}{5} - x_1^3 - x_2^5\right) \cdot e^{\left(-x_1^2 - x_2^2\right)} - \frac{1}{3} \cdot e^{\left(-(x_1+1)^2 - x_2^2\right)}$$

$$-3 \leq x_1 \leq 3$$

Subject to: $$\tag{1.16}$$

$$-3 \leq x_2 \leq 3$$

Under this formulation, a two-dimensional function $f(x_1, x_2)$ with a search space defined on the interval $[-1, 1]$ for each decision variable x_1 and x_2 is considered. Figure 1.7 shows a representation of the objective function $f(x_1, x_2)$.

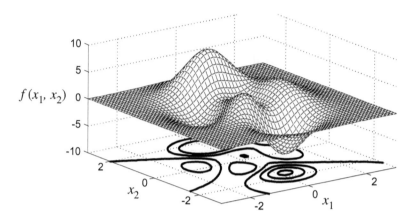

FIGURE 1.7 Graphical representation of the function $f(x_1, x_2)$.

As it can be seen, the function $f(x_1,x_2)$ can be derived twice. However, it is multimodal (several local optima). For these reasons, the function $f(x_1,x_2)$ does not fulfill the requirements to be minimized under the gradient descent method. Under these circumstances, it is maximized by the random search method.

The operation of the random search method over the maximization of $f(x_1,x_2)$ is presented in the form of a pseudocode in Algorithm 1.2. The procedure starts by randomly selecting a candidate solution $\mathbf{x}^k$ ($k=0$), within the search space defined on the interval $[-3,3]$ for each variable x_1 and x_2. Then, a new solution candidate $\mathbf{x}^{k+1}$ through the inclusion of random disturbance $\Delta\mathbf{x}$ is calculated. Once $\mathbf{x}^{k+1}$ is obtained, it is verified whether it belongs to the search space. If it is not included in $\mathbf{X}$, it is assigned to $\mathbf{x}^{k+1}$ a very low-quality value $\left(f\left(\mathbf{x}^{k+1}\right)=-\infty\right)$. The idea is that points outside the search space cannot be promoted their production. Finally, it is decided if the new point $\mathbf{x}^{k+1}$ presents an improvement compared with its predecessor $\mathbf{x}^k$. Therefore, if the quality of $\mathbf{x}^{k+1}$ is better than $\mathbf{x}^k$, the value of $\mathbf{x}^{k+1}$ is accepted as the new candidate; otherwise, solution $\mathbf{x}^k$ remains unchanged. This process is repeated iteratively until a maximum number of iterations $Niter$ has been reached.

From the point of view of implementation, the most critical part is the computation of $\Delta\mathbf{x}=(\Delta x_1,\Delta x_2)$. These values are obtained by a Gaussian probability distribution. In MATLAB, a random sample r which comes from a population with Gaussian distribution is calculated as follows:

$$r = \mu + \sigma \cdot \text{randn};$$

where μ and σ represent the average value and standard deviation of the population, respectively.

Algorithm 1.2 Random Search Method

1. $k \leftarrow 0$
2. $x_1^k \leftarrow$ Random $[-3,3]$, $x_2^k \leftarrow$ Random $[-3,3]$
3. **while** $(k < Niter)$ {
4. $\Delta x_1 = N(0,1)$, $\Delta x_2 = N(0,1)$
5. $x_1^{k+1} = x_1^k + \Delta x_1$, $x_2^{k+1} = x_2^k + \Delta x_2$
6. $\mathbf{x}^k = \left(x_1^k, x_2^k \right)$, $\mathbf{x}^{k+1} = \left(x_1^{k+1}, x_2^{k+1} \right)$
7. **If** $\left(\mathbf{x}^{k+1} \notin \mathbf{X} \right) \left\{ f\left(\mathbf{x}^{k+1} \right) = -\infty \right\}$
8. **If** $\left(f\left(\mathbf{x}^{k+1} \right) < f\left(\mathbf{x}^k \right) \right) \left\{ \mathbf{x}^{k+1} = \mathbf{x}^k \right\}$
9. $k \leftarrow k+1$}

Program 1.3 shows the implementation of Algorithm 1.2 in MATLAB. In the operation of Program 1.3, first, the function $f(x_1, x_2)$ is plotted in order to visualize its characteristics. Then, iteratively, the set of candidate solutions generated from its initial value $\mathbf{x}^0$ is shown until the optimum value $\mathbf{x}^*$ is found. Figure 1.8 shows an example of the set of solutions produced during the optimization process.

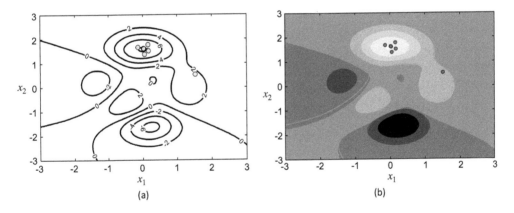

FIGURE 1.8   Solution map drawn on (a) the function contours and (b) the grayscale regions.

Program 1.3 Random Search Method

```
%%%%%%%%%%%%%%%%%%%%%%%%%%%%%%%%%%%%%%%%%%%%%%%%%%%%%%%%%%%%%%%%
% Random search algorithm
%%%%%%%%%%%%%%%%%%%%%%%%%%%%%%%%%%%%%%%%%%%%%%%%%%%%%%%%%%%%%%%%
% Erik Cuevas, Alma Rodríguez
%%%%%%%%%%%%%%%%%%%%%%%%%%%%%%%%%%%%%%%%%%%%%%%%%%%%%%%%%%%%%%%%
% Clear memory
clear all
% Definition of the objective function
funstr='3*(1-x).^2.*exp(-(x.^2)-(y+1).^2)-10*(x/5-x.^3-
y.^5).*exp(-x.^2-y.^2)-3*exp(-(x+1).^2 -y.^2)';
f=vectorize(inline(funstr));
range=[-3 3 -3 3];
% Draw the objective function
Ndiv=50;
dx=(range(2)-range(1))/Ndiv; dy=(range(4)-range(3))/Ndiv;
[x,y] =meshgrid(range(1):dx:range(2),range(3):dy:range(4));
z=f(x,y);
figure(1);  surfc(x,y,z);
% Definition of the number of iterations
Niter=3000;
k=0;
% Initialization of the candidate solution
xrange=range(2)-range(1);
yrange=range(4)-range(3);
xn=rand*xrange+range(1);
yn=rand*yrange+range(3);
figure
% Starting point of the Optimization process
while(k<Niter)
    % It is tested if the solution falls inside the search space
    if ((xn>=range(1))&(xn<=range(2))&(yn>=range(3))&(yn<=
    range(4)))
        %If yes, it is evaluated
        zn1=f(xn,yn);
    else
        % If not, it is assigned a low quality
        zn1=-1000;
    end
    % The produced solution is drawn
    contour(x,y,z,15); hold on;
    plot(xn,yn,'.','markersize',10,'markerfacecolor','g');
    drawnow;
    hold on;
    % A new solution is produced
    xnc=xn+randn*1;
```

```
ync=yn+randn*1;
% It is tested if the solution falls inside the search space
if ((xnc>=range(1))&(xnc<=range(2))&(ync>=range(3))&(ync<=
range(4)))
        % If yes, it is evaluated
        zn2=f(xnc,ync);
else
        % If not, it is assigned a low quality
        zn2=-1000;
end
% It is analyzed if the new solution is accepted
if (zn2>zn1)
        xn=xnc;
        yn=ync;
end
k=k+1;
end
```

1.7 SIMULATED ANNEALING

Simulated annealing (Kirkpatrick, Gelatt, & Vecchi, 1983) is an optimization technique that emulates the tempered process in metallic materials. The idea with this process is to cool metallic material in a controlled way so that the crystal structures can orient themselves and avoid defects in metal structures.

The use of this process as an inspiration for the formulation of optimization algorithms was first proposed by Kirkpatrick et al. (1983). Since then, several studies and applications to analyze the scope of this method have been suggested. Different from the gradient-based algorithms which have the disadvantage of stuck in local minima, the simulated annealing method presents a great ability to avoid this difficulty.

In simulated annealing, the objective function to optimize is analogous to the energy of a thermodynamic system. At high temperatures, the algorithm allows the exploration of very distant points within the search space. Under these circumstances, the probability with which bad-quality solutions are accepted is very large.

On the other hand, at low temperatures, the algorithm allows the generation of points in neighbor locations. In this stage, the probability of accepting bad-quality solutions is also reduced. Therefore, only new solutions that enhance their previous value will be considered.

The simulated annealing maintains only one candidate solution (x^k) during its operation. This solution is modified in each iteration using a procedure similar to the random search method, where each point is updated through the generation of a random vector Δx. The simulated annealing algorithm does not only accept changes that improve the objective function. It also incorporates a probabilistic mechanism that allows accepting solutions with lower quality (worse solutions). The idea with this mechanism is to accept bad solutions in order to avoid getting trapped in local minima.

Under these circumstances, assuming as an example a maximization problem, a new solution $\mathbf{x}^{k+1}$ will be accepted considering two different alternatives:

1. If its quality is superior to its previous value $\mathbf{x}^k$, this is $f(\mathbf{x}^{k+1}) > f(\mathbf{x}^k)$.

2. Under an acceptance probability p_a.

In the second option, although the quality of $\mathbf{x}^{k+1}$ is not superior to $\mathbf{x}^k\left(f(\mathbf{x}^{k+1}) < f(\mathbf{x}^k)\right)$, the new solution $\mathbf{x}^{k+1}$ will be accepted according to an acceptance probability p_a defined as

$$p_a = \mathrm{e}^{-\frac{\Delta f}{T}}, \tag{1.17}$$

where T represents the temperature that controls the cooling process, while Δf symbolizes the energy difference between the point $\mathbf{x}^{k+1}$ and $\mathbf{x}^k$, which is defined as

$$\Delta f = f(\mathbf{x}^{k+1}) - f(\mathbf{x}^k) \tag{1.18}$$

Therefore, the acceptance or not of a new position $\mathbf{x}^{k+1}$ is performed under the following procedure. First, a random number r_1 uniformly distributed between [0,1] is produced. Then, if $r_1 < p_a$, the point $\mathbf{x}^{k+1}$ is accepted as the new solution.

For a given energy difference Δf, if T is large, then $p_a \to 1$, which means that all the suggested values of $\mathbf{x}^{k+1}$ will be accepted regardless of their quality in comparison with the previous candidate solution $\mathbf{x}^k$. If T is very small, then $p_a \to 0$, which means that only the values of $\mathbf{x}^{k+1}$ that improve the quality of $\mathbf{x}^k$ will be accepted. When this happens, the search strategy of simulated annealing is similar to the random search method.

Thus, if T is large, the algorithm simulates a system with high thermal energy. Under these conditions, the search space $\mathbf{X}$ is explored extensively. On the other hand, if T is very small, the system allows refining around the position already known locally.

From the parameter description, it is clear that the most important element in simulated annealing is the cooling control. This factor specifies the process in which the temperature is varied from high to low. Since this process depends on the specific application, it requires a calibration stage performed by trial and error. There are several ways to control the cooling process from an initial temperature T_{ini} to a final temperature T_{fin}. For this task, two methods, the linear and the geometrical, are known.

In the linear scheme, the temperature reduction is modeled using the following formulation:

$$T(k) = T_{ini} - \beta \cdot k, \tag{1.19}$$

where β is the cooling rate. It should be chosen so that $T \to 0$ when $k \to Niter$ (maximum number of iterations). This means that $\beta = (T_{ini} - T_{fin})/Niter$. On the other hand, in the geometric scheme, the temperature is decremented by the use of a cooling factor defined on the interval [0,1]. Therefore, the geometric cooling strategy is modeled using the following expression:

$$T(k) = T_{ini} \eta^k, \tag{1.20}$$

The advantage of the geometrical model is that $T \rightarrow 0$ when $k \rightarrow \infty$. In practice, $\eta \in [0.7, 0.95]$. Algorithm 1.3 shows the full computational procedure of the simulated annealing method in the form of a pseudocode.

The simulated annealing method generically begins with a configuration of its parameters T_{ini}, T_{fin}, β, and Niter. Then, an initial point within the search space $\mathbf{X}$ is randomly generated. Afterward, the evolution process begins. This process remains either until the number of iterations has been reached or until the temperature has achieved its projected final value T_{fin}. During the process, a new candidate solution $\mathbf{x}^{k+1}$ is produced by applying a perturbation $\Delta\mathbf{x}$ over the original solution $\mathbf{x}^k$. Such modification $\Delta\mathbf{x}$ is used in a similar way to the random search algorithm described in Section 1.6. Once $\mathbf{x}^{k+1}$ is generated, it is analyzed whether this new solution will be accepted or not. Two possibilities are considered for this purpose. (1) If the new solution $\mathbf{x}^{k+1}$ improves the previous one, $\mathbf{x}^{k+1}$ is accepted. Otherwise, if there is no improvement, (2) the acceptance of $\mathbf{x}^{k+1}$ is tested with a probability p_a. If the test is positive, $\mathbf{x}^{k+1}$ is accepted. Otherwise, it is discarded and $\mathbf{x}^k$ is maintained. Additionally, in each iteration, the temperature is decreased by a factor β in order to reduce the degree of acceptance for new solutions that do not present better quality than their predecessors.

For the generation of new candidate solutions $\mathbf{x}^{k+1}$, the simulated annealing algorithm considers a random modification $\Delta\mathbf{x}$. Because of this, many new solutions could fall outside the search space $\mathbf{X}$. The random search algorithm avoids this problem by assigning to the new solution $\mathbf{x}^{k+1}$ a very bad quality, with the objective that $\mathbf{x}^{k+1}$ can never be selected. As the simulated annealing scheme allows a probabilistic acceptance of solutions that have poor quality, solutions outside the search space $\mathbf{X}$ could also be accepted. To avoid this problem, the algorithm of simulated annealing implements a mechanism of generation of solutions, which does not consider solutions out the limits of the search space $\mathbf{X}$. This mechanism is implemented through a **while** cycle that is continually running until a feasible solution belonging to the search space $\mathbf{X}$ has been reached (see lines 5–7 of Algorithm 1.3).

An improvement often implemented in the method of simulated annealing is the gradual reduction of random perturbations $\Delta\mathbf{x}$. The idea is that in first iterations, large random jumps are permitted in order to explore the search space extensively. However, as the algorithm evolves, this ability is reduced so that in the last iterations, only local perturbation around a solution is performed (with very small values of $\Delta\mathbf{x}$). The disturbances $\Delta\mathbf{x}$ are calculated by using a Gaussian distribution such as $\Delta\mathbf{x} \leftarrow N(0, \sigma \cdot T)$. Therefore, this behavior is easily implemented by multiplying the standard deviation with the current value of the temperature T. Under these conditions, as the temperature decreases $(T \rightarrow 0)$ during the optimization process, the perturbation magnitude also diminishes $(\Delta\mathbf{x} \rightarrow 0)$.

TABLE 1.3   Parameter Values Used by Simulated Annealing in Program 1.4

Parameter	Value
T_{ini}	1
T_{fin}	1×10^{-10}
β	0.95
Niter	150
σ	2.5

Algorithm 1.3 Simulated Annealing Algorithm

1. Initialize T_{ini}, T_{fin}, β, σ and Niter.
2. $k \leftarrow 0$, $T = T_{ini}$
3. $\mathbf{x}^k \leftarrow$ Random $[\mathbf{X}]$
4. **while** $\left(\left(T > T_{fin} \right) \textbf{ and } (k < Niter) \right)\{$
5. **while** $\left(\mathbf{x}^{k+1} \notin \mathbf{X} \right)\{$
6. $\Delta \mathbf{x} \leftarrow N(0, \sigma \cdot T)$
7. $\mathbf{x}^{k+1} \leftarrow \mathbf{x}^k + \Delta \mathbf{x} \}$
8. **If** $\left(\mathbf{x}^{k+1} \text{ is worse than } \mathbf{x}^k \right)$
9. $\left\{ \Delta f \leftarrow f\left(\mathbf{x}^{k+1} \right) - f\left(\mathbf{x}^k \right) \right.$
10. $p_a \leftarrow e^{-\frac{\Delta f}{T}}$
11. **If** $\left(p_a < \text{rand} \right) \left\{ \mathbf{x}^{k+1} = \mathbf{x}^k \right\}\}$
12. $k \leftarrow k + 1$
13. $T \leftarrow \beta \cdot T \}$

1.7.1 Computational Example in MATLAB

To illustrate the operation of the simulated annealing algorithm and its practical implementation in MATLAB, in this section, the simulated annealing method is used to solve the maximization problem formulated in Eq. 1.16. Program 1.4 shows the implementation of Algorithm 1.3 in MATLAB. In its operation, the parameters of the simulated annealing approach have been configured as shown in Table 1.3.

Simulated annealing method significantly reduces the number of iterations to find the optimal solution $\mathbf{x}^*$ in comparison with the random search algorithm. In metaheuristic schemes, there is always the problem of finding the number of appropriate iterations to solve a particular optimization task. If too few iterations are performed, there is a risk that the global optimum is never found. On the other hand, if the number of iterations is exaggerated, the solution converges to the optimal value, but at high computational expense.

Program 1.4 Simulated Annealing Algorithm

```
%%%%%%%%%%%%%%%%%%%%%%%%%%%%%%%%%%%%%%%%%%%%%%%%%%%%%%%%%%
% Simulated annealing
%%%%%%%%%%%%%%%%%%%%%%%%%%%%%%%%%%%%%%%%%%%%%%%%%%%%%%%%%%
% Erik Cuevas, Alma Rodríguez
%%%%%%%%%%%%%%%%%%%%%%%%%%%%%%%%%%%%%%%%%%%%%%%%%%%%%%%%%%
% Clear memory
clear all
% Definition of the objective function
funstr='3*(1-x).^2.*exp(-(x.^2)-(y+1).^2)-10*(x/5-x.^3-
y.^5).*exp(-x.^2-y.^2)-1/3*exp(-(x+1).^2 -y.^2)';
f=vectorize(inline(funstr));
range=[-3 3 -3 3];
% Draw the Function as reference
Ndiv=50;
dx=(range(2)-range(1))/Ndiv; dy=(range(4)-range(3))/Ndiv;
[x,y] =meshgrid(range(1):dx:range(2),range(3):dy:range(4));
z=f(x,y);
figure(1);  surfc(x,y,z);
% Definition of the number of iterations
k=1;
valid=0;
Niter=150;
% Define initial temperature
T_init =1.0;
% Define final temperature
T_fin = 1e-10;
% Cooling rate
beta=0.95;
% Initialization of the candidate solution
xrange=range(2)-range(1);
yrange=range(4)-range(3);
xn=rand*xrange+range(1);
yn=rand*yrange+range(3);
% Temperature initialization
T = T_init;
% Starting point of the Optimization process
while (k<Niter)
        % The produced solution is drawn
        contour(x,y,z); hold on;
        plot(xn,yn,'.','markersize',10,'markerfacecolor','g');
        drawnow;
        hold off;
        % It is evaluated the fitness of x(k)
        E_old = f(xn,yn);
        % A new solution x(k+1) is produced
```

```
% The cycle while is Applied until a feasible point has been
reached
while(valid==0)
        % The magnitude of the perturbation is modified
        xnc=xn+randn*2.5*T;
        ync=yn+randn*2.5*T;
        if((xnc>=range(1))&(xnc<=range(2))&(ync>=range(3))
        &(ync<=range(4)))
                valid=1;
        end
end
valid=0;
% The current temperature is stored
data(k)=T;
% It is evaluated the fitness of x(k+1)
E_new=f(xnc,ync);
% The fitness difference is computed
DeltaE=E_new-E_old;
% Acceptance for fitness quality
if (DeltaE>0)
        xn=xnc;
        yn=ync;
end
% Probabilistic Acceptance
if (DeltaE<0 & exp(DeltaE/T)>rand);
        xn=xnc;
        yn=ync;
end
% Update Temperature
T = beta*T;
if (T<T_fin)
        T=T_fin;
end
k=k+1;
end
```

In the operation of Program 1.4, first, the objective function $f(x_1, x_2)$ is plotted in order to appreciate its main characteristics. Then, iteratively, the set of solutions generated from its initial value $\mathbf{x}^0$ to the optimum value $\mathbf{x}^*$ is shown. Figure 1.9a presents an example of the set of solutions produced during the evolution process when Program 1.4 is executed. Figure 1.9b shows the cooling process experimented during the evolution process.

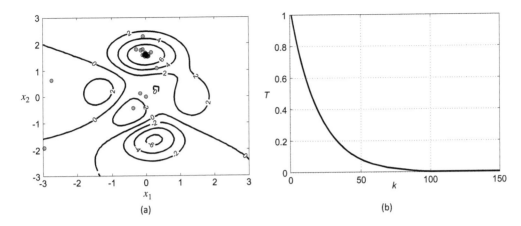

FIGURE 1.9 (a) Produced solution map over the function contour and (b) cooling process experimented during the optimization process.

EXERCISES

1.1 Assuming the minimization of $f(\mathbf{x})$, where

$$f(\mathbf{x}) = \sum_{i=1}^{4} -x_i \operatorname{sen}\left(\sqrt{|x_i|}\right)$$

Determine

a. which are the decision variables,

b. the number of dimensions.

1.2 Using the graphical method presented in Section 1.1. Find the minimum optimum and local optima, according to the following formulation:

$$\text{Minimize} \quad f(x) = x^4 - 15x^2 + 10x + 24$$
$$\text{Subject to:} \quad x \in [-4, 3]$$

1.3 Reformulate the optimization problem 1.2 as a process of maximization. Then find the maximum global and local, using the graphical method.

1.4 Modify the Program 1.1 (gradient descent method) so that it solves the following minimization problem:

$$\text{Minimize} \quad f_1(x_1, x_2) = x_1 \cdot e^{\left(-x_1^2 - x_2^2\right)}$$

$$-2 \leq x_1 \leq 2$$

Subject to:

$$-2 \leq x_2 \leq 2$$

Then, analyze the performance of gradient descent method considering that the parameter α assumes the following values: 0.05, 0.1, and 0.5.

1.5 Rewrite Program 1.1 so that it can solve the following minimization problem:

$$\text{Minimize} \quad f_2(x_1, x_2) = \text{sen}(x_1) \cdot \text{sen}(x_2)$$

$$0 \leq x_1 \leq 6$$

Subject to:

$$0 \leq x_2 \leq 6$$

a. Determine the number of local minima.

b. Analyze the performance of gradient descent method considering that the parameter α assumes the following values: 0.05, 0.1, and 0.5.

c. Explain the behavior of the algorithm in the presence of more than one global minimum.

1.6 Adapt Program 1.1 so that it can solve the following minimization problem:

$$\text{Minimize} \quad f_3(x_1, x_2) = \text{floor}\left(10 \cdot \left(10 - e^{-\left(x_1^2 + 3x_2^2\right)}\right)\right)$$

$$-1 \leq x_1 \leq 1$$

Subject to:

$$-1 \leq x_2 \leq 1$$

a. Analyze the effects of the round function **floor** on the shape of the objective function.

b. Discuss the characteristics of this problem that don't allow the operation of gradient descent method.

1.7 Execute Program 1.2 considering the following number of iterations: 500, 1,000, and 5,000. Analyze the effect of these changes in the number of times that is executed the action **A**. Then, determine the minimum number of necessary iterations so that the action **A** reaches 70%.

1.8 Assuming a population $\mathbf{P}^k$ with four elements, whose qualities (fitness values) are represented by the following table:

Solution	$f(\cdot)$
$\mathbf{x}_1^k$	$f(\mathbf{x}_1^k)=1$
$\mathbf{x}_2^k$	$f(\mathbf{x}_2^k)=2$
$\mathbf{x}_3^k$	$f(\mathbf{x}_3^k)=5$
$\mathbf{x}_4^k$	$f(\mathbf{x}_4^k)=2$

Considering the probabilistic selection method, determine the probability of choosing the element $\mathbf{x}_3^k$ over the other.

1.9 Assuming the random search method (Section 1.6), modify Program 1.3 so that it can solve the following problem of maximization:

$$\text{Maximize} \quad f_4(x_1,x_2)=e^{-\left(\left((x_1-\pi)^2+(x_2-\pi)^2\right)/30\right)}$$

$$-100\le x_1 \le 100$$

$$\text{Subject to:}$$

$$-100\le x_2 \le 100$$

a. Determine the global maximum.

b. Determine which characteristics of f_4 difficult the performance of the search method.

1.10 Using the simulated annealing method (Section 1.7), modify Program 1.4 so that it can solve the following problem of maximization:

$$\text{Maximize} \quad f_5(x_1,x_2)=20\cdot e^{\left(-0.2\sqrt{0.5\left(x_1^2+x_2^2\right)}\right)}+e^{\left(0.5\left(\cos(2\pi x_1)+\cos(2\pi x_2)\right)\right)}-20$$

$$-5\le x_1 \le 5$$

$$\text{Subject to:}$$

$$-5\le x_2 \le 5$$

a. Determine the global maximum.

b. Analyze the multimodal characteristics of the function f_5.

1.11 Considering the same formulation as Exercise 1.10, analyze the performance of the simulated annealing method when the cooling rate assumes the following values: 0.01, 0.1, 0.5, 0.8, and 0.99.

REFERENCES

Baldick, R. (2006). *Applied optimization: Formulation and algorithms for engineering systems.* Cambridge: Cambridge University Press.

Bartholomew-Biggs, M. (2008). *Nonlinear optimization with engineering applications.* US: Springer.

Deb, K. (2001). *Multi-objective optimization using evolutionary algorithms.* John Wiley & Sons, Inc.

Dennis, J. E. (1978) A brief introduction to quasi-Newton methods. In G. H. Golub & J. Öliger (Eds.), *Numerical Analysis: Proceedings of Symposia in Applied Mathematics* (pp. 19–52). Providence, RI: American Mathematical Society.

Hocking, L. (1991). *Optimal control: An introduction to the theory with applications.* US: Oxford University Press.

Kirkpatrick, S., Gelatt, C., & Vecchi, P. (1983). Optimization by simulated annealing. *Science, 220*(4598), 671–680.

Mathews, J., & Fink, K. (2000). *Métodos numéricos con MATLAB.* Madrid: Prentice Hall.

Matyas, J. (1965). Random optimization. *Automation and Remote Control, 26,* 246–253.

Reinhardt, R., Hoffmann, A., & Gerlach, T. (2013). *Nichtlineare Optimierung.* Heidelberg, Berlin: Springer.

Simon, D. (2013). *Evolutionary optimization algorithms, biologically inspired and population-based approaches to computer intelligence.* Hoboken, New Jersey: John Wiley & Sons, Inc.

Venkataraman, P. (2009). *Applied optimization with MATLAB programming* (2nd ed.). Hoboken, New Jersey: John Wiley & Sons, Inc.

Yang, X.-S. (2010). *Engineering optimization.* Hoboken, New Jersey: John Wiley & Sons, Inc.

CHAPTER 2

Genetic Algorithms (GA)

2.1 INTRODUCTION

The initial concept of a genetic algorithm (GA) was first introduced by John Holland at the University of Michigan (Holland, 1975). Nowadays, there exist several GA variants where the original structure has been changed or combined with other computational schemes. Such new GA approaches can be found in recent publications contained in specialized journals such as *Evolutionary Computation, Transactions on Evolutionary Computation, Swarm and Evolutionary Computation, Applied Soft Computing, Soft Computing, Evolutionary Intelligence, Memetic Computing,* and *Neural Computing and Applications,* to name a few.

GAs use natural genetics as a computational principle (Back, Pogel, & Michalewicz, 1997). In this chapter, we will discuss the characteristics in the operation of GAs.

GAs represent search strategies that have been extracted from the principles of natural selection. Therefore, the central concepts of genetics are adopted and adapted artificially to produce search schemes. These schemes maintain high robustness and minimal information requirements.

GAs define three important operators (Vose, 1999):

- Selection

- Crossover

- Mutation

In its operation, a GA starts its strategy by producing a set of random solutions, instead of considering only one candidate solution. Once the initial population of solutions is produced, each of them is evaluated in terms of the optimization problem symbolized by a cost function. The value of this cost function is known in the metaheuristic context as a fitness value assigned to each candidate solution. The evaluation of a solution corresponds to combining its cost function value and its respective constraint violation. The result of this combination represents the relative score that reflexes the way in which this solution solves the optimization problem.

Then, the population of the solutions is changed by using three main operations, namely selection, crossover, and mutation. The operations of crossover and mutation are stochastic schemes that are executed according to a certain probability. The crossover operator is applied with a probability p_c which normally is high. Crossover allows exchanging spatial information among candidate solutions. On the other hand, the mutation process is executed with a probability p_m. In general, the value of p_m is low. The mutation is an operator that modifies the original candidate solution in order to avoid local optima or to improve the solution accuracy. The idea of both operators is to develop a search strategy that is able to localize promising regions within the solution space. Afterward, an iteration counter is incremented to register that one more cycle has been completed.

Finally, a termination criterion is evaluated. If this condition is not fulfilled, a new GA cycle is conducted. Otherwise, the algorithm finishes its execution. The complete execution step of a GA is illustrated in the form of flowchart in Figure 2.1.

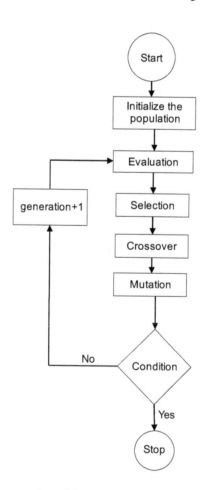

FIGURE 2.1   Flowchart of the operation of GA.

2.2 BINARY GA

To exhibit their processing method, we consider a hand-simulation of one generation of GAs in terms of a two-variable problem. The problem has been taken from Deb (1999). Then, a theoretical discussion of the different GA parameters with their interactions is conducted.

We discuss the fundamental operating principles of a GA by considering a simple design of a can. In the optimization problem, it is assumed that the cylindrical can involves two parameters, height h and diameter d. Suppose that the can must contain a volume of at least 500 ml, while the design goal is to minimize the cost of the metal employed in its production. Therefore, the optimization problem can be formulated as follows:

$$\text{Minimize} \quad f(d,h)=c\left(\frac{\pi d^2}{2}+\pi dh\right)$$

$$g(d,h)=\frac{\pi d^2 h}{4}\geq 500 \tag{2.1}$$

$$\text{Subject to} \quad d_{min}\leq d\leq d_{max}$$

$$h_{min}\leq h\leq h_{max}$$

where c corresponds to the cost of the can metal per cm^2. On the other hand, the design variables h and d maintain value within the range $\left[d_{min},d_{max}\right]$ and $\left[h_{min},h_{max}\right]$ in cm, respectively.

The first step to use GAs in finding the optimal variable values d and h is to represent them as binary strings. Assuming that we consider five bits to represent both of the decision variables, it is necessary to combine ten bits to symbolize a complete chromosome. Under such conditions, a solution that corresponds to a can of diameter 8 cm and height 10 cm is represented in Figure 2.2.

In this representation, the lower and upper limits of both design variables are considered within the range [0,31]. Assuming five bits to code a decision variable, several candidate solutions can be tested in order to find the optimal solution.

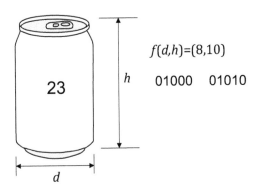

FIGURE 2.2 Candidate solution representation for the can optimization problem. The cost associated with the can is marked as 23 units.

Once a candidate solution in the form of binary string is produced, the next step is to evaluate the solution in terms of the cost function and constraint violations. In case constraints are not defined, the fitness value assigned to the candidate solution depends only on the cost function. For our example, the cost function and restriction are evaluated as follows:

$$f(d,h) = 0.065 \left(\frac{\pi \cdot 8^2}{2} + \pi \cdot 8 \cdot 10 \right) = 23 \tag{2.2}$$

$$g(d,h) = \frac{\pi \cdot 8^2 \cdot 10}{4} = 502.656 \tag{2.3}$$

where $c = 0.065$ corresponds to the cost of the can metal per cm².

The objective of our optimization problem is to minimize the total material cost but assuring that the minimal value of the can is not lower than 300 ml. Therefore, in the comparison, it is to be noted that a solution with a smaller fitness value is better than another solution.

Figure 2.3 illustrates a set of six random solutions to the can problem. Feasible solutions correspond to solutions that fulfill the constraint requirements (for example, the can contains at least 300 ml). Unfeasible solutions represent solutions that violate to some extent the constraints limits imposed by $g(d,h)$. Feasible solutions are qualified in terms of the cost function $f(d,h)$. On the other hand, the fitness value of unfeasible solutions is a combination of the cost function plus the penalty magnitude as a consequence of a constraint violation. In the example, two solutions do not contain an internal volume of 300 ml. For this reason, they are penalized by including an extra constraint cost. This extra cost must be calculated depending on the violation level of the respective constraint. However, this value must be large enough so that all infeasible solutions have a worse fitness value than any other feasible solution. In Figure 2.3, cans A, B, D, and E are feasible solutions since they are able to contain at least 300 ml. Therefore, they are qualified considering only the cost function $f(d,h)$. In contrast, candidate solutions corresponding to cans C and F are infeasible solutions since they are not able to contain at least 300 ml. Under such

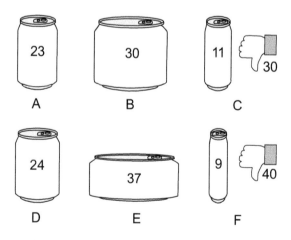

FIGURE 2.3 A random population of six cans (a–f) and the computation of their respective quality.

conditions, these solutions must be penalized. In consequence, the quality of both solutions is calculated adding their corresponding cost function $f(d,h)$ (11 and 9, for C and F, respectively) and their violation value $g(d,h)$ (30 and 40, for C and F, respectively).

2.2.1 Selection Operator

The main objective of the selection process is to proliferate good solutions and avoid bad solutions in a population, while it maintains the number of candidate solutions constant (Goldberg & Deb, 1991). During its operation, the selection operator performs the following tasks:

1. Determine the good solutions in a population in terms of quality.

2. Reproduce good solutions.

3. Avoid the selection of bad solutions from the population so that new copies of good solutions replace bad solutions in the population.

There are several schemes for selection. The most common methods are tournament selection (Blickle & Thiele, 1996), proportional selection (Holland, 1975), ranking selection (Darrell, 1989), and pure random selection.

Under the tournament method, two solutions are randomly chosen. Then, a contest is verified between both solutions. Finally, the best solution is selected for a further process. If this process is repeated several times, the best solutions in a population will be selected several times. On the other hand, the worst solutions will be eliminated as a consequence of lost tournaments. An important aspect of the tournament selection method is that the minimization and maximization problems can be handled easily. This is possible just by modifying the comparison operator. The proportional selection method chooses a solution x_i under the probability P_i which is proportional to its fitness value $f(x_i)$. Assume that the average fitness of all population members is f_{avg}. If the process of proportional selection is executed several times, a solution x_i with a fitness $f(x_i)$ is approximately chosen $\left(f(x_i)/f_{avg} \right)$ times. This selection operation can be implemented through the use of a Roulette-Wheel Selection (RWS) mechanism. Under this process, a wheel is divided into N different divisions which correspond to the number of solutions in the population. The area of each solution x_i in the wheel is assigned in proportion to its fitness value $f(x_i)$. The selection process implies to roll the wheel and choose the solution indicated by the pointer as a consequence of the stochastic final result. As an example, Figure 2.4 presents a roulette wheel for five candidate solutions with different fitness values. According to Figure 2.4, the third solution maintains the highest fitness value in comparison with the

i	$f(x_i)$	$P_i(x_i)$
1	25.0	0.25
2	5.0	0.05
3	40.0	0.40
4	10.0	0.10
5	20.0	0.20

FIGURE 2.4 A roulette wheel for five solutions according to their fitness values.

other four elements. Under such conditions, it is expected that RWS scheme will select the third solution more often than any other solution. The RWS approach can also be easily emulated as a computer program.

To emulate the RWS process, the probability to select the solution x_i among N elements is determined as follows:

$$P_i(x_i) = \frac{f(x_i)}{\sum_{j=1}^{N} f(x_j)} \tag{2.4}$$

Once the probabilities of all solutions are calculated, the cumulative probability P_i^A of each element x_i can be obtained by combining the individual probabilities from the first solution x_1 to the respective element x_i, such as

$$P_i^A(x_i) = \sum_{j=1}^{i} P_j(x_j) \tag{2.5}$$

Therefore, the cumulative probability P_N^A of the last element x_N is equal to one. Under such circumstances, the cumulative probability of the solution P_i^A models the occurrences between the probabilities of solutions P_{i-1} and P_i. One special case is the cumulative probability of the solution P_1^A which corresponds to the probabilities between 0 and P_1.

To select a solution emulating the RWS process, a random number u uniformly distributed is generated. Then, the solution which is the most similar in the cumulative probability range with regard to the number u is selected.

Figure 2.5 presents the cumulative probability map (with values from 0 to 1) of the five solutions for the example illustrated in Figure 2.4. Therefore, a random number u uniformly distributed is generated. Since the probability P_3 of solution x_3 is the highest of all five elements, there is a high likelihood that the number u corresponds to the area between P_2 and P_3. One disadvantage of the proportional selection method is that requires the average fitness of all population members. Therefore, it is slow compared with the tournament selection method.

In some metaheuristic methods, it is necessary to select a set of N elements from an initial population of M individuals, where $M \geq N$. Selecting several individuals in a single process is more efficient and robust than selecting only one individual. This is the case of Evolutionary Strategies in which a set of μ elements are selected in a single process from the original population. In this process, the number of copies N_i selected by each solution x_i in the final set is computed as follows:

$$N_i = int(N \cdot P_i) \tag{2.6}$$

where $int(\cdot)$ delivers the integer part of its argument. If the number of copies of all solutions $\left(\sum_{j=1}^{N} N_j < N \right)$ does not fulfill the complete set of N elements, the rest $\left(N - \sum_{j=1}^{N} N_j \right)$ is computed by the RWS method.

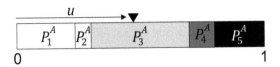

FIGURE 2.5   Implementation of the RWS operator.

In spite of effective results, the proportional selection scheme has a critical flaw. According to its processing model, the proportional selection approach assumes that all fitness values are positive. Under these conditions, Eq. 2.3 delivers valid probability values. If the fitness values are negative, the probabilities assigned to each solution is no longer valid. This problem can be solved by adding to each fitness value enough positive θ value so that it guarantees positive values for all involved solutions. The determination of θ is a difficult task since the nature of the optimization problem normally is unknown.

Under the ranking selection method, all the solutions are organized according to their fitness values. Therefore, the worst solution is assigned rank 1, while the best element corresponds to the rank N. With this new rank assignation, the proportionate selection operator is applied considering the rank numbers instead of the fitness values. This selection method presents the advantage that it does not consider negative values (only the rank). For this reason, it does not present the inconsistencies of the proportional method which considers the fitness values. However, an important disadvantage of the ranking scheme is the lack of selection pressure. This effect is produced by a difference in the scale between rank and fitness values. It could be that two solutions maintain a big difference in fitness results but holding a difference of only one rank. Although both solutions have significant differences, the two solutions are considered with a similar probability to be selected.

The pure random selection represents the easiest way to choose solution from a population. In this method, a solution is randomly selected without considering rank or fitness information. For this reason, this method does not produce good results since it does not allow the proliferation of good solutions and the elimination of bad elements.

2.2.2 Binary Crossover Operator

The crossover operation is used to exchange information between solutions (Eshelman, Caruana, & Schaffer, 1989). The idea is to change spatial information among elements of the population with the objective to use it as a search strategy. It is important to remark that the selection operator is not used to produce any new solutions in the population. The selection scheme only allows reproducing copies of good solutions, while it avoids not-so-good solutions.

Crossover and mutation operators are the binary operators that are used to produce new candidate solutions. Under the crossover operation, two solutions, called parents, are randomly selected from the original population. Then, a portion of the binary strings is exchanged between both solutions to produce two new strings.

The crossover operators for binary schemes involve a combination of two selected parents $\mathbf{p}_1$ and $\mathbf{p}_2$. In order to illustrate this process easily, it is also defined a mask $\mathbf{m}$ that specifies the bits of the parents that should be swapped or combined. The bits of **m** that are defined as one will be swapped, while those defined as zero remain without change. From crossover, two new elements are produced, c_1 and c_2. Three crossover schemes for binary representations will be discussed in this book: One-point crossover, two-point crossover, and uniform crossover.

The operation of crossover is a stochastic scheme that is executed according to a certain probability p_c. The crossover operator is applied with a probability p_c which normally is high.

One-point crossover

Under the one-point crossover, the segments of bits are swapped between the parents p_1 and p_2 to produce their offspring c_1 and c_2. For the operation, a bit position b is randomly selected. Then, the binary strings after that point are swapped between the two parents. An example of the one-point crossover is exhibited in Figure 2.6a. This crossover operation can also be defined in terms of the mask **m** which is configured with zeros and ones distributed around the crossover point b .

Two-point crossover

In this operation, two-bit positions are randomly chosen. Then, the binary strings among such points are swapped. Its process is very similar to the case of the one-point crossover, but considering the two-bit positions b_1 and b_2 instead of one. Under this operation, the mask **m** contains two chains of ones within the complete bit string. Figure 2.6b illustrates the process of the two-point crossover operation.

Uniform crossover

Under uniform crossover, the combination of bits between parents is randomly performed. The probability of conducting a combination in a certain bit is 0.5. Therefore, each bit of the mask **m** is produced by generating a random number r uniformly distributed. Then, if $r > 0.5$, the bit i is set to one. Otherwise, it is set to zero. Figure 2.6c illustrates the process of the two-point crossover operation.

2.2.3 Binary Mutation

Under the operation of mutation, one or more bits from the binary string are randomly changed by their opposite values. The objective of this process is to add diversity in the

FIGURE 2.6 Different crossover operators: (a) one-point crossover, (b) two-point crossover, and (c) uniform crossover.

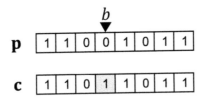

FIGURE 2.7 Mutation operation.

population by modifying the candidate solution. The mutation is also applied to avoid that solution to get trapped in local minima. Similar to crossover, the mutation is a stochastic operation which is executed according to a mutation probability p_m. The value of p_m is small to guaranty that good candidate solutions are not completely distorted.

The most popular mutation operation is the uniform mutation. Under this scheme, a bit position b or several $b_1 \ldots b_m$ from the binary string $\mathbf{p}$ are randomly selected. Then, a new solution $\mathbf{c}$ is produced by inverting these bits. In other words, if the bit is one, it is set to zero, otherwise, it is set to one. Figure 2.7 illustrates the uniform mutate process.

2.2.4 Computational Procedure

In this section, the complete process of the binary GA is integrated and implemented. In order to illustrate its construction, it is considered to minimize the following problem:

$$\text{Minimize} \quad f(x) = (x-2)^4 + 5(x-2)^3 + 4(x-2)^2 - 4(x-2) + 1$$
$$\text{Subject to} \quad -2 \le x \le 3 \tag{2.7}$$

The graphical representation of this cost function is shown in Figure 2.8. According to Figure 2.8, the cost function has two minima, one global minimum $x_g \approx -1$ and one local

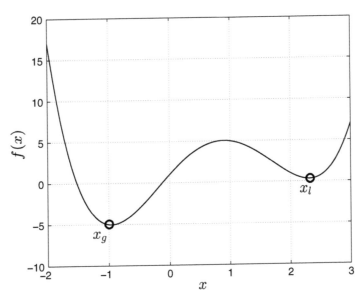

FIGURE 2.8 Cost function example for the implementation of the binary GA.

minima $x_l \approx 2.25$. Since GAs are global optimization schemes, it is expected that they find the solution x_g. This cost function has also negative fitness values; for this reason, the use of proportional selection method is not recommended.

Program 2.1 shows the complete implementation of the binary GA. The implementation also contains several functions considered in order to make its analysis easy. The optimization process can be divided into five sections which correspond to each function: initialization, conversion from binary to decimal value, ranking selection, crossover, and mutation.

Program 2.1 Implementation of the Binary GA in MATLAB®

```
%%%%%%%%%%%%%%%%%%%%%%%%%%%%%%%%%%%%%%%%%%%%%%%%%%%%%%%%%%%%%%%%
% Binary GA implementation
% Erik Cuevas, Alma Rodríguez
%%%%%%%%%%%%%%%%%%%%%%%%%%%%%%%%%%%%%%%%%%%%%%%%%%%%%%%%%%%%%%%%
clear all
global solnew sol pop popnew fitness fitold f range;
%% Objective function
funstr='(x-2)^4+5*(x-2)^3+4*(x-2)^2-4*(x-2)+1';
%% Search space range
range=[-2 3];
f=vectorize(inline(funstr));
%% Parameter Initialization
popsize=10;     % Population size N
MaxGen=120;     % maximal number of generations
nsite=2;        % bits to be mutated
pc=0.95;        % Crossover probability
pm=0.05;        % Mutation probability
nsbit=16;       % Binary string size (bits)
%%The initial population is generated
popnew=init_genA(popsize,nsbit); % Section 1
fitness=zeros(1,popsize);    % Memory is kept
%% Binary string is converted into a decimal value
for i=1:popsize
     solnew(i)=bintodecA(popnew(i,:)); % Section 2
     fitness(i)=f(solnew(i));
end
%% The optimization process begins
for i=1:MaxGen,
     fitold=fitness; pop=popnew; sol=solnew;
     %% A new population is generated applying the ranking
     selection
     for z=1:popsize
          e=selectionR(fitold); % Section 3
          MP(z,:)=pop(e,:);
     end
```

```
    for z1=1:2:popsize
          %% The parents p1 and p2 are selected
          p1=floor(popsize*rand)+1;
          p2=floor(popsize*rand)+1;
          %% Crossover is applied
          if pc>rand,
                  % Products c1 and c2 are generated
                  % Section 4
                  [NP(z1,:),NP(z1+1,:)]=crossoverA(MP(p1,:),MP
                  (p2,:)) ;
          else
                  % Otherwise the parents remain
                  NP(z1,:)=MP(p1,:);
                  NP(z1+1,:)=MP(p2,:);
          end
          %% Mutation is executed
          if pm>rand
                  %% Products n1 y n2 are generated
                  mu1=NP(z1,:);
                  mu2=NP(z1+1,:);
                  NP(z1,:)=mutate(mu1,nsite); % Section 5
                  NP(z1+1,:)=mutate(mu2,nsite);
          end
    end
    %% The binary strings are converted into decimal
    for i=1:popsize
          solnew(i)=bintodecA(NP(i,:)); % Section 2
          fitness(i)=f(solnew(i));
    end
    popnew=NP;
end
%% The final results are shown
x=range(1):0.001:range(2);
plot(x,f(x));
hold on
plot(solnew,fitness,'or');
```

Section 1

The optimization process begins with an initial population. In the absence of information, the best way to create an initial set of candidate solutions is generating random binary strings. For this particular case, a bit string of 17 bits is used. From them, 16 bits correspond to the numeric value, while one represents the sign. To randomly assign the 17 bits in the string, a set of 17 random numbers uniformly distributed are generated. Since such numbers are in the range of [0,1], the numbers with a value higher than 0.5 will be set to one. Otherwise, they will be set to zero. This process is coded in function **init_genA** shown in Program 2.2.

Program 2.2 Implementation of the Function init_genA

```
function pop=init_genA(np,nsbit)
        % np solutions with nsbits to describe the numerical value
        % an extra bit is also defined to indicate the sign
        pop=rand(np,nsbit+1)>0.5;
end
```

Section 2

The binary GA performs the optimization process considering binary strings. Under such conditions, a routine to convert a binary string in decimal data is necessary. The idea with this conversion is to evaluate each candidate solution in terms of the cost function. This routine is repeated in each part of the implementation where it is required for this operation. This process is coded in function **bintodecA** shown in Program 2.3.

Program 2.3 Implementation of the Function bintodecA

```
function [dec]=bintodecA(bin)
        global range;
        % The size of the string is evaluated
        % this part corresponds to the numeric part
        nn=length(bin)-1;
        num=bin(2:end);
        % This is the part that determines the sign
        sign=1-2*bin(1);
        % Accumulator is initialized
        dec=0;
        % The maximal number to represent is determined
        dp=floor(log2(max(abs(range))));
        % Here, the number is converted
        for i=1:nn,
                dec=dec+num(i)*2^(dp-i);
        end
        dec=dec*sign;
```

Section 3

The first genetic operator used in the implementation is the selection operation. The main objective of the selection process is to proliferate good solutions and avoid bad solutions in a population, while it maintains the number of candidate solutions constant. In the problem to solve, the cost function has also negative fitness values; for this reason, the use of a proportional selection method is not recommended. Therefore, the ranking selection method is employed. Under this scheme, all the solutions are organized according to their fitness values. Therefore, the worst solution is assigned rank 1, while the best element corresponds to the rank N. For this propose, the following segment of MATLAB® code is used:

```
1.  [D I] = sort(fP,'descend');
2.  r = 1:length(D);
3.  r(I) = r;
```

In the code, the first line organizes the elements of fP in descending order. Then, lines 2 and 3 assign the appropriate rank to each element. With this new rank assignation, the proportionate selection operator is applied considering the rank numbers instead of the fitness values. To conduct the proportional selection process, the probabilities of selection P_i for each solution i is evaluated. Then, the cumulative probability P_i^A of each element x_i is obtained. To select a solution emulating the proportional selection process, a random number u uniformly distributed is generated. Then, the solution which is the most similar in the cumulative probability range with regard to the number u is selected. This process is coded in function **selectionR** shown in Program 2.4.

Program 2.4 Implementation of the Function selectionR

```
function [iE] = selectionR(fP)
      % It is assigned a rank to each solution
      % The worst has rank 1
      % the best the rank N
      Ps=length(fP);
      [D I] = sort(fP,'descend');
      r = 1:length(D);
      r(I) = r;
      fP=r;
      suma=0;
      % The roulette-wheel process
      for k=1:Ps
            P(k)=fP(k)/(sum(fP));
            suma=suma+P(k);
            A(k)=suma; % cumulative probability
      end
      R=rand;
      for u=1:Ps
            if (A(u)>=R)
      break
            end
      end
      % iE is the selected element
      iE=u;
      end
```

Section 4

In the crossover operation, two candidate solutions **a** and **b** are randomly selected. They act as parents during the process. Then, a number (**cpoint**) from 1 to 17 is also selected randomly. It represents the crossover point from which the string parts will be swapped. This process is coded in function **crossoverA** shown in Program 2.5.

Program 2.5 Implementation of the Function crossoverA

```
function [c,d]=crossoverA(a,b)
        nn=length(a);
        % two new individuals are generated by crossover
        % cpoint represents the point where both
        % solutions are swapped
        cpoint=floor(nn*rand)+1;
        c=[a(1:cpoint) b(cpoint+1:end)];
d=[b(1:cpoint) a(cpoint+1:end)];
```

Section 5

Under the mutation operation, the number of mutations **nsite** is first fixed. It corresponds to the number of bits that will be changed from the original binary string. Then, a cycle that is repeated **nsite** times is initialized. Afterward, in each repetition the following operations are conducted. First, a random bit position from 1 to 17 is selected. Second, this bit is changed to its opposite logic. This process is coded in function **mutate** shown in Program 2.6.

Program 2.6 Implementation of the Function mutate

```
function anew=mutate(a,nsite)
        nn=length(a); anew=a;
        % A new solution is generated with nsite modifications
        % from the original binary string
        for i=1:nsite
                j=floor(rand*nn)+1;
                anew(j)=mod(a(j)+1,2);
        end
```

After running Program 2.1, the system delivers the final solution, such as that shown in Figure 2.9.

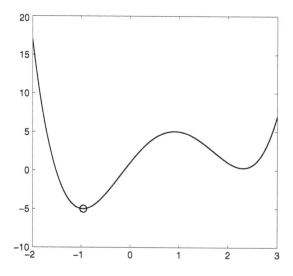

FIGURE 2.9   The result delivered after running Program 2.1.

2.3 GA WITH REAL PARAMETERS

The binary GA presents several difficulties when they face the optimization of continuous cost functions. Binary GAs consider a fixed coding scheme to represent all decision variables. Under such conditions, the binary strings must be devised such that a minimum value of the cost function can fall within their variable values. Since this information is not usually known a priori, this may cause some accuracy errors in the application of binary GAs.

There are several implementations of GA with real parameters. In these implementations, the mutation and crossover operations are directly manipulated through real parameter values. During the operation of a GA with real parameters, real values are considered without using a string coding. Therefore, solving continuous optimization problems, these schemes avoid the use of a conversion step accelerating their execution when they are compared with binary-coded GAs. Different from binary-coded GAs, GA with real parameters allows also to evaluate directly a candidate solution in terms of the cost function.

In spite of these advantages, the main difficulty represents the adaptation of the original binary operators in other that can operate with real values. Crossover and mutation operations are search mechanisms easy to visualize and understand in the binary context. The idea is to design operations that use real-parameter candidate solutions to produce new solutions so that they can be conceived as a search strategy. Therefore, the operation crossover does not represent any more information swapping. It can be interpreted in terms of real parameters as a blending operator.

In this section, the most popular operators for crossover and mutation in terms of real parameters will be discussed.

2.3.1 Real-Parameter Crossover Operator

Linear crossover

One of the first and simple floating-point crossover operators is the linear crossover (Michalewicz, 1996). Under this scheme, two n-dimensional parents $\mathbf{p}_1 = \left\{ p_1^1, \ldots, p_1^n \right\}$ and $\mathbf{p}_2 = \left\{ p_1^1, \ldots, p_1^n \right\}$ are linearly combined to produce three different candidate solutions $\mathbf{c}_1, \mathbf{c}_2$, and $\mathbf{c}_3$ as offspring. These solutions are computed as follows:

$$\mathbf{c}_1 = \mathbf{p}_1 + \mathbf{p}_2$$

$$\mathbf{c}_2 = 1.5\mathbf{p}_1 - 0.5\mathbf{p}_2 \qquad (2.8)$$

$$\mathbf{c}_3 = -0.5\mathbf{p}_1 + 1.5\mathbf{p}_2$$

From the three solutions, the two that maintain the best value in terms of the objective function are selected as the crossover offspring (new candidate solutions).

Arithmetic crossover

In the arithmetic crossover (Michalewicz, 1996), two candidate solutions $\mathbf{p}_1$ and $\mathbf{p}_2$, considered as parents, are blended producing a new solution according to the following model:

$$\mathbf{c}_1 = (1 - \gamma)\mathbf{p}_1 + \gamma\mathbf{p}_2 \qquad (2.9)$$

where $\gamma \in [0,1]$. The new solution c_1 represents the weighted sum of its parents $\mathbf{p}_1$ and $\mathbf{p}_2$.

Blend crossover (BLX-α)

As a result of the blend crossover (BLX-α) (Eshelman & Schaffer, 1993), a new solution c_1 is produced from the combination of two parents $\mathbf{p}_1$ and $\mathbf{p}_2$ so that its results present the following behavior:

$$\mathbf{c}_1 = (1-\rho)\mathbf{p}_1 + \rho\mathbf{p}_2 \qquad (2.10)$$

Different from the arithmetic crossover, the value of ρ is determined as follows:

$$\rho = (1-2\alpha)U(0,1)-\alpha \qquad (2.11)$$

where $U(0,1)$ corresponds to a random number uniformly distributed from 0 to 1. α represents a constant between [0,1].

The BLX-α produces a new solution in the first dimension c_1^1 which corresponds to a random position within the interval $\left[p_1^1 - \alpha\left(p_2^1 - p_1^1\right), p_2^1 - \alpha\left(p_2^1 - p_1^1\right)\right]$. In the BLX-$\alpha$, it is also assumed that $p_1^1 < p_2^1$.

The BLX-α blending operator has the characteristic that the position of the new solution c_1 is located in function on the distance $d(\mathbf{p}_1, \mathbf{p}_2)$ between the parents $\mathbf{p}_1$ and $\mathbf{p}_2$. If $d(\mathbf{p}_1, \mathbf{p}_2)$ is long, then the distances of $d(\mathbf{c}_1, \mathbf{p}_1)$ and $d(\mathbf{c}_1, \mathbf{p}_2)$ between the new solution c_1 and its parents $\mathbf{p}_1$ and $\mathbf{p}_2$ are also large. Under such conditions, the BLX-α allows a better exploration of the search space than the weighted mechanism of the arithmetic crossover. This fact is a consequence of the stochastic component incorporated in Eq. 2.11.

Simulated binary crossover (SBX)

The simulated binary crossover (SBX) (Deb & Agrawal, 1995) scheme emulates the operation of the one-point crossover for binary representations. In SBX, two parents $\mathbf{p}_1$ and $\mathbf{p}_2$ are considered to generate two new solutions c_1 and c_2 as offspring. In the SBX process, a dispersion factor n_c controls the effect of the crossover operation. For large values of n_c, there is a higher probability that the new solutions will be located near the parents $\mathbf{p}_1$ and $\mathbf{p}_2$. For small n_c values, the new solutions c_1 and c_2 will be produced far from the parents. The new solutions c_1 and c_2 in SBX are produced by the following process. First, a quasi-random factor β is generated by the following formulation:

$$\beta = \begin{cases} (2r)^{\frac{1}{n_c+1}} & \text{if } r \leq 0.5 \\ \left(\dfrac{1}{2(1-r)}\right)^{\frac{1}{n_c+1}} & \text{otherwise} \end{cases} \qquad (2.12)$$

where r is random number uniformly distributed $U(0,1)$. Once β is computed, the new solutions c_1 and c_2 are generated as follows:

$$\mathbf{c}_1 = 0.5\big[(1+\beta)\mathbf{p}_1 + (1-\beta)\mathbf{p}_2\big]$$

$$\mathbf{c}_2 = 0.5\big[(1-\beta)\mathbf{p}_1 + (1+\beta)\mathbf{p}_2\big]$$

(2.13)

In order to illustrate the effects of SBX in the production of new individuals, an experiment has been designed. In the experiment, a set of 1,000 crossover operations are executed considering different values of the dispersion factor n_c. Then, the probability density of the new solutions is computed through a histogram of 100 bins. In the experiment, it is assumed that the parents $\mathbf{p}_1$ and $\mathbf{p}_2$ are fixed in positions 2 and 5, respectively. Program 2.7 shows the implementation of SBX and the environment of the experiment in MATLAB.

Program 2.7 Implementation of the SBX Crossover Operation

```
%%%%%%%%%%%%%%%%%%%%%%%%%%%%%%%%%%%%%%%%%%%%%%%%%%%%%%%%%%%%%%%%%%%
% SBX crossover effect experiments
% Erik Cuevas, Alma Rodríguez
%%%%%%%%%%%%%%%%%%%%%%%%%%%%%%%%%%%%%%%%%%%%%%%%%%%%%%%%%%%%%%%%%%%
clear all
% Initialization
nc=2; % Dispersion factor
p1=2; % Parent 1
p2=5; % Parent 2
% Cycle of 1000 executions
for k=1:1000
% Random number U[0,1]
r=rand;
% SBX crossover
if r<=0.5
    mu=(2*r)^(1/(nc+1));
else
    mu=(1/(2*(1-r)))^(1/(nc+1));
end
c1(k)=((1+mu)*p1+(1-mu)*p2)*0.5;
c2(k)=((1-mu)*p1+(1+mu)*p2)*0.5;
end
CT=[c1 c2];
% Histogram of 100 bins
hist(CT,100)
```

Figure 2.10a and b shows the result of the execution of Program 2.7 for the cases of $n_c = 2$ and $n_c = 5$, respectively. According to Figure 2.10, when the value of $n_c = 2$, the solutions are distributed far from the values of their parents. On the other hand, when the value of $n_c = 5$, the solutions are distributed near the values of their parents.

Another remarkable effect of the SBX crossover depends on the parent positions. When the parents are close each other, the new candidate solutions produced are also close to the parents. Conversely, when the parents are distant, the new solutions are generated far from

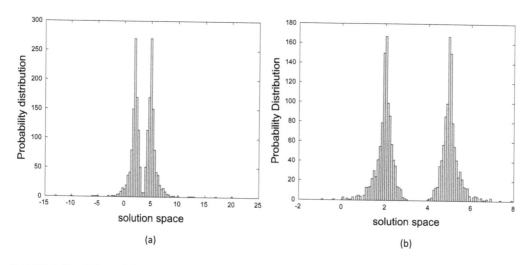

FIGURE 2.10 Effect of the SBX crossover operation for (a) $n_c = 2$ and (b) $n_c = 5$.

the parents. Such conditions happen considering the same dispersion factor n_c. To illustrate this effect, a new experiment has also been designed. In the experiment, a set of 1,000 crossover operations are executed considering the same value of the dispersion factor $n_c = 2$. Then, the probability density of the new solutions is computed through a histogram of 100 bins. In the experiment, it is assumed that the parents $\mathbf{p}_1$ and $\mathbf{p}_2$ are fixed in two positions: (a) $\mathbf{p}_1 = 2$, $\mathbf{p}_2 = 2.5$ and (b) $\mathbf{p}_1 = 2$, $\mathbf{p}_2 = 8$. Program 2.7 is modified to run this experiment. Figure 2.11 shows the distribution of the solutions for both cases.

According to Figure 2.11, it is clear that the new solutions in (b) are distributed near the parents. On the other hand, the new solutions and (b) are distributed far from the original solutions. Therefore, it can be concluded that the distribution of the new solutions has a high implication in relation to the distance of the parents. This effect can be interpreted as an exploration or exploitation mechanism depending on the distance of the parents. When

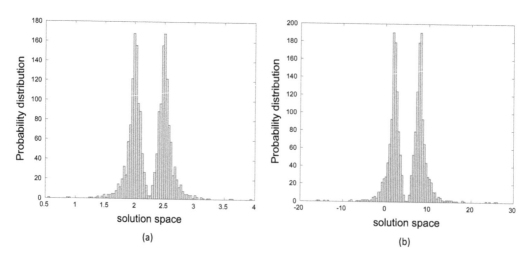

FIGURE 2.11 Effect of the SBX crossover operation for (a) $\mathbf{p}_1 = 2$, $\mathbf{p}_2 = 2.5$ and (b) $\mathbf{p}_1 = 2$, $\mathbf{p}_2 = 8$.

the parents are far from each other, the search mechanism can be considered an exploration of the search space. However, when the parents are near each other, the mechanism corresponds to an exploitation operator.

Unimodal Distributed (UNDX) Operator

The previous crossover operations consider in their process the blending of two parents in order to produce other new solutions. The next part discusses a number of crossover operators where more than two parents are used for the blending process. The use of multi-parent operators allows intensifying the explorative capabilities compared with two-parent operators. With the combination of multi-parent data, a better interchange of spatial information can be reached to produce new solutions in promising areas of the search space.

The unimodal distributed (UNDX) operator (Ono & Kobayashi, 1997) requires three parents for producing new individuals. The new candidate solutions are generated considering an ellipsoidal probability distribution. Such a distribution presents two axes. One axis (**A**) is formed along the line that connects two of the parents. The other axis (**B**) corresponds to the orthogonal direction which is determined from the perpendicular distance of the third parent to the axis **A**. Although the UNDX can be operated with more than three parents, its common use in practical approaches is with three parents. In the process to produce new solutions by the UNDX method, n_μ parents are randomly selected (normally $n_\mu = 3$). Then, the mean that considers only $n_\mu - 1$ parents are computed as follows.

$$\bar{\mathbf{p}} = \frac{1}{n_\mu - 1} \sum_{i=1}^{n_\mu - 1} \mathbf{p}_i \qquad (2.14)$$

Then, the direction vectors $\mathbf{d}_i$ for all these $n_\mu - 1$ parents are calculated as follows $\mathbf{d}_i = \mathbf{p}_i - \bar{\mathbf{p}}$. Afterward, the direction cosines are computed by the following formulation:

$$\mathbf{e}_i = \frac{\mathbf{e}_i}{|\mathbf{e}_i|} \qquad (2.15)$$

where $|\mathbf{e}_i|$ corresponds to the magnitude of the vector $\mathbf{e}_i$. With these vectors, one of the axes is built from the ellipsoid probability distribution. Then, the last (third) parent n_μ is considered to evaluate the other orthogonal axis D whose value is calculated considering three parents $\mathbf{p}_1$, $\mathbf{p}_2$, and $\mathbf{p}_3$ as follows:

$$D = |\mathbf{p}_3 - \mathbf{p}_1| \cdot \left(1 - \left(\frac{(\mathbf{p}_3 - \mathbf{p}_1)^T (\mathbf{p}_2 - \mathbf{p}_1)}{|\mathbf{p}_3 - \mathbf{p}_1| |\mathbf{p}_2 - \mathbf{p}_1|} \right) \right)^{\frac{1}{2}} \qquad (2.16)$$

Figure 2.12 presents an illustration of the ellipsoid probability distribution. In Figure 2.12, square points correspond to parents $\mathbf{p}_1$ and $\mathbf{p}_2$, while the cross point symbolizes the parent $\mathbf{p}_3$. According to Figure 2.12, the probability distribution involves two axes. The first one corresponds to the major axis represented by the vectors $\mathbf{p}_1 - \bar{\mathbf{p}}$ and $\mathbf{p}_2 - \bar{\mathbf{p}}$. The second one represents the minor axis which involves the orthogonal vector D.

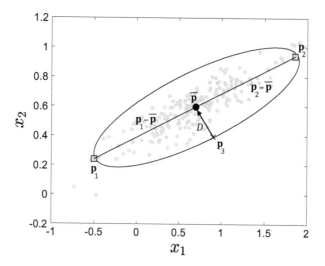

FIGURE 2.12 The ellipsoid probability distribution of the UNDX.

Once the ellipsoid probability distribution is defined, new solutions are produced according to the following model:

$$\mathbf{c}_i = \overline{\mathbf{p}} + \sum_{j=1}^{n_\mu-1} N(0,\sigma_1^2)\big|\mathbf{d}_j\big|\mathbf{e}_j + N\big(0,\sigma_2^2\big)D\mathbf{e}_{n_\mu}, \qquad (2.17)$$

where

$$\sigma_1 = \frac{0.30}{\sqrt{n_\mu-2}}, \qquad \sigma_2 = \frac{0.35}{\sqrt{n_\mu-2}},$$

In order to illustrate the effects of UNDX in the production of new individuals, an experiment has been designed. In the experiment, a set of 500 new individuals are generated considering that the parents are randomly selected from the search space. In the experiment, a two-dimensional case is assumed. Program 2.8 shows the implementation of UNDX and the environment of the experiment in MATLAB.

Program 2.8 Implementation of the UNDX Crossover Operation

```
%%%%%%%%%%%%%%%%%%%%%%%%%%%%%%%%%%%%%%%%%%%%%%%%%%%%%%%%%%%
% UNDX crossover effect experiments
% Erik Cuevas, Alma Rodríguez
%%%%%%%%%%%%%%%%%%%%%%%%%%%%%%%%%%%%%%%%%%%%%%%%%%%%%%%%%%%
clear all
% Number of new solutions generated
Npts=500;
% Selection of parents
p1=randn(1,2);
p2=randn(1,2);
```

```
p3=randn(1,2);
% The parents are highlighted
plot(p1(1),p1(2),'or');
hold on
plot(p2(1),p2(2),'or');
% The mean of the first two parents
m=(p1+p2)/2;
% Directions vectors
d1=p1-m;
d2=p2-m;
d3=p3-m;
% Direction cosines
e1=d1/(norm(d1));
e2=d2/(norm(d2));
e3=d3/(norm(d3));
% The orthogonal axis
D= norm(p3-p1)*((1-((((p3-p1)*(p2-p1)')/
(norm(p3-p1)*norm(p2-p1)))^2))^0.5);
for it=1:Npts
    t1=0.30*randn*norm(d1)*e1+0.30*randn*norm(d2)*e2;
    t2=0.35*randn*D*e3;
    c(it,:)=m+t1+t2;
end
% The solutions are shown
plot(p1(1),p1(2),'o','MarkerSize',10,'MarkerFaceColor','r');
hold on
plot(p2(1),p2(2),'o','MarkerSize',10,'MarkerFaceColor','k');
plot(p3(1),p3(2),'o','MarkerSize',10,'MarkerFaceColor','g');
plot(c(:,1),c(:,2),'ob');
```

Figure 2.13 presents several executions of Program 2.8 where some interesting configurations are illustrated. In this figure, the square points represent parents $\mathbf{p}_1$ and $\mathbf{p}_2$, while the

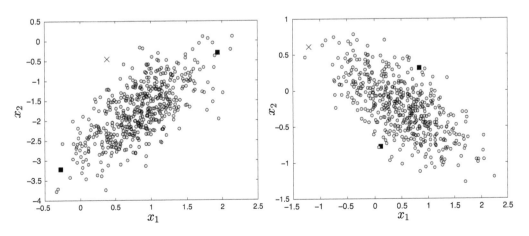

FIGURE 2.13   (a and b) Two different generations of solutions through the UNDX crossover.

cross point symbolizes the parent $\mathbf{p}_3$. In Figure 2.13a, the new solutions are distributed along the major axis that involves the vector of the parents $\mathbf{p}_1$ and $\mathbf{p}_2$. On the other hand, in Figure 2.13b, the produced solutions are scattered in the direction of the D axis.

Parent-centric crossover (PCX)

The parent-centric crossover (PCX) (Deb, Joshi, & Anand, 2002) is a multi-parent crossover operation where new solutions are generated around a selected parent. Although in PCX several parents can be used, its standard application is with only three parents. Under this operation, n_μ parents are randomly selected (normally $n_\mu = 3$) from the current population. Then, one parent $\mathbf{p}_i$ from the existent n_μ is randomly chosen. Therefore, the new individual $\mathbf{c}_i$ is produced near $\mathbf{p}_i$. The process of production is conducted in five stages. In the first step, the central point $\bar{\mathbf{p}}$ of all parents is calculated. In the second step, a direction vector between the selected parent $\mathbf{p}_i$ and central point $\bar{\mathbf{p}}$ is computed as follows $\mathbf{d}_i = \mathbf{p}_i - \bar{\mathbf{p}}$. Afterward, the direction cosines are calculated for all parents as follows $\mathbf{e}_i = \mathbf{e}_i / |\mathbf{e}_i|$

In the fourth step, the orthogonal distances $\delta_j \left(j \in 1,\ldots,n_\mu, \; j \neq i \right)$ of the other $n_\mu - 1$ parents to the vector $\mathbf{d}_i$ are calculated. Then, the average orthogonal distance is assessed as follows:

$$\bar{\delta} = \frac{\sum_{j=1, j \neq i}^{n_\mu} \delta_j}{n_\mu - 1} \tag{2.18}$$

Finally, in the fifth step, a new solution is produced by the following model:

$$\mathbf{c}_k = \mathbf{p}_i + N\left(0, \sigma_1^2\right) |\mathbf{d}_i| + \sum_{j=1, j \neq i}^{n_\mu} N\left(0, \sigma_2^2\right) \bar{\delta} \mathbf{e}_j \tag{2.19}$$

where σ_1 and σ_2 correspond to two factors that determine the size of the dispersion. Figure 2.14 presents an illustration of the generation of 500 new individuals. In Figure 2.12, square points correspond to parents $\mathbf{p}_1$, $\mathbf{p}_2$, and $\mathbf{p}_3$. In this figure, the parent $\mathbf{p}_1$ is always

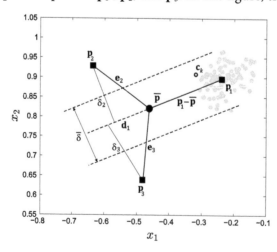

FIGURE 2.14 Generation of solutions under the PCX crossover.

selected to produce new candidate solutions. Therefore, in order to compute a new individual $\mathbf{c}_k$, the orthogonal distances δ_2 and δ_3 are computed with regard to the vector $\mathbf{d}_i$. Then, once the average orthogonal distance $\bar{\delta}$ is computed, the position of $\mathbf{c}_i$ is computed according to the following model:

$$\mathbf{c}_k = \mathbf{p}_1 + N\left(0,\sigma_1^2\right)|\mathbf{d}_1| + N\left(0,\sigma_2^2\right)\bar{\delta}\mathbf{e}_2 + N\left(0,\sigma_2^2\right)\bar{\delta}\mathbf{e}_3 \qquad (2.20)$$

In order to illustrate the effects of PCX in the production of new individuals, an experiment has been designed. In the experiment, a set of 300 crossover operations are executed considering a random parent selection. Then, the position of the computed solutions is plotted. In the experiment, three parents along with $\sigma_1 = 0.15$ and $\sigma_2 = 0.15$ are assumed. Program 2.9 shows the implementation of PCX in MATLAB considering a two-dimensional case.

Program 2.9 Implementation of the PCX Crossover Operation

```
%%%%%%%%%%%%%%%%%%%%%%%%%%%%%%%%%%%%%%%%%%%%%%%%%%%%%%%%%%%%%%%%
% PCX crossover effect experiments
% Erik Cuevas, Alma Rodríguez
%%%%%%%%%%%%%%%%%%%%%%%%%%%%%%%%%%%%%%%%%%%%%%%%%%%%%%%%%%%%%%%%
clear all
% Number of generated points
Npts=300;
% Dispersion factors sigma 1 and sigma 2
sigma1=0.15;
sigma2=0.15;
% Parents are randomly produced
p1=randn(1,2);
p2=randn(1,2);
p3=randn(1,2);
% Calculate the parent central point
m=(p1+p2+p3)/3;
% Direction vector
d1=p1-m;
d2=p2-m;
d3=p3-m;
% Direction cosines
e1=d1/(norm(d1));
e2=d2/(norm(d2));
e3=d3/(norm(d3));
% Cycle of 300 executions
for it=1:Npts
    % One parent is randomly selected
    N = randi(3);
    % If the selected parent is one
    if N==1
        % Orthogonal distance is computed
```

```
                D2= norm(p3-p1)*((1-((((p3-p1)*(m-p1)')/(norm(p3-p1)
                *norm(m-p1)))^2))^0.5);
                D3= norm(p2-p1)*((1-((((p2-p1)*(m-p1)')/
                (norm(p2-p1)*norm(m-p1)))^2))^0.5);
                % The average orthogonal value
                D=(D2+D3)/2;
                c(it,:)=p1+sigma1*randn*d1+sigma2*randn*D*e2+sigma2*randn
                *D*e3;
        end
        % If the selected parent is two
        if N==2
                D1= norm(p3-p2)*((1-((((p3-p2)*(m-p2)')/
                (norm(p3-p2)*norm(m-p2)))^2))^0.5);
                D3= norm(p1-p2)*((1-((((p1-p2)*(m-p2)')/
                (norm(p1-p2)*norm(m-p2)))^2))^0.5);
                D=(D1+D3)/2;
                c(it,:)=p2+sigma1*randn*d2+sigma2*randn*D*e1+sigma2*randn
                *D*e3;
        end
        % If the selected parent is three
        if N==3
                D1= norm(p2-p3)*((1-((((p2-p3)*(m-p3)')/
                (norm(p2-p3)*norm(m-p3)))^2))^0.5);
                D2= norm(p1-p3)*((1-((((p1-p3)*(m-p3)')/
                (norm(p1-p3)*norm(m-p3)))^2))^0.5);
                D=(D1+D2)/2;
                c(it,:)=p3+sigma1*randn*d3+sigma2*randn*D*e1+sigma2*randn
                *D*e2;
        end
end
% Results are shown
plot(c(:,1),c(:,2),'ob');
hold on
plot(p1(1),p1(2),'o','MarkerSize',10,'MarkerFaceColor','r');
plot(p2(1),p2(2),'o','MarkerSize',10,'MarkerFaceColor','k');
plot(p3(1),p3(2),'o','MarkerSize',10,'MarkerFaceColor','g');
```

Figure 2.15 presents several executions of Program 2.9 where some interesting configurations are illustrated. In this figure, the square points represent parents $\mathbf{p}_1$, $\mathbf{p}_2$, and $\mathbf{p}_3$, while points symbolize the new individuals. In Figure 2.15a, the new solutions are produced considering as dispersion factors $\sigma_1 = 0.15$ and $\sigma_2 = 0.15$. On the other hand, in Figure 2.15b, the solutions produced are generated considering as dispersion factors $\sigma_1 = 0.35$ and $\sigma_2 = 0.35$. According to Figure 2.15, when the values of σ_1 and σ_2 are low, the solutions are produced near the parents. However, if the values of σ_1 and σ_2 are high, the solutions are produced far from the parents.

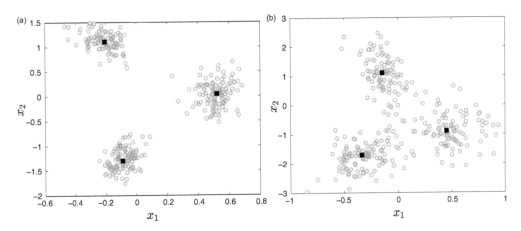

FIGURE 2.15 Two different generation of solutions through the PCX crossover with (a) $\sigma_1 = 0.15$, $\sigma_2 = 0.15$ and (b) $\sigma_1 = 0.35, \sigma_2 = 0.35$.

2.3.2 Real-Parameter Mutation Operator

One important operation in GA is mutation. The main idea of mutation is to modify candidate solutions to increase the population diversity. With this search mechanism, it is possible to avoid local minima. In this sub-section, the main mutation operators for real-parameter approaches are discussed.

Uniform mutation

The simplest mutation approach corresponds to create a solution c_1^U in the neighborhood of the parent solution $\mathbf{p}_1$ with a uniform probability distribution (Michalewicz, 1996). Therefore,

$$c_1^U = \mathbf{p}_1 + (r - 0.5)\delta \tag{2.21}$$

where δ is a calibration factor which represents the magnitude of the allowed perturbation. Through the mutation operation, it is possible that the value of c_1^U can be located outside the specified lower and upper limits. Under such conditions, it is important to protect the code in its implementation to avoid this action.

Normal mutation

Perhaps, the most popular mutation method is to use a zero-mean Gaussian probability distribution (Michalewicz, 1996). Under this scheme, a new solution c_1^N is generated from $\mathbf{p}_1$ through the addition of a random number extracted from a normal Gaussian distribution. For this purpose, the following model is used:

$$c_1^N = \mathbf{p}_1 + N(0, \sigma) \tag{2.22}$$

where σ corresponds to a user-defined parameter. $N(0, \sigma)$ is a normal Gaussian distribution. The parameter σ represents the size of the modification that experiments $\mathbf{p}_1$. σ can also be adaptively adjusted in each iteration according to a determined predefined rule. This factor maintains a big similarity with the mutation operation used commonly in the evolution strategy (ES).

In order to analyze the effect of both mutation operators, a MATLAB program has been implemented to visualize the mutation results. The program is shown in Program 2.10. In the program, it is considered that the parent $\mathbf{p}_1$ is located in 1. For the case of uniform mutation, the parameter δ is set to 0.7, while σ for the case of normal mutation is configured to 0.1. Under such conditions, several mutations will be executed and stored in a vector. The number of mutations needs to be huge to guaranty an appropriate convergence to a certain distribution. Finally, distributions as a form of a histogram are displayed.

Program 2.10 Implementation of Uniform and Normal

```
%%%%%%%%%%%%%%%%%%%%%%%%%%%%%%%%%%%%%%%%%%%%%%%%%%%%%%%%%%%%%%%%
% Uniform and normal mutation
% Erik Cuevas, Alma Rodríguez
%%%%%%%%%%%%%%%%%%%%%%%%%%%%%%%%%%%%%%%%%%%%%%%%%%%%%%%%%%%%%%%%
clear all
% Parent location
p1=1;
% Parameter configuration
delta=0.7; % For uniform
sigma=0.1; % For normal
% Cycle of mutations
for i=1:1000000
        c1(i)=p1+(rand-0.5)*delta; % For uniform
        c2(i)=p1+randn*sigma; % For normal
end
% Histograms for both cases
hist(c1,50)
figure
hist(c2,50)
```

From Program 2.10, the use of the MATLAB functions **rand** and **randn** can be seen for producing random numbers in case of uniform and Gaussian distributions, respectively. Figure 2.16 shows the histograms delivered once Program 2.10 is executed.

Simulated binary mutation

Similar to the SBX, the simulated binary mutation aims to emulate the binary mutation (Hinterding, 1995) but considering a real-parameter scheme. Under this approach, a new solution $\mathbf{c}_1^B$ is produced through the adjustment of a parent solution $\mathbf{p}_1$. It is assumed that the solution space has defined minimal v_{min} and maximal v_{max} values. Since this mutation

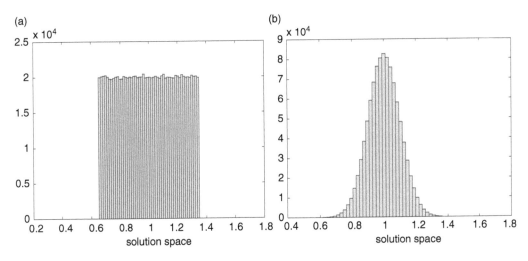

FIGURE 2.16   Effect of the mutation operations for the case of (a) uniform and (b) normal.

operation modifies the parent solutions depending on a binary value, this factor is emulated probabilistically through the parameter p_B. Therefore, the simulated binary mutation is conducted by the following operation:

$$
c_1^B = \begin{cases} \mathbf{p}_1 + (1 - 2 \cdot rand(\cdot)) \cdot (v_{max} - \mathbf{p}_1) & rand(\cdot) \le p_B \\ \mathbf{p}_1 + (1 - 2 \cdot rand(\cdot)) \cdot (\mathbf{p}_1 - v_{min}) & \text{otherwise} \end{cases} \tag{2.23}
$$

where $rand(\cdot)$ corresponds to a random number uniformly distributed. In order to analyze the effect of the simulated binary mutation, a MATLAB program has been implemented to visualize its mutation results. The program is shown in Program 2.11. In the program, it is considered that the parent $\mathbf{p}_1$ is located in 1. It is considered that the solution space of $\mathbf{p}_1$ is defined by the interval $[-3,3]$. Furthermore, the binary probability p_B is set to 0.5. The number of mutations needs to be huge to guaranty an appropriate convergence to a certain distribution. Finally, distributions as a form of a histogram are displayed. Figure 2.17 shows the histograms delivered once Program 2.11 is executed considering four cases (a) $p_B = 0.1$, (b) $p_B = 0.25$, (c) $p_B = 0.5$, and (d) $p_B = 0.9$.

Program 2.11 Implementation of the Simulated Binary Mutation

```
%%%%%%%%%%%%%%%%%%%%%%%%%%%%%%%%%%%%%%%%%%%%%%%%%%%%%%%%%%%%%
% Simulated binary mutation and normal mutation
% Erik Cuevas, Alma Rodríguez
%%%%%%%%%%%%%%%%%%%%%%%%%%%%%%%%%%%%%%%%%%%%%%%%%%%%%%%%%%%%%
clear all
% Parent location
p1=1;
```

```
% Parameter configuration
rangeMax=3; % Max value
rangeMin=-3; % Min Value
pB=0.5; % Binary probability
% Cycle of mutations
for i=1:1000000
        if rand<=pB
                c1(i)=p1+(1-2*rand)*(rangeMax-p1);
        else
                c1(i)=p1+(1-2*rand)*(p1-rangeMin);
        end
end
% Histograms for both cases
hist(c1,50)
```

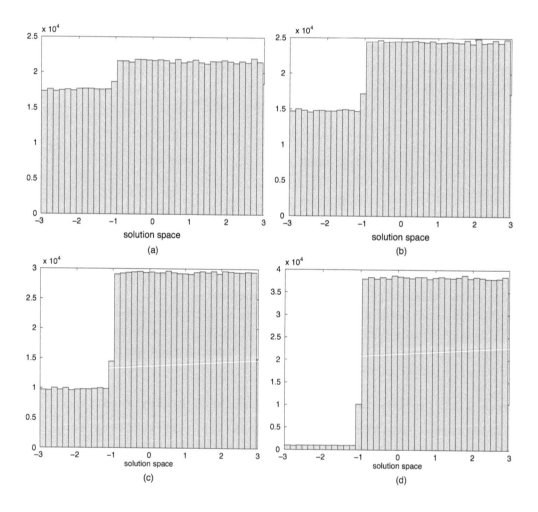

FIGURE 2.17 Effect of the simulated binary mutation operations for the case of (a) $p_B = 0.1$, (b) $p_B = 0.25$, (c) $p_B = 0.5$, and (d) $p_B = 0.9$.

According to Figure 2.17, it is clear that the value of p_B has a big impact on the generation of a new solution. Therefore, as the binary probability p_B increases, the probability that the solution $\mathbf{c}_1^B$ falls within the interval $[-3,-1]$ is higher.

2.3.3 Computational Procedure

In this section, the complete process of the real-parameter GA is integrated and implemented. In order to illustrate its construction, it is considered to maximize the following two-dimensional problem:

$$\text{Maximize} \quad f(x_1,x_2) = 3(1-x_1)^2 e^{-\left(x_1^2 - x_2^2\right)} - 10\left(\frac{x_1}{5} - x_1^3 - x_2^5\right)e^{\left(-x_1^2 - x_2^2\right)} - 1/3e^{\left(-(x_1+1)^2 - x_2^2\right)}$$

$$\text{Subject to} \quad -3 \leq x_1, x_2 \leq 3$$

$$(2.24)$$

The graphical representation of this cost function is shown in Figure 2.18. According to Figure 2.18, the cost function has three maxima, one global maximum in $x_g \approx (0.0, 1.5)$ and two local maxima. Since GAs are global optimization schemes, it is expected that they find the solution x_g. This cost function has also negative fitness values; for this reason, the use of proportional selection method is not recommended.

Program 2.12 shows the complete implementation of the real-parameter GA. The implementation also contains several functions considered in order to make easy its analysis.

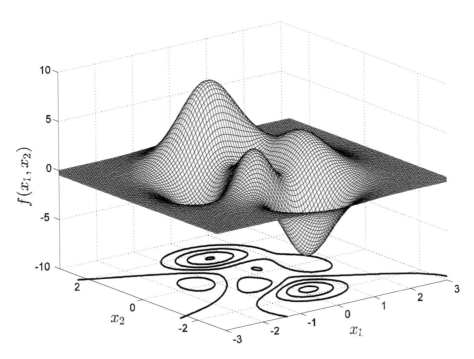

FIGURE 2.18   Cost function example for the implementation of the real-parameter GA.

The optimization process can be divided into five sections which correspond to each function: initialization, conversion from binary to decimal value, ranking selection, crossover, and mutation.

Program 2.12 Implementation of the Real-Parameter GA in MATLAB®

```
%%%%%%%%%%%%%%%%%%%%%%%%%%%%%%%%%%%%%%%%%%%%%%%%%%%%%%%%%%%%%%%%%%%
% Real-parameter GA implementation
% Erik Cuevas, Alma Rodríguez
%%%%%%%%%%%%%%%%%%%%%%%%%%%%%%%%%%%%%%%%%%%%%%%%%%%%%%%%%%%%%%%%%%%
clear all
% Two-dimensional objective function
funstr='3*(1-x).^2.*exp(-(x.^2)-(y+1).^2)-10*(x/5-x.^3-
y.^5).*exp(-x.^2-y.^2)- 1/3*exp(-(x+1).^2 - y.^2)';
% Search space range
range=[-3 3 -3 3];
f=vectorize(inline(funstr));
% Parameter initialization
n=20;               %Population size N
MaxGen=300;         % Maximal number of generations
pc=0.95;            % Crossover probability
pm=0.05;            % Mutation probability
% The objective function is shown
Ndiv=100;
dx=(range(2)-range(1))/Ndiv; dy=(range(4)-range(3))/Ndiv;
[x,y]=meshgrid(range(1):dx:range(2),range(3):dy:range(4));
zin=f(x,y);
figure(1);   surfc(x,y,zin); figure(2);
% Generation of the first population (Section 1)
xrange=range(2)-range(1);
yrange=range(4)-range(3);
xn=rand(1,n)*xrange+range(1);
yn=rand(1,n)*yrange+range(3);
% The optimization process begins
for i=1:MaxGen,
      contour(x,y,zin,15); hold on;
      % Fitness evaluation
      zn=f(xn,yn);
      % A new population is generated applying the ranking
      selection
      for z=1:n
          selectionRM(zn);   % Section 2
          MP(z,1)=xn(e);
          MP(z,2)=yn(e);
      end
```

```
    for z1=1:2:n
        %The parents p1 and p2 are selected
            p1=floor(n*rand)+1;
            p2=floor(n*rand)+1;
            %Crossover is applied (simulated binary crossover SBX)
            if pc>rand,
                % Section 3
                [NP(z1,:),NP(z1+1,:)]=crossoverRE(MP(p1,:),M
                P(p2,:)) ;
            else
                %Otherwise the parents remain
            NP(z1,:)=MP(p1,:);
            NP(z1+1,:)=MP(p2,:);
            end
            % Mutation is executed (Normal mutation)
            if pm>rand,
                mu1=NP(z1,:);
                mu2=NP(z1+1,:);
                % Section 4
                NP(z1,:)=mutateRE(mu1);
                NP(z1+1,:)=mutateRE(mu2);
            end
    end
    % The new population is integrated
    xn=NP(:,1);
    yn=NP(:,2);
    % The final results are shown
    plot(xn,yn,'.','markersize',22,'markerfacecolor','g');
    drawnow;
    hold off;
end
```

Section 1

The optimization process begins with an initial population. In the absence of information, the best way to create an initial set of candidate solutions is generating random numbers within the interval range of each variable. For this particular case, every variable is defined in the range from −3 to 3. Therefore, the population of n individuals is generated by executing the code shown in Program 2.13.

Program 2.13 Implementation of the Population Initialization

```
% Generation of the first population
xrange=range(2)-range(1);
yrange=range(4)-range(3);
xn=rand(1,n)*xrange+range(1);
yn=rand(1,n)*yrange+range(3);
```

Section 2

Similar to the case of binary implementation, the first genetic operator used in the real-parameter program is the selection operation. The main objective of the selection process is to proliferate good solutions and avoid bad solutions in a population, while it maintains the number of candidate solutions constant. In the problem to solve, the cost function has also negative fitness values; for this reason, the use of proportional selection method is not recommended. Therefore, the ranking selection method is employed. Under this scheme, all the solutions are organized according to their fitness values. Therefore, the worst solution is assigned rank 1, while the best element corresponds to the rank N. Different from the binary case in which a minimization operation is considered, in this implementation, the maximization of the objective function is considered. This change modifies the selection operator such that the order of the elements is acquired in ascended order. Under such conditions, the solutions with a bigger value have a higher probability of being selected. The instructions that make the difference for this effect are presented below:

```
1. [D I] = sort(fP,'ascend');
2. r = 1:length(D);
3. r(I) = r;
```

The final process is coded in function **selectionRM** shown in Program 2.14.

Program 2.14 Implementation of the Function selectionRM

```
function [iE] = selectionRM(fP)
        % It is assigned a rank to each solution
        % The worst has rank 1
        % the best the rank N
        Ps=length(fP);
        [D I] = sort(fP,'ascend'); % Configured for maximization
        r = 1:length(D);
        r(I) = r;
        fP=r;
        suma=0;
        % The roulette-wheel process
        for k=1:Ps
                P(k)=fP(k)/(sum(fP));
                suma=suma+P(k);
                A(k)=suma; % cumulative probability
        end
        R=rand;
        for u=1:Ps
                if (A(u)>=R)
                break
                end
        end
```

```
        % iE is the selected element
        iE=u;
end
```

Section 3

The crossover operation is applied under the crossover probability p_m. As a crossover operation, the SBX scheme is implemented. In SBX, two parents $\mathbf{p}_1$ and $\mathbf{p}_2$ are considered to generate two new solutions $\mathbf{c}_1$ and $\mathbf{c}_2$ as offspring. In the SBX process, a dispersion factor n_c controls the effect of the crossover operation. In the suggested program, it has been set as $p_c = 0.95$ and $n_c = 1$. The crossover process is coded in function **crossoverRE** shown in Program 2.15.

Program 2.15 Implementation of the Function crossoverRE

```
function [c,d]=crossoverRE(a,b)
        % Dispersion factor
        nc=1;
        % Random number U[0,1]
        r=rand;
        % SBX crossover
        if r<=0.5
                mu=(2*r)^(1/(nc+1));
        else
                mu=(1/(2*(1-r)))^(1/(nc+1));
        end
        % Generation of individuals for each dimension
        c1x=((1+mu)*a(1)+(1-mu)*b(1))*0.5;
        c1y=((1+mu)*a(2)+(1-mu)*b(2))*0.5;
        c2x=((1-mu)*a(1)+(1+mu)*b(1))*0.5;
        c2y=((1-mu)*a(2)+(1+mu)*b(2))*0.5;

        c(1)=c1x;
        c(2)=c1y;
        d(1)=c2x;
        d(2)=c2y;
end
```

Section 4

The operation of mutation is executed stochastically according to the mutation probability p_m. There exist several mutation schemes. Nevertheless, for the sake of easiness, the normal mutation has been used in this implementation. Under this scheme, a new solution $\mathbf{c}_1^N$ is generated from $\mathbf{p}_1$ through the addition of a random number extracted from a normal Gaussian distribution. In the operation, it is necessary to define the parameter σ which represents the size of the modification that experiments $\mathbf{p}_1$. In the implementation, the parameters p_m and σ are set to 0.05 and 0.1, respectively. This process is coded in function **mutateRE** shown in Program 2.16.

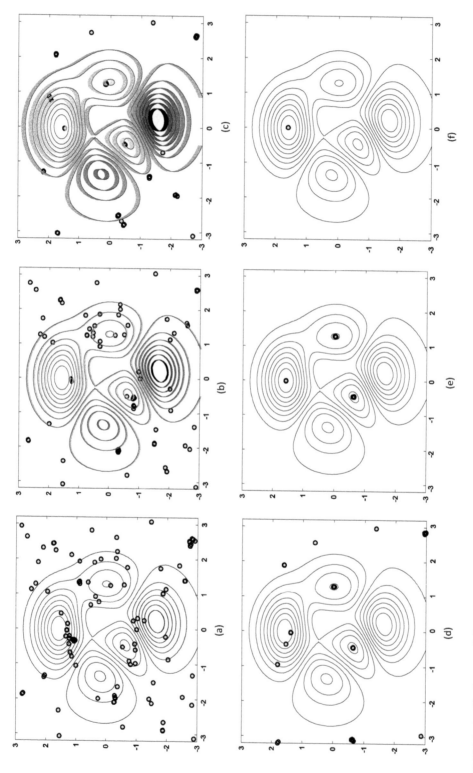

FIGURE 2.19   Evolution of the optimization process performed by the GA. The solution distributions consider (a) initial population, (b) 40 iterations, (c) 100 iterations, (d) 180 iterations, (e) 230 iterations, and (f) 300 iterations.

Program 2.16 Implementation of the Function mutateRE

```
function anew=mutateRE(a)
        % Perturbation size
        sigma=0.1;
        % Two-dimensional mutation
        mx=a(1)+randn*sigma;
        my=a(2)+randn*sigma;
        anew(1)=mx;
        anew(2)=my;
end
```

Figure 2.19 shows the evolution of the optimization process performed by the GA when it tries to solve the problem formulated in Eq. 2.7. In this figure, the solution distributions for different iterations are considered. They present the distribution in the generations (a) initial population, (b) 40 iterations, (c) 100 iterations, (d) 180 iterations, (e) 230 iterations, and (f) 300 iterations. As can be seen from Figure 2.19, as the iterations increase, the algorithm finds the best solutions until it reaches the maximum global value. The performance of GA can be changed if several of its configuration parameters are adjusted.

REFERENCES

Back, T., Pogel, D., & Michalewicz, Z. (Eds.) (1997). *Handbook of evolutionary computation.* Bristol/New York, NY: Institute of Physics Publishing/Oxford University Press.

Blickle, T., & Thiele, L. (1996, December). A comparison of selection schemes used in evolutionary algorithms. *Evolutionary Computation, 4*(4), 361–394.

Darrell, L. W. (1989). The GENITOR algorithm and selection pressure: Why rank-based allocation of reproductive trials is best. In J. D. Schaffer (Ed.), *Proceedings of the 3rd International Conference on Genetic Algorithms* (pp. 116–123). San Francisco, CA: Morgan Kaufmann Publishers Inc.

Deb, K. (1999). An introduction to genetic algorithms. *Sadhana, 24*(4), 293–315.

Deb, K., & Agrawal, R.B. (1995). Simulated binary crossover for continuous space. *Complex Systems, 9*, 115–148.

Deb, K., Joshi, D., & Anand, A. (2002). Real-coded evolutionary algorithms with parent-centric recombination. In K. Deb, D. Joshi, & A. Anand (Eds.) *Proceedings of the IEEE Congress on Evolutionary Computation* (pp. 61–66). Honolulu, HI: IEEE.

Eshelman, L. J., Caruana, R.A., & Schaffer, J. D. (1989). Biases in the crossover landscape. In J. D. Schaffer (Ed.), *Proceedings of the Third International Conference on Genetic Algorithms* (pp. 10–19). San Francisco, CA: Morgan Kaufmann Publishers Inc.

Eshelman, L. J., & Schaffer, J. D. (1993). Real-coded genetic algorithms and interval schemata. In D. Whitley (Ed.), *Foundations of genetic algorithms* (Vol. 2, pp. 187–202). San Mateo, CA: Morgan Kaufmann.

Goldberg, D. E., & Deb, K. (1991). A comparison of selection schemes used in genetic algorithms. In D. E. Goldberg & K. Deb (Ed.) *Foundations of genetic algorithms 1 (FOGA-1)* (pp. 69–93). Elsevier.

Hinterding, R. (1995). Gaussian mutation and self-adaption for numeric genetic algorithms. In R. Hinterding *Proceedings of the International Conference on Evolutionary Computation* (Vol. 1, p. 384). Perth, WA, Australia: IEEE.

Holland, J. H. (1975). *Adaptation in natural and artificial systems.* Ann Arbor, MI: MIT Press.

Michalewicz, Z. (1996). *Genetic algorithms + data structures = evolutionary programs* (3rd ed.). Berlin, Germany: Springer.

Ono, I., Kita, H., & Kobayashi, S. (2003). A real-coded genetic algorithm using the unimodal normal distribution crossover. In A. Ghosh & S. Tsutsui (Eds.), Advances in Evolutionary Computing: Theory and Applications (pp. 213–237). https://doi.org/10.1007/978-3-642-18965-4_8

Ono, I., & Kobayashi, S. (1997). A real-coded genetic algorithm for function optimization using unimodal normal distribution crossover. In T. Back (Ed.), *Proceedings of the Seventh International Conference on Genetic Algorithms* (pp. 246–253). San Francisco, CA: Morgan Kaufmann Publishers Inc.

Vose, M. D. (1999). *Simple genetic algorithm: Foundation and theory*. Ann Arbor, MI: MIT Press.

CHAPTER 3

Evolutionary Strategies (ES)

3.1 INTRODUCTION

In the 1960s, three students of the Technical University of Berlin (Ingo Rechenberg, Hans-Paul Schwefel, and Peter Bienert) tried to solve a problem analytically without obtaining satisfactory results. The problem was difficult to solve, so they came up with trying random solutions. Then, the performance of the solutions was experimentally evaluated. In this way, the students selected those random solutions that worked best for solving the problem. These solutions were modified and re-evaluated to verify if they improved. These modifications were called mutations. If the solutions improved, then they were selected and mutated again. If they did not improve, then the mutated solutions were discarded. The students repeated this process until they managed to find satisfactory results.

The idea and design of this algorithm was based on biological processes. If the species mutated to improve and adapt to changes in the evolutionary process, then the solutions could be improved if they were mutated to evolve. Under this reasoning arises the idea that gave the name of ES to this algorithm.

An interesting fact of the emergence of this method is that its implementation was done experimentally because there were not enough computational resources for its simulation. In the problem, the students tried to modify the shape of a wing, so that the drag in a field of air flow was minimized (Rechenberg, 1965). The solutions they tried were different wing shapes, and they evaluated its performance experimentally.

The first version of the evolution strategy (ES) algorithm, known as $(1 + 1)$ ES (Rechenberg, 1965, 1973), used a simple parent solution that mutated to generate another solution that was called offspring or son. Hence, the name $(1 + 1)$ refers to a father and a son. According to the algorithm, if the offspring were better than the parent solution, then the offspring was selected to be a father and the original father was discarded. Otherwise, the offspring was discarded. The solution that passed the selection process was mutated to generate a new offspring. In this way, the process was repeated until some stop condition was reached.

Another important feature of this first method is that it was designed for discrete problems, so that particle mutations were made in discrete spaces. Because of this, the method tended to stagnate in local optimum. For this reason, the original algorithm $(1 + 1)$ ES was modified by Beyer and Schwefel (2002) to operate in continuous spaces.

Later, other versions of the first method $(1 + 1)$ ES emerged. These new versions included, in addition to the mutation, another operator known as recombination. Additionally, some of the new approaches used a population of solutions instead of a single particle as in the case of the $(1 + 1)$ ES. Furthermore, different forms of mutation, recombination, and selection were also included in the new methods.

Throughout this chapter, the first version of the ES method and its most representative variants will be described in detail, such as the adaptive $(1 + 1)$ ES, the $(\mu + 1)$ ES, the $(\mu + \lambda)$ ES, the (μ, λ) ES, the $(\mu, \alpha, \lambda, \beta)$ ES, the adaptive $(\mu + \lambda)$ ES, and the (μ, λ) ES adaptive.

3.2 THE $(1 + 1)$ ES

As it was stated before, the $(1 + 1)$ ES algorithm implements a parent $\mathbf{x}_p$ in the search process. This particle is randomly initialized. Later, it is mutated to generate a new particle $\mathbf{x}_o$ that represents its offspring. If the new particle $\mathbf{x}_o$ is better than the parent $\mathbf{x}_p$, then $\mathbf{x}_o$ will take the place of $\mathbf{x}_p$. Otherwise, the new particle will be discarded. This evolution process will be described in more detail below.

3.2.1 Initialization

In the initialization stage of the algorithm $(1 + 1)$ ES, a particle $\mathbf{x}_p^0 = \{x_1^0, \ldots, x_d^0\}$ is randomly created with values located within the lower lb and upper ub limits of the d-dimensional search space. Equation 3.1 describes the way in which the particle is initialized.

$$x_j^0 = lb_j + r_j\left(ub_j - lb_j\right) \quad j = 1, 2, \ldots, d \tag{3.1}$$

where x_j^0 corresponds to the initialization of the particle in the dimension j. The lower and upper limits for each dimension are bounded with lb_j and ub_j, respectively. In addition, r_j is a random value within the range $[0, 1]$. Normally, the random value of r_j is generated using a uniform distribution function. However, any other distribution can be used.

In addition to the initialization of the particle $\mathbf{x}_p^0$, the variance σ^2 is also defined. The variance is used to mutate the parent and is a tuning parameter. The value of σ^2 must be chosen in such a way that it maintains a compromise between the exploration and exploitation of the search space. A very large variance value would cause over exploitation, slow convergence, and solutions with poor precision. On the other hand, a small variance value would cause stagnation in local optimum, difficulties in finding solutions, and also slow convergence.

3.2.2 Mutation

In the search strategy of the method $(1 + 1)$ ES, the particle moves in the solution space through a disturbance caused by the mutation operator. In this process, each element of $\mathbf{x}_p$ is mutated with a random value ρ_j that is generated using a normal distribution with zero mean and variance σ^2. Under such conditions, the particle is mutated as defined below:

$$\mathbf{x}_o = \mathbf{x}_p + \rho \tag{3.2}$$

where $\rho = \{\rho_1, \ldots, \rho_d\}$ is a vector of normally distributed random values. In addition, each of its elements is defined as

$$\rho_j = N(0, \sigma^2) \quad j = 1, 2, \ldots, d \tag{3.3}$$

According to Eq. 3.3, the mutation is isometric since the variance used for the mutation of each element of $\mathbf{x}_p$ is the same. This means that the covariance information is ignored, resulting in a standard multivariate normal distribution with zero mean and a covariance matrix Σ defined as

$$\Sigma = \begin{bmatrix} \sigma_1^2 & 0 & \cdots & 0 \\ 0 & \sigma_2^2 & \cdots & 0 \\ \vdots & \vdots & \ddots & \vdots \\ 0 & 0 & \cdots & \sigma_d^2 \end{bmatrix} \tag{3.4}$$

where Σ is a symmetric matrix of size $d \times d$. The main diagonal is formed by the variances associated with each decision variable, whose values are equivalent to σ^2. The symmetry of a normal distribution of this nature can be clearly observed in Figure 3.1, which illustrates a standard bivariate normal distribution.

The normal distribution of Figure 3.1a has a circular shape because the variance is the same for all decision variables. Under these conditions of mutation, the offspring $\mathbf{x}_o$ can be located anywhere in that circular contour, but more likely to be positioned at the center, near the particle $\mathbf{x}_p$. Figure 3.2 illustrates some possible positions where the mutated particle can be located around $\mathbf{x}_p$.

3.2.3 Selection

After the particle $\mathbf{x}_p$ is mutated to generate the offspring $\mathbf{x}_o$, the algorithm (1 + 1) ES uses an elitist selection method to choose the best particle that will pass to the next generation. In the selection, both elements are compared in terms of their quality as a solution.

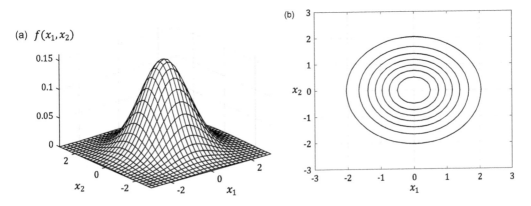

FIGURE 3.1　(a) Standard bivariate normal distribution and (b) its top view.

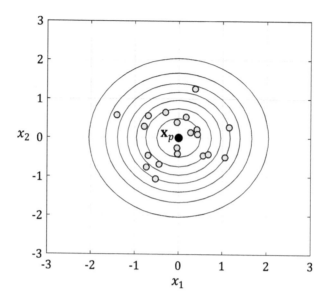

FIGURE 3.2   Distribution of mutated particles in the $(1 + 1)$ ES algorithm.

In this way, if $\mathbf{x}_o$ has a better fitness value, then $\mathbf{x}_o$ will be the new $\mathbf{x}_p$ in the next generation. Otherwise, the original $\mathbf{x}_p$ will remain as the parent element in the next generation. Thus, the selection process is formulated as

$$\mathbf{x}_p^{k+1} = \begin{cases} \mathbf{x}_p^k, & f\left(\mathbf{x}_o^k\right) < f\left(\mathbf{x}_p^k\right) \\ \mathbf{x}_o^k, & f\left(\mathbf{x}_o^k\right) \geq f\left(\mathbf{x}_p^k\right) \end{cases} \tag{3.5}$$

3.3 COMPUTATIONAL PROCEDURE OF THE $(1 + 1)$ ES

So far, the operators of the algorithm $(1 + 1)$ ES have been established, and the method has been generally described. However, in this section, all the details of the algorithm for its computational implementation will be described in greater depth.

3.3.1 Description of the Algorithm $(1 + 1)$ ES

The $(1 + 1)$ ES begins with a randomly generated particle $\mathbf{x}_p^0$ within the limits of the search space using Eq. 3.1. Additionally, the variance σ^2 is initialized. Then, $\mathbf{x}_p^0$ is evaluated in the objective function to determine its quality as a solution.

Subsequently, the iterative process begins, where the mutation vector ρ is generated from Eq. 3.3 to modify the element $\mathbf{x}_p^k$ according to Eq. 3.2 and thereby generate the element $\mathbf{x}_o^k$. Then, the offspring is evaluated in the objective function. Finally, the most suitable individual is selected according to Eq. 3.5. This process is repeated until a stop criterion is reached. The flowchart of the algorithm $(1 + 1)$ ES is shown in Figure 3.3. In addition, the general procedure of the method is presented in Algorithm 3.1.

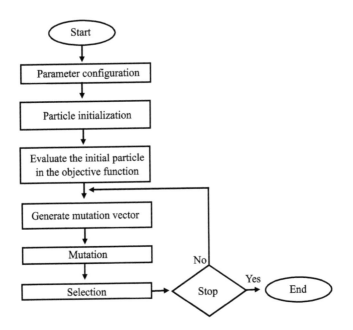

FIGURE 3.3   Flowchart of the algorithm (1 + 1) ES.

Algorithm 3.1 General Procedure of Algorithm (1 + 1) ES

Step 1: Parameter configuration

$$d, lb, ub, k \leftarrow 0, k_{max}, \sigma^2$$

Step 2: Particle initialization

$$\mathbf{x}_p^k \leftarrow \mathbf{r} \cdot (\mathbf{ub} - \mathbf{lb}) + \mathbf{lb}$$

Step 3: Evaluation of the initial particle in the objective function

$$\mathbf{fx}_p^k \leftarrow f\left(\mathbf{x}_p^k\right)$$

Step 4: Generate mutation vector

$$\rho \leftarrow N\left(0, \sigma^2\right)$$

Step 5: Mutation

$$\mathbf{x}_o^k \leftarrow \mathbf{x}_p^k + \rho$$

Step 6: Evaluation of the offspring in the objective function

$$\mathbf{fx}_o^k \leftarrow f\left(\mathbf{x}_o^k\right)$$

Step 7: Selection
if $\text{fx}_o^k < \text{fx}_p^k$

$$\mathbf{x}_p^k \leftarrow \mathbf{x}_o^k$$

$$\text{fx}_p^k \leftarrow \text{fx}_o^k$$

end
Step 8: Verify stop condition

$$\text{if } k == k_{max}$$

$$Best\ solution \leftarrow \mathbf{x}_p^k$$

End the search process
else

$$k \leftarrow k+1$$

Go to Step **4**
end

3.4 MATLAB IMPLEMENTATION OF ALGORITHM (1 + 1) ES

The algorithm (1 + 1) ES has been implemented in the MATLAB® environment with the intention of illustrating the search procedure, which can be observed in Program 3.1.

In the example, it is intended to minimize the objective Rastringin function, whose definition is given by

$$f(\mathbf{x}) = 10d + \sum_{i=1}^{d}\left[x_i^2 - 10\cos(2\pi x_i)\right] \quad x_i \in [-5.12,\ 5.12]; i \in \{1,\ldots,d\} \tag{3.6}$$

where d is the number of dimensions. The Rastringin function has a global optimum $f(\mathbf{x}*) = 0$ at $\mathbf{x}* = \{0,\ldots,0\}$. Therefore, considering $d = 2$, the Rastringin function has a global minimum of zero at $x_1 = 0$ and $x_2 = 0$. The shape of this function is illustrated in Figure 3.4, in which it can be seen that the Rastringin function has a surface with multiple local optimum.

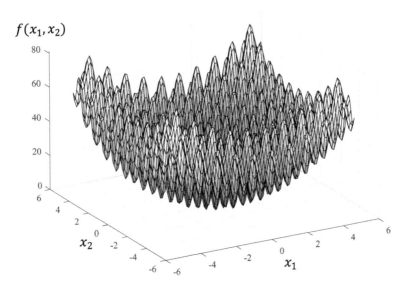

FIGURE 3.4   The Rastringin function considering two dimensions.

Program 3.1 MATLAB® Implementation of the Algorithm (1 + 1) ES

```
%%%%%%%%%%%%%%%%%%%%%%%%%%%%%%%%%%%%%%%%%%%%%%%%%%%%%%%%%%%%%%
%%%%%%%%%%%
% Evolution Strategies algorithm (1+1) ES
% Erik Cuevas, Alma Rodríguez
%%%%%%%%%%%%%%%%%%%%%%%%%%%%%%%%%%%%%%%%%%%%%%%%%%%%%%%%%%%%%%
%%%%%%%%%%%

%% Clear memory and close windows
clear all
close all
%% Parameter configuration
d = 2;                % Number of dimensions
lb = [-5.12 -5.12];% Lower bound
ub = [5.12 5.12];  % Upper bound
k = 0;                % Iteration counter
kmax = 500;           % Maximum number of iterations
sigma = 2;            % Standard deviation
sigma2 = sigma^2;  % Variance
%% Optimization problem (minimization), definition of the
objective function
f = @(x) 10*d + sum(x.^2 - 10*cos(2*pi.*x));
%% Particle initialization
Xp = rand(1,d).*(ub-lb)+lb;
%% Evaluation of the initial particle in the objective function
fXp = f(Xp);
%% Definition of the search space
xAxis=linspace(min(lb),max(ub),85);
```

```
yAxis=xAxis;
zAxis=[];
for i = 1:length(xAxis)
      for j = 1:length(yAxis)
            zAxis(i,j) = f([xAxis(i) yAxis(j)]);
      end
end
[yAxis,xAxis] = meshgrid(xAxis,yAxis);
%% Iterative process
while k<kmax
      %% Generate mutation vector
      rho = normrnd(0,sigma,1,d);
      %% Mutation
      Xo = Xp + rho;
      %% Verify search space limits
      for j=1:d
            if Xo(j) < lb(j)
                  Xo(j) = rand*(ub(j)-lb(j))+lb(j);
            elseif Xo(j) > ub(j)
                  Xo(j) = rand*(ub(j)-lb(j))+lb(j);
            end
      end
      %% Evaluation of the offspring in the objective function
      fXo = f(Xo);
      %% Draw the search space
      figure(1);
      surf(xAxis,yAxis,zAxis)
      hold on
      %% Draw particles Xp and Xo
      plot3(Xp(1),Xp(2),fXp,'o','MarkerFaceColor','m','Marker
      Size',10)
      plot3(Xo(1),Xo(2),fXo,'o','MarkerFaceColor','y','Marker
      Size',10)
      pause(0.01)
      hold off
      %% Draw the contour space
      figure(2)
      contour(xAxis,yAxis,zAxis,20)
      hold on
      %% Draw Xp and Xo in the contour space
      plot(Xp(1),Xp(2),'o','MarkerFaceColor','m');
      plot(Xo(1),Xo(2),'o','MarkerFaceColor','y');
      pause(0.01)
      hold off
      %% Selection
      if fXo < fXp
            Xp = Xo;
```

```
        fXp = fXo;
    end
    k=k+1;
end
%% Show results
display(['Best solution: x1= ',num2str(Xp(1)),', x2= ',
num2str(Xp(2))])
display([' f(X)= ',num2str(fXp)])
```

In the implementation described in Program 3.1, the Rastringin function has been considered in two dimensions, 500 iterations, and variance $\sigma^2 = 4$. In addition, the code needed to draw the search process has been included. At the end of the execution of Program 3.1, it is possible to observe that the solution found by the algorithm (1 + 1) ES approximates the expected solution. However, the method does not always reach or approach the global minimum due to the complexity of the objective function. For this reason, other variants arise with the idea of outperforming the algorithm, and thereby obtain better solutions with greater accuracy in less time.

3.5 ES VARIANTS

In the algorithm (1 + 1) ES, the value of the parameter σ is decisive in the search process. It is desirable that this value is not fixed, since in the first iteration, its value is required to be large enough to achieve a broad exploration of the solution space. However, as the search progresses, its value should decrease to refine the solution. Thus, it is important to determine the initial value of σ and define how to decrease it over the course of the iterations. Due to these observations, Rechenberg proposes an improved version of the (1 + 1) ES known as adaptive (1 + 1) ES, and this version will be described in the next section.

3.5.1 Adaptive (1 + 1) ES

Adaptive (1 + 1) ES improves the search strategy by modifying σ in such a way that its value adjusts automatically over the time. This method is based on the theory that 20% of the mutations should be successful (in terms of improving the quality of the solution) in order to conclude that the value of σ is adequate. If the percentage of improvement is greater than 20%, then the mutations are very small, that is, the value of σ is small. This causes small improvements and long convergence time. On the other hand, if the percentage of improvement is less than 20%, then the mutations are very large, so the value of σ is big and the improvements are large, but infrequent. This also causes a lot of time to converge to an acceptable solution.

The rule of the $\frac{1}{5}$ proposed by Rechenberg derives from the explanation above. This rule states that if the success rate of mutations is less than $\frac{1}{5}$, then the value of the standard deviation σ must be decreased. Otherwise, if the success rate is greater than $\frac{1}{5}$, then the value of σ must be increased.

With this rule it is possible to establish a guide that indicates when the standard deviation σ should be modified. However, another question arises about how much σ should be modified based on this rule. For this, Schwefel proposes a factor that allows to increase or decrease the value of σ according to the $\frac{1}{5}$ rule. This factor is a constant c whose suggested value is 0.817. Then, using the c factor, it is possible to adapt the sigma value as follows:

$$\sigma = c\sigma \tag{3.7}$$

$$\sigma = \frac{\sigma}{c} \tag{3.8}$$

The expression given by Eq. 3.7 makes possible to decrease the sigma value, while Eq. 3.8 allows to increase its value.

To calculate the percentage of success, it is necessary to determine a range of analysis to measure the success of mutations. The objective is to establish a time window w to analyze the mutations, given a constant sigma value during that period of time. The range of analysis should be large enough, so that it is possible to obtain sufficient information to determine the success of mutations. However, it is desired that this analysis window is not too large to hinder the sigma adaptation process. An acceptable recommendation is to set the window w under the following considerations:

$$w = \min(d, 30) \tag{3.9}$$

where d is the number of dimensions in the optimization problem. Considering the value of w and the number of times nm that the solution improved during that interval of time, the success percentage is determined as

$$\varphi = \frac{nm}{w} \tag{3.10}$$

Thus, the sigma adaptation is carried out as follows:

$$\sigma = \begin{cases} c\sigma, & \varphi < \dfrac{1}{5} \\[2mm] \dfrac{\sigma}{c}, & \varphi > \dfrac{1}{5} \end{cases} \tag{3.11}$$

The general procedure of adaptive $(1 + 1)$ ES is presented in Algorithm 3.2.

Algorithm 3.2 General Procedure of the Adaptive (1+1) ES

Step 1: Parameter configuration

$$d, lb, ub, k \leftarrow 0, k_{max}, \sigma^2, w, c$$

Step 2: Particle initialization

$$\mathbf{x}_p^k \leftarrow \mathbf{r} \cdot (\mathbf{ub} - \mathbf{lb}) + \mathbf{lb}$$

Step 3: Evaluation of the initial particle in the objective function

$$\mathbf{fx}_p^k \leftarrow f\left(\mathbf{x}_p^k\right)$$

Step 4: Generate mutation vector

$$\rho \leftarrow N\left(0, \sigma^2\right)$$

Step 5: Mutation

$$\mathbf{x}_o^k \leftarrow \mathbf{x}_p^k + \rho$$

Step 6: Evaluation of the offspring in the objective function

$$\mathbf{fx}_o^k \leftarrow f\left(\mathbf{x}_o^k\right)$$

Step 7: Selection
if $\mathbf{fx}_o^k < \mathbf{fx}_p^k$

$$\mathbf{x}_p^k \leftarrow \mathbf{x}_o^k$$

$$\mathbf{fx}_p^k \leftarrow \mathbf{fx}_o^k$$

end
Step 8: Sigma adaptation

$$\varphi \leftarrow \frac{nm}{w}$$

$$\text{if } \varphi < \frac{1}{5}$$

$$\sigma \leftarrow c\sigma$$

$$\text{else if } \varphi > \frac{1}{5}$$

$$\sigma \leftarrow \frac{\sigma}{c}$$

end

Step 9: Verify stop condition

if $k == k_{max}$

$$Best\ solution \leftarrow \mathbf{x}_p^k$$

End of the search process

else

$$k \leftarrow k+1$$

Go to **Step 4**

end

The adaptive $(1 + 1)$ ES algorithm has been implemented in the MATLAB environment with the intention of illustrating the search procedure, which can be observed in Program 3.2. As in Program 3.1, the Rastringin function was used considering two dimensions, 500 iterations, and an initial sigma σ equal to 2. In addition, a factor $c = 0.817$ and a time window $w = 20$ have been contemplated.

Program 3.2 MATLAB® Implementation of the Adaptive (1+1) ES

```
%%%%%%%%%%%%%%%%%%%%%%%%%%%%%%%%%%%%%%%%%%%%%%%%%%%%%%%%%%%%%%%%%
%%%%%%%%%%%%
% Adaptive (1+1) ES algorithm
% Erik Cuevas, Alma Rodríguez
%%%%%%%%%%%%%%%%%%%%%%%%%%%%%%%%%%%%%%%%%%%%%%%%%%%%%%%%%%%%%%%%%
%%%%%%%%%%%%
%% Clear memory and close windows
clear all
close all
%% Parameter configuration
d = 2;                 % Number of dimensions
lb = [-5.12 -5.12];% Lower bound
ub = [5.12 5.12];  % Upper bound
k = 0;                 % Iteration counter
kmax = 500;            % Maximum number of iterations
sigma=2;               % Standard deviation
sigma2= sigma^2;       % Variance
w = 20;                % Window
c = 0.817;             % Constant factor
phi = 0;               % Mutation rate
nm = 0;                % Number of successful mutations
cont=0;                % Counter
```

```
%% Optimization problem (minimization), objective function
definition
f = @(x) 10*d + sum(x.^2 - 10*cos(2*pi.*x));
q%% Particle initialization
Xp = rand(1,d).*(ub-lb)+lb;
%% Evaluation of the initial particle in the objective function
fXp = f(Xp);
%% Determine the search space
xAxis=linspace(min(lb),max(ub),85);
yAxis=xAxis;
zAxis=[];
for i = 1:length(xAxis)
      for j = 1:length(yAxis)
              zAxis(i,j) = f([xAxis(i) yAxis(j)]);
      end
end
[yAxis,xAxis] = meshgrid(xAxis,yAxis);
%% Iterative process
while k<kmax
   %% Generate mutation vector
   rho = normrnd(0,sigma,1,d);
   %% Mutation
   Xo = Xp + rho;
   %% Verify the limits of the search space
   for j=1:d
            if Xo(j) < lb(j)
                 Xo(j) = rand*(ub(j)-lb(j))+lb(j);
            elseif Xo(j) > ub(j)
                 Xo(j) = rand*(ub(j)-lb(j))+lb(j);
            end
   end
   %% Evaluate the offspring in the objective function
   fXo = f(Xo);
   %% Draw the search space
   figure(1);
   surf(xAxis,yAxis,zAxis)
   hold on
   %% Draw particles Xp y Xo
   plot3(Xp(1),Xp(2),fXp,'o','MarkerFaceColor','m','Marker
   Size',10)
   plot3(Xo(1),Xo(2),fXo,'o','MarkerFaceColor','y','Marker
   Size',10)
   pause(0.01)
   hold off
   %% Draw the contour contorno of the search space
   figure(2)
   contour(xAxis,yAxis,zAxis,20)
```

```
      hold on
      %% Draw Xp y Xo in the contour
      plot(Xp(1),Xp(2),'o','MarkerFaceColor','m');
      plot(Xo(1),Xo(2),'o','MarkerFaceColor','y');
      pause(0.01)
      hold off
      %% Selection
      if fXo < fXp
            Xp = Xo;
            fXp = fXo;
            nm = nm + 1;
      end
      %% Sigma adaptation
      if k > 30
            cont = cont + 1;
            if cont == w
                  phi = nm/w;
                  if phi < 1/5
                        sigma = c*sigma;
                  elseif phi > 1/5
                        sigma = sigma/c;
                  end
                  cont = 0;
                  nm = 0;
            end
      end
      k=k+1;
end
%% Show results
display(['Best solution: x1= ',num2str(Xp(1)),', x2= ',
num2str(Xp(2))])
display([' f(X)= ',num2str(fXp)])
```

After the execution of Program 3.2, it is notable that the obtained result is closer to the expected solution than the one found by the algorithm (1 + 1) ES. The adaptive method achieves greater precision and requires less time to find the solution than the method (1 + 1) ES. However, the adaptive (1 + 1) ES does not always manage to approach the global optimum due to the complexity of the Rastringin function. Occasionally, the adaptive method stagnates in local optimum due to the randomness and the gradual reduction of the standard deviation. Over the course of the time, the adaptation of sigma causes smaller mutations that prevent scaping from local solutions. Thus, it is not possible to continue exploring potential solutions. However, it allows to refine the potential solutions already found.

To contrast the performance of the (1 + 1) ES against the adaptive (1 + 1) ES, both methods have been executed 100 times using the Rastringin function in 30 dimensions. In each execution, 500 iterations and a standard deviation equal to two have been considered. In addition, a factor $c = 0.817$ and a time window $w = 30$ have been considered for the adaptive

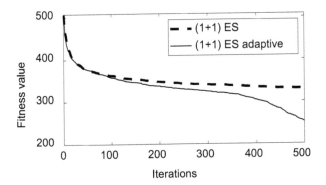

FIGURE 3.5 Convergence analysis of algorithm (1 + 1) ES and adaptive (1 + 1) ES. Performance comparison of both methods for the Rastringin function in 30 dimensions, considering the average result of 100 independent executions.

method. The average of the results obtained by both algorithms in each iteration is illustrated in Figure 3.5.

In Figure 3.5, it can be seen that the adaptive (1 + 1) ES algorithm achieves a lower cost than the (1 + 1) ES. In addition, the adaptive method converges faster. However, the $\frac{1}{5}$ rule does not always work for all problems. The success of the adaptive method depends on several factors, such as the number of dimensions of the problem, the type of surface of the objective function, the proper selection of the initial value of σ, and the determination of the time window. Thus, if the same comparative exercise in Figure 3.5 is performed using the same parameters, but with another objective function, it will be possible to observe that the performance of the adaptive (1 + 1) ES method is not superior to the (1 +1) ES. To verify this, the performance of both methods is illustrated in Figure 3.7. For this, the average of the results obtained during 100 independent executions and the optimization of the Salomon function have been considered. This function is illustrated in Figure 3.6, and its definition is given by

$$f(\mathbf{x})=1-\cos\left(2\pi\sqrt{\sum_{i=1}^{d}x_i^2}\right)+0.1\sqrt{\sum_{i=0}^{d}x_i^2} \quad x_i \in[-100,\,100];i \in\{1,\ldots,d\} \qquad (3.12)$$

Like the Rastringin function, the Salomon function has a global optimum $f(\mathbf{x}^*)=0$ at $\mathbf{x}^*=\{0,\ldots,0\}$ and has a surface with multiple local optimal observed in Figure 3.6.

Figure 3.7 shows how the adaptive (1 + 1) ES method tends to stagnate in sub-optimal solutions, while the (1 + 1) ES manages to get closer to the optimal solution. By not having the same scanning capacity as the (1 + 1) ES, the adaptive method can easily get stuck in a sub-optimal solution when the objective function is highly complex and the initial sigma value and the size window are not appropriate.

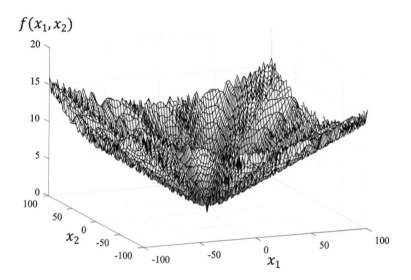

FIGURE 3.6   Salomon function considering two dimensions.

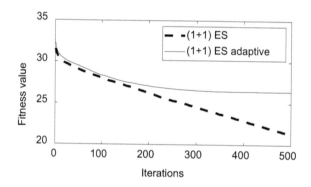

FIGURE 3.7   Convergence analysis of the (1 + 1) ES and the adaptive (1 + 1) ES algorithm. Performance comparison of both methods for the Salomon function in 30 dimensions, considering the average result of 100 independent executions.

Although the $\frac{1}{5}$ rule does not always generate optimal results and requires some ability to properly configure the necessary parameters, it is certainly a guide that allows a functional and general implementation of the ES algorithm.

3.5.2 $(\mu+1)$ ES

A population version arises after the $(1 + 1)$ ES. This method uses a set of individuals for the search process instead of just one particle. The main objective of using a population is to accelerate the search by exchanging information between the particles. The difference from previous versions is that the $(\mu+1)$ ES algorithm implements μ parents in each generation, where every parent $\mathbf{x}_{pi}$ has a vector $\boldsymbol{\sigma}_{pi}$ that controls the magnitude of its movements in

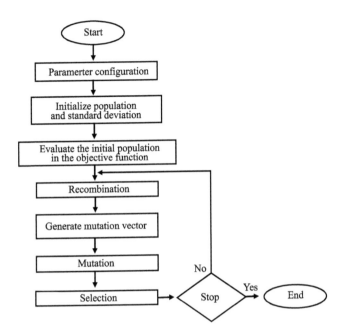

FIGURE 3.8   Flowchart of the $(\mu+1)$ ES algorithm.

each dimension. In each iteration, two parents $\mathbf{x}_{pa}$ and $\mathbf{x}_{pb}$ are randomly selected and then recombined to generate a single offspring $\mathbf{x}_o$. Subsequently, the son $\mathbf{x}_o$ is mutated. Finally, the best μ individuals are selected from the μ parents and the child to create the new population of μ parents who become part of the next generation.

The flowchart that represents the $(\mu+1)$ ES algorithm is illustrated in Figure 3.8. By contrasting the flowchart from Figure 3.3 against the one from Figure 3.8 (corresponding to the methods $(1 + 1)$ ES and $(\mu+1)$ ES, respectively), it is possible to detect two important differences: The first corresponds to the fact that the $(\mu+1)$ ES is a population algorithm, while the second points to the recombination operator, which was not considered in the algorithm $(1 + 1)$ ES.

In the recombination method, the information is exchanged between the parents. The objective of this mechanism is to generate an offspring that includes a combination of the parents' characteristics. In the recombination used by the $(\mu+1)$ ES, not only is the information of the position of the parent exchanged to generate the child, but their standard deviation vectors are also recombined to obtain the $\boldsymbol{\sigma}_o$ vector of the offspring.

There are several methods of recombination, such as discrete sexual, intermediate, global or panmitic, global discrete, and global intermediate recombination. In discrete sexual recombination, the offspring $\mathbf{x}_o$ is formed by randomly taking elements from each parent $\mathbf{x}_{pa}$ and $\mathbf{x}_{pb}$. Similarly, the vector of standard deviations $\boldsymbol{\sigma}_o$ associated with the child is formed by randomly taking elements from the vectors of standard deviations $\boldsymbol{\sigma}_{pa}$ and $\boldsymbol{\sigma}_{pb}$ of each parent. An example of discrete sexual recombination is illustrated in Figure 3.9.

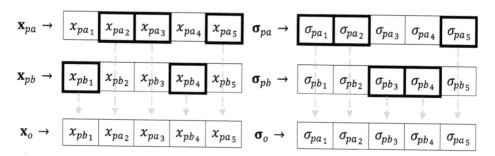

FIGURE 3.9 Example of discrete sexual recombination considering a five-dimensional problem, where each element of $\mathbf{x}_o$ is randomly chosen from the parents $\mathbf{x}_{pa}$ and $\mathbf{x}_{pb}$, which are also randomly chosen from the entire population.

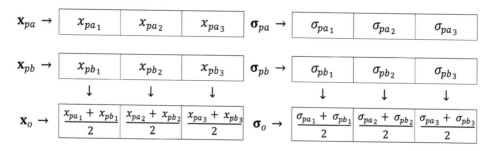

FIGURE 3.10 Example of intermediate sexual recombination considering a three-dimensional problem, where each element of $\mathbf{x}_o$ is determined with the average of the information of the parents $\mathbf{x}_{pa}$ and $\mathbf{x}_{pb}$, which are chosen randomly from the entire population.

In the intermediate sexual recombination, it is characterized by taking the average information of both parents for the generation of the child. Figure 3.10 illustrates this process more clearly. In the case of global or panmitic recombination, the construction of the child is done considering all the parents as potential participants in the recombination process. In such a way that, not only are two parents considered as in the discrete sexual recombination method but also any parent can provide information for the generation of the offspring.

By joining discrete sexual recombination with global or panmitic, global discrete recombination arises. In this kind of recombination, each element of the child is formed with the information of a randomly selected parent from the entire population. An example of this type of recombination can be seen in Figure 3.11.

Also, it is possible to mix the intermediate sexual recombination with the global one, resulting in the global intermediate recombination. In this type of recombination, each element of the offspring is determined with the average of the information of two parents, who are randomly chosen from the entire population. The difference between the sexual intermediate and the global intermediate recombination is that, in the sexual intermediate, two parents are randomly chosen and with the average of their information all the elements of the offspring are generated, while in the global intermediate, a couple of parents is randomly chosen each time an element of the offspring is determined. An example

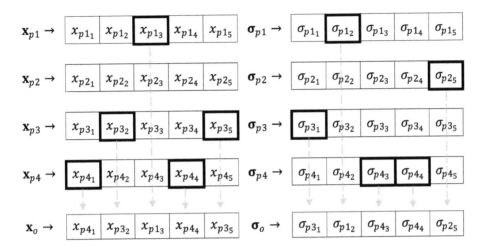

FIGURE 3.11 Example of global discrete recombination considering a population of $\mu = 4$ individuals and a five-dimensional problem, where each element of $\mathbf{x}_o$ is randomly chosen from the entire population.

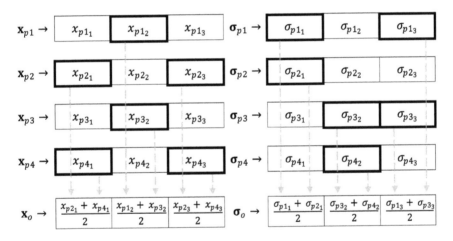

FIGURE 3.12 Example of global intermediate recombination considering a population of $\mu = 4$ individuals and a three-dimensional problem, where each element of $\mathbf{x}_o$ is determined with the average of the information of two parents randomly chosen from the entire population.

of global intermediate recombination is illustrated in Figure 3.12. There are other types of recombination that have been proposed. However, these methods are beyond the scope of this chapter.

Another difference between the $(1 + 1)$ ES and the $(\mu + 1)$ ES is that in the $(\mu + 1)$ ES the particles move in the solution space under a disturbance caused by a non-isometric mutation. In addition, in the $(\mu + 1)$ ES method, the particle that mutates is the offspring, instead of the father. Also, the variance of each element of the offspring $\mathbf{x}_o$ is not the same. Under these conditions, the mutation of each child in the $(\mu + 1)$ ES is defined as

$$\mathbf{x}_o = \mathbf{x}_o + \rho \tag{3.13}$$

where $\rho = \{\rho_1, \ldots, \rho_d\}$ is a vector of normally distributed random values, and each of its elements is defined as follows:

$$\rho_j = N(0, \Sigma) \quad j = 1, 2, \ldots, d \tag{3.14}$$

According to Eq. 3.14, the mutation operation uses a multivariate normal distribution with zero mean and a covariance matrix Σ defined as

$$\Sigma = \begin{bmatrix} \sigma_{o_1}^2 & 0 & \cdots & 0 \\ 0 & \sigma_{o_2}^2 & \cdots & 0 \\ \vdots & \vdots & \ddots & \vdots \\ 0 & 0 & \cdots & \sigma_{o_d}^2 \end{bmatrix} \tag{3.15}$$

where Σ is a $d \times d$ symmetric matrix and the main diagonal is formed by the variances corresponding to each element of σ_o. The shape of a normal distribution of this nature can be clearly observed in Figure 3.13, which illustrates a normal non-isometric bivariate distribution.

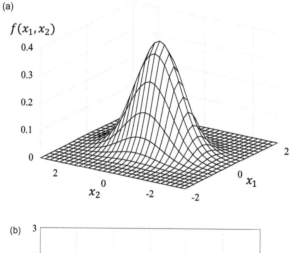

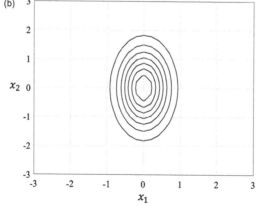

FIGURE 3.13   (a) Normal non-isometric bivariate distribution and (b) its top view.

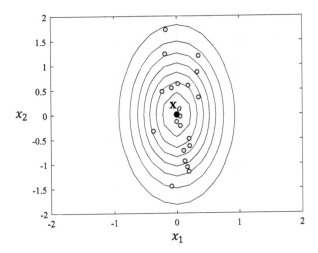

FIGURE 3.14 Distribution of mutated particles in the algorithm $(\mu+1)$ ES.

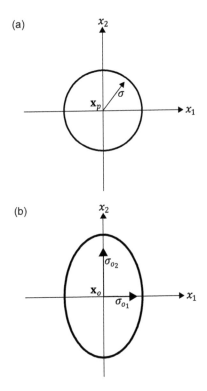

FIGURE 3.15 Mutation distribution of (a) the (1+1) ES and (b) the $(\mu+1)$ ES.

Figure 3.14 illustrates some possible positions where the mutated particle can be located around $\mathbf{x}_o$, while Figure 3.15 shows a comparison between the mutation distribution of the (1 + 1) ES method and the $(\mu+1)$ ES.

The general procedure of the $(\mu+1)$ ES is presented in Algorithm 3.3, in which a discrete sexual recombination has been used. In addition, its implementation in the MATLAB environment can be observed in Program 3.3, where the Rastringin function has been used in two dimensions, with a population $\mu = 3$ and 500 iterations.

As can be seen in Algorithm 3.3, the $(\mu + 1)$ ES method does not include the adaptive strategy based on the $\frac{1}{5}$ rule used by the adaptive (1+1) ES. Instead, the $(\mu + 1)$ ES uses the recombination of the standard deviation vectors associated with each individual. With this mechanism, the variances are modified in each direction, and thereby the size of the particle's movements. However, the variances do not decrease progressively and adaptively over the course of iterations. However, at the end they all tend to converge towards a single value due to the recombination that occurs between the same elements.

When executing Program 3.3 it is notable that the solution obtained approximates the global minimum, although it does not always achieve the expected result. With the idea of improving the algorithm $(\mu + 1)$ ES, other very similar variants arise, which will be studied in the following sections.

Algorithm 3.3 General Procedure of the $(\mu + 1)$ ES Method

Step 1: Parameter configuration

$$\mu, d, lb, ub, k \leftarrow 0, k_{max}$$

Step 2: Initialize particles and standard deviations
for $i = 1; i \leq \mu; i++$

$$\mathbf{x}_{pi}^k \leftarrow \mathbf{r} \cdot (\mathbf{ub} - \mathbf{lb}) + \mathbf{lb}$$

$$\sigma_{pi}^k \leftarrow rand(); \ \sigma_{pi}^k \in \mathbb{R}^d$$

end
Step 3: Evaluate initial particles in the objective function
for $i = 1; i \leq \mu; i++$

$$\mathbf{fx}_{pi}^k \leftarrow f\left(\mathbf{x}_{pi}^k\right)$$

end
Step 4: Select parents

$$\left(\mathbf{x}_{pa}^k, \sigma_{pa}^k\right) \leftarrow rand\left(\mathbf{x}_p^k, \sigma\varpi_p^k\right)$$

$$\left(\mathbf{x}_{pb}^k, \sigma_{pb}^k\right) \leftarrow rand\left(\mathbf{x}_p^k, \sigma_p^k\right)$$

Step 5: Recombination

$$\mathbf{x}_o^k \leftarrow recombination\left(\mathbf{x}_{pa}^k, \mathbf{x}_{pb}^k\right)$$

$$\sigma_o^k \leftarrow recombination\left(\sigma_{pa}^k, \sigma_{pb}^k\right)$$

Step 6: Generate mutation vector

$$\Sigma \leftarrow diag\left(\left(\sigma_{o_1}^k\right)^2, \ldots, \left(\sigma_{o_d}^k\right)^2\right) \in \mathbb{R}^{d \times d}$$

$$\rho \leftarrow N\left(0, \Sigma\right)$$

Step 7: Mutation

$$\mathbf{x}_o^k \leftarrow \mathbf{x}_o^k + \rho$$

Step 8: Evaluate the offspring in the objective function

$$fx_o^k \leftarrow f\left(\mathbf{x}_o^k\right)$$

Step 9: Select the best μ individuals

$$\mathbf{x}_p^k \leftarrow best\left(\left\{\mathbf{x}_p^k \bigcup \mathbf{x}_o^k\right\}, \mu\right)$$

Step 10: Verify stop condition

$$if\ k == k_{max}$$

$$Best\ solution \leftarrow best\left(\mathbf{x}_p^k\right)$$

End the search process
else

$$k \leftarrow k+1$$

Go to **Step 4**
end

Program 3.3 Implementation of the (μ+1) ES Algorithm in MATLAB®
```
%%%%%%%%%%%%%%%%%%%%%%%%%%%%%%%%%%%%%%%%%%%%%%%%%%%%%%%%%%%%%%
%%%%%%%%%%%
% (µ+1) ES algorithm
% Erik Cuevas, Alma Rodríguez
%%%%%%%%%%%%%%%%%%%%%%%%%%%%%%%%%%%%%%%%%%%%%%%%%%%%%%%%%%%%%%
%%%%%%%%%%%
```

```
%% Clear memory and close windows
clear all
close all
%% Parameter configuration
mu = 3;                % Number of particles
d = 2;                 % Dimensions
lb = [-5.12 -5.12];% Lower bound
ub = [5.12 5.12];  % Upper bound
k = 0;                 % Iteration counter
kmax = 500;            % Maximum number of iterations
%% Optimization problem (minimization), objective function
definition
f = @(x) 10*d + sum(x.^2 - 10*cos(2*pi.*x));
%% Initialize particles and standard deviations
for i = 1:mu
        Xp(i,:) = rand(1,d).*(ub-lb)+lb;
        sigma_p(i,:) = rand(1,d)*2;
end
%% Evaluate initial particles in the objective function
for i = 1:mu
        fXp(i,1) = f(Xp(i,:));
end
%% Definition of the search space
xAxis=linspace(min(lb),max(ub),85);
yAxis=xAxis;
zAxis=[];
for i = 1:length(xAxis)
        for j = 1:length(yAxis)
                zAxis(i,j) = f([xAxis(i) yAxis(j)]);
        end
end
[yAxis,xAxis] = meshgrid(xAxis,yAxis);
%% Iterative process
while k<kmax
        %% Parents selection
        % Parent 1
        a = randi(mu);
        Xpa  = Xp(a,:);
        sigma_pa = sigma_p(a,:);
        % Parent 2
        b = randi(mu);
        Xpb  = Xp(b,:);
        sigma_pb = sigma_p(b,:);
        %% Recombination
        for i=1:d
                if rand<0.5
                        Xo(1,i) = Xpa(i);
```

```
                sigma_o(1,i) = sigma_pa(i);
        else
                Xo(1,i) = Xpb(i);
                sigma_o(1,i) = sigma_pb(i);
        end
end
%% Generate mutation vector
rho = normrnd(0,sigma_o);
%% Mutation
Xo = Xo + rho;
%% Verify bounds
for j=1:d
        if Xo(j) < lb(j)
                Xo(j) = rand*(ub(j)-lb(j))+lb(j);
        elseif Xo(j) > ub(j)
                Xo(j) = rand*(ub(j)-lb(j))+lb(j);
        end
end
%% Evaluate the offspring in the objective function
fXo = f(Xo);
%% Draw the search space
figure(1);
surf(xAxis,yAxis,zAxis)
hold on
%% Draw particles Xp y Xo
plot3(Xp(:,1),Xp(:,2),fXp,'o','MarkerFaceColor','m','Marker
Size',10)
plot3(Xo(1),Xo(2),fXo,'o','MarkerFaceColor','y','Marker
Size',10)
pause(0.01)
hold off
%% Draw contour
figure(2)
contour(xAxis,yAxis,zAxis,20)
hold on
%% Draw Xp y Xo in contour
plot(Xp(:,1),Xp(:,2),'o','MarkerFaceColor','m');
plot(Xo(1),Xo(2),'o','MarkerFaceColor','y');
pause(0.01)
hold off
%% Select the best mu individuals
Xpo = [Xp;Xo];
sigma_po = [sigma_p;sigma_o];
fXpo = [fXp;fXo];
[fXpo, ind] = sort(fXpo);
Xpo = Xpo(ind,:);
sigma_po = sigma_po(ind,:);
```

```
        Xp = Xpo(1:mu,:);
        sigma_p = sigma_po(1:mu,:);
        fXp = fXpo(1:mu);
        k=k+1;
end
%% Show results
display(['Best solution: x1= ',num2str(Xp(1,1)),', x2= ',num2str
(Xp(1,2))])
display([' f(X)= ',num2str(fXp(1))])
```

3.5.3 $(\mu+\lambda)$ ES

Like the algorithm $(\mu+1)$ ES, the method $(\mu+\lambda)$ ES uses an initial population of μ parents. The difference is that the $(\mu+\lambda)$ ES does not generate a single child in each iteration, but generates λ individuals resulting from recombination between parents. Once the offspring have been generated, $\mu+\lambda$ individuals will be merged considering the parents and children. From this set of particles, only the best μ elements will be selected to form the new population of parents, who will become part of the next generation.

The general procedure of $(\mu+\lambda)$ ES is presented in Algorithm 3.4, in which a discrete sexual recombination has been used. In addition, its implementation in the MATLAB environment can be observed in Program 3.4. Where the Rastringin function has been used in two dimensions, with a population $\mu=3$, an offspring $\lambda=6$, and 500 iterations.

Algorithm 3.4 describes how, in each generation, two parents are randomly selected and recombined to create a child that later will be mutated. Then, two new parents are randomly selected and recombined to obtain another individual who will be mutated. This process is repeated until the λ elements have been produced. Then, the selection is made, in which the λ descendants and the μ parents are gathered in a single set to choose the most suitable μ individuals who will become the parents of the next generation.

Algorithm 3.4 General Procedure of the $(\mu+\lambda)$ ES Method

Step 1: Parameter configuration

$$\mu,\lambda,d,lb,ub,k \leftarrow 0,k_{max}$$

Step 2: Initialize particles and standard deviations
for $i=1;i\leq\mu;i++$

$$\mathbf{x}_{pi}^{k} \leftarrow \mathbf{r}\cdot(\mathbf{ub}-\mathbf{lb})+\mathbf{lb}$$

$$\sigma_{pi}^{k} \leftarrow rand();\ \sigma_{pi}^{k} \in \mathbb{R}^{d}$$

end
Step 3: Evaluate initial particles in the objective function
for $i=1;i\leq\mu;i++$

$$\mathbf{fx}_{pi}^k \leftarrow f\left(\mathbf{x}_{pi}^k\right)$$

end

Step 4: Parents selection

$$\left(\mathbf{x}_{pa}^k, \sigma_{pa}^k\right) \leftarrow rand\left(\mathbf{x}_{p}^k, \sigma_{p}^k\right)$$

$$\left(\mathbf{x}_{pb}^k, \sigma_{pb}^k\right) \leftarrow rand\left(\mathbf{x}_{p}^k, \sigma_{p}^k\right)$$

Step 5: Recombination

$$\mathbf{x}_{on}^k \leftarrow recombination\left(\mathbf{x}_{pa}^k, \mathbf{x}_{pb}^k\right)$$

$$\sigma_{on}^k \leftarrow recombination\left(\sigma_{pa}^k, \sigma_{pb}^k\right)$$

Step 6: Generate mutation vector

$$\Sigma \leftarrow diag\left(\left(\sigma_{on_1}^k\right)^2, \ldots, \left(\sigma_{on_d}^k\right)^2\right) \in \mathbb{R}^{d \times d}$$

$$\rho \leftarrow N\left(0, \Sigma\right)$$

Step 7: Mutation

$$\mathbf{x}_{on}^k \leftarrow \mathbf{x}_{on}^k + \rho$$

Step 8: Evaluate the offspring in the objective function

$$\mathbf{fx}_{on}^k \leftarrow f\left(\mathbf{x}_{on}^k\right)$$

Step 9: Verify the number of generated particles

$$\text{if } n == \lambda$$

Go to **Step 10**

else

$$n \leftarrow n+1$$

Go to **Step 4**

end

Step 10: Select the best μ individuals

$$\mathbf{x}_p^k \leftarrow best\left(\left\{\mathbf{x}_p^k \bigcup \mathbf{x}_o^k\right\}, \mu\right)$$

Step 11: Verify stop condition

$$\text{if } k == k_{max}$$

$$Best \ soluton \leftarrow best\left(\mathbf{x}_p^k\right)$$

End the search process
else

$$k \leftarrow k+1$$

Go to **Step 4**
end

Program 3.4 MATLAB® Implementation of the $(\mu+\lambda)$ ES Algorithm

```
%%%%%%%%%%%%%%%%%%%%%%%%%%%%%%%%%%%%%%%%%%%%%%%%%%%%%%%%%%%%%%%%%%%%%
%%%%%%%%%%%%
% (μ+λ) ES method
% Erik Cuevas, Alma Rodríguez
%%%%%%%%%%%%%%%%%%%%%%%%%%%%%%%%%%%%%%%%%%%%%%%%%%%%%%%%%%%%%%%%%%%%%
%%%%%%%%%%%%

%% Clear memory and close windows
clear all
close all
%% Parameter configuration
mu = 3;                % Number of particles
lambda = 6;            % Number of children
d = 2;                 % Dimension
lb = [-5.12 -5.12];%   Lower bound
ub = [5.12 5.12];      % Upper bound
k = 0;                 % Iteration counter
kmax = 500;            % Maximum number of iterations
%% Optimization problem (minimization), objective function
definition
f = @(x) 10*d + sum(x.^2 - 10*cos(2*pi.*x));
%% Initialize particles and standard deviations
for i = 1:mu
        Xp(i,:) = rand(1,d).*(ub-lb)+lb;
        sigma_p(i,:) = rand(1,d)*2;
end
%% Evaluate initial particles in the objective function
for i = 1:mu
        fXp(i,1) = f(Xp(i,:));
end
%% Definition of the search space
xAxis=linspace(min(lb),max(ub),85);
yAxis=xAxis;
zAxis=[];
for i = 1:length(xAxis)
        for j = 1:length(yAxis)
                zAxis(i,j) = f([xAxis(i) yAxis(j)]);
```

```matlab
        end
end
[yAxis,xAxis] = meshgrid(xAxis,yAxis);
%% Iterative process
while k<kmax
        for n=1:lambda
                %% Parents selection
                % Parent 1
                a = randi(mu);
                Xpa  = Xp(a,:);
                sigma_pa = sigma_p(a,:);
                % Parent 2
                b = randi(mu);
                Xpb  = Xp(b,:);
                sigma_pb = sigma_p(b,:);
                %% Recombination
                for i=1:d
                        if rand<0.5
                                Xo(n,i) = Xpa(i);
                                sigma_o(n,i) = sigma_pa(i);
                        else
                                Xo(n,i) = Xpb(i);
                                sigma_o(n,i) = sigma_pb(i);
                        end
                end
                %% Generate mutation vector
                rho = normrnd(0,sigma_o(n,:));
                %% Mutation
                Xo(n,:) = Xo(n,:) + rho;
                %% Verify bounds
                for j=1:d
                        if Xo(n,j) < lb(j)
                                Xo(n,j) = rand*(ub(j)-lb(j))+lb(j);
                        elseif Xo(n,j) > ub(j)
                                Xo(n,j) = rand*(ub(j)-lb(j))+lb(j);
                        end
                end
                %% Evaluate the offspring in the objective function
                fXo(n,1) = f(Xo(n,:));
        end
        %% Draw the search space
        figure(1);
        surf(xAxis,yAxis,zAxis)
        hold on
        %% Draw particles Xp y Xo
        plot3(Xp(:,1),Xp(:,2),fXp,'o','MarkerFaceColor','m','Marker
        Size',10)
```

```
plot3(Xo(:,1),Xo(:,2),fXo,'o','MarkerFaceColor','y','Marker
Size',10)
pause(0.1)
hold off
%% Draw contour
figure(2)
contour(xAxis,yAxis,zAxis,20)
hold on
%% Draw Xp y Xo in contour
plot(Xp(:,1),Xp(:,2),'o','MarkerFaceColor','m');
plot(Xo(:,1),Xo(:,2),'o','MarkerFaceColor','y');
pause(0.1)
hold off
%% Select the best mu individuals
Xpo = [Xp;Xo];
sigma_po = [sigma_p;sigma_o];
fXpo = [fXp;fXo];
[fXpo, ind] = sort(fXpo);
Xpo = Xpo(ind,:);
sigma_po = sigma_po(ind,:);
Xp = Xpo(1:mu,:);
sigma_p = sigma_po(1:mu,:);
fXp = fXpo(1:mu);
k=k+1;
end
%% Show results
display(['Best solution: x1= ',num2str(Xp(1,1)),',
x2= ',num2str(Xp(1,2))])
display([' f(X)= ',num2str(fXp(1))])
```

3.5.4 (μ,λ) ES

The (μ,λ) ES is based on the same principle as the $(\mu+\lambda)$ ES. The difference between both algorithms is that they use different selection operators. While the $(\mu+\lambda)$ ES merges the μ parents with the λ children to select the best μ elements from the entire population, the (μ,λ) ES does not merge the parents with the children. Instead, it selects the best μ individuals from the λ descendants to form the new population. This means that each generation of parents can only survive one iteration, forcing all individuals to change in each generation and allowing only the best children to remain in the population.

The general procedure of the (μ,λ) ES is presented in Algorithm 3.5, in which a discrete sexual recombination has been used. In addition, its implementation in the MATLAB environment can be observed in Program 3.5, where the Rastringin function in two dimensions has been used, with a population $\mu=3$, an offspring of $\lambda=6$, and 500 iterations.

Algorithm 3.5 General Procedure of the (μ, λ) ES Method

Step 1: Parameter configuration

$$\mu, \lambda, d, lb, ub, k \leftarrow 0, k_{max}$$

Step 2: Initialize particles and standard deviations
for $i = 1; i \le \mu; i++$

$$\mathbf{x}_{pi}^{k} \leftarrow \mathbf{r} \cdot (\mathbf{ub} - \mathbf{lb}) + \mathbf{lb}$$

$$\sigma_{pi}^{k} \leftarrow rand(); \sigma_{pi}^{k} \in \mathbb{R}^{d}$$

end
Step 3: Evaluate initial particles in the objective function
for $i = 1; i \le \mu; i++$

$$\mathbf{fx}_{pi}^{k} \leftarrow f\left(\mathbf{x}_{pi}^{k}\right)$$

end
Step 4: Parents selection

$$\left(\mathbf{x}_{pa}^{k}, \sigma_{pa}^{k}\right) \leftarrow rand\left(\mathbf{x}_{p}^{k}, \sigma_{p}^{k}\right)$$

$$\left(\mathbf{x}_{pb}^{k}, \sigma_{pb}^{k}\right) \leftarrow rand\left(\mathbf{x}_{p}^{k}, \sigma_{p}^{k}\right)$$

Step 5: Recombination

$$\mathbf{x}_{on}^{k} \leftarrow recombination\left(\mathbf{x}_{pa}^{k}, \mathbf{x}_{pb}^{k}\right)$$

$$\sigma_{on}^{k} \leftarrow recombination\left(\sigma_{pa}^{k}, \sigma_{pb}^{k}\right)$$

Step 6: Generate mutation vector

$$\Sigma \leftarrow diag\left(\left(\sigma_{on_{1}}^{k}\right)^{2}, \ldots, \left(\sigma_{on_{d}}^{k}\right)^{2}\right) \in \mathbb{R}^{d \times d}$$

$$\rho \leftarrow N(0, \Sigma)$$

Step 7: Mutation

$$\mathbf{x}_{on}^{k} \leftarrow \mathbf{x}_{on}^{k} + \rho$$

Step 8: Evaluate the offspring in the objective function

$$\mathbf{fx}_{on}^{k} \leftarrow f\left(\mathbf{x}_{on}^{k}\right)$$

Step 9: Verify the number of generated children

$$\text{if } n == \lambda$$

Go to **Step 10**
else

$$n \leftarrow n+1$$

Go to **Step 4**
end
Step 10: Select the best μ individuals

$$\mathbf{x}_p^k \leftarrow best\left(\mathbf{x}_o^k, \mu\right)$$

Step 11: Verify the stop condition

$$\text{if } k == k_{max}$$

$$Best\ solution \leftarrow best\left(\mathbf{x}_p^k\right)$$

End the search space
else

$$k \leftarrow k+1$$

Go to **Step 4**
end

Program 3.5 MATLAB® Implementation of the (μ, λ) ES Algorithm

```
%%%%%%%%%%%%%%%%%%%%%%%%%%%%%%%%%%%%%%%%%%%%%%%%%%%%%%%%%%%%%%%%%%
%%%%%%%%%%
% (μ,λ) ES method
% Erik Cuevas, Alma Rodríguez
%%%%%%%%%%%%%%%%%%%%%%%%%%%%%%%%%%%%%%%%%%%%%%%%%%%%%%%%%%%%%%%%%%
%%%%%%%%%%%
%% Clear memory and close windows
clear all
close all
%% Parameter configuration
mu = 3; % Number of particles
lambda = 6; % Number of children
d = 2; % Dimensions
lb = [-5.12 -5.12]; % Lower bound
ub = [5.12 5.12]; % Upper bound
k = 0; % Iteration counter
```

```matlab
kmax = 500; % Maximum number of iterations
%% Optimization problem (minimization), objective function
definition
f = @(x) 10*d + sum(x.^2 - 10*cos(2*pi.*x));
%% Initialize particles and standard deviation
for i = 1:mu
     Xp(i,:) = rand(1,d).*(ub-lb)+lb;
     sigma_p(i,:) = rand(1,d)*2;
end
%% Evaluate initial particles in the objective function
for i = 1:mu
     fXp(i,1) = f(Xp(i,:));
end
%% Definition of the search space
xAxis=linspace(min(lb),max(ub),85);
yAxis=xAxis;
zAxis=[];
for i = 1:length(xAxis)
     for j = 1:length(yAxis)
          zAxis(i,j) = f([xAxis(i) yAxis(j)]);
     end
end
[yAxis,xAxis] = meshgrid(xAxis,yAxis);
%% Iterative process
while k<kmax
     for n=1:lambda
          %% Parents selection
          % Parent 1
          a = randi(mu);
          Xpa  = Xp(a,:);
          sigma_pa = sigma_p(a,:);
          % Parent 2
          b = randi(mu);
          Xpb  = Xp(b,:);
          sigma_pb = sigma_p(b,:);
          %% Recombination
          for i=1:d
               if rand<0.5
                    Xo(n,i) = Xpa(i);
                    sigma_o(n,i) = sigma_pa(i);
               else
                    Xo(n,i) = Xpb(i);
                    sigma_o(n,i) = sigma_pb(i);
               end
          end
          %% Generate mutation vector
          rho = normrnd(0,sigma_o(n,:));
```

```
            %% Mutation
            Xo(n,:) = Xo(n,:) + rho;
            %% Verify bounds
            for j=1:d
                if Xo(n,j) < lb(j)
                        Xo(n,j) = rand*(ub(j)-lb(j))+lb(j);
                elseif Xo(n,j) > ub(j)
                        Xo(n,j) = rand*(ub(j)-lb(j))+lb(j);
                end
            end
            %% Evaluate offspring in the objective function
            fXo(n,1) = f(Xo(n,:));
        end
        %% Draw search space
        figure(1);
        surf(xAxis,yAxis,zAxis)
        hold on
        %% Draw particles Xp y Xo
        plot3(Xo(:,1),Xo(:,2),fXo,'o','MarkerFaceColor','y','Marker
        Size',10)
        plot3(Xp(:,1),Xp(:,2),fXp,'o','MarkerFaceColor','m','Marker
        Size',10)
        pause(0.01)
        hold off
        %% Draw contour
        figure(2)
        contour(xAxis,yAxis,zAxis,20)
        hold on
        %% Draw Xp y Xo in contour
        plot(Xo(:,1),Xo(:,2),'o','MarkerFaceColor','y');
        plot(Xp(:,1),Xp(:,2),'o','MarkerFaceColor','m');
        pause(0.01)
        hold off
        %% Select the best mu individual
        [fXo, ind] = sort(fXo);
        Xo = Xo(ind,:);
        sigma_o = sigma_o(ind,:);
        Xp = Xo(1:mu,:);
        sigma_p = sigma_o(1:mu,:);
        fXp = fXo(1:mu);
        k=k+1;
end
%% Show results
display(['Best solution: x1= ',num2str(Xp(1,1)),',
x2= ',num2str(Xp(1,2))])
display([' f(X)= ',num2str(fXp(1))])
```

Normally, the method $(\mu + \lambda)$ ES works better than the (μ, λ) ES, especially in discrete problems with restricted and not very noisy search spaces. This is because the (μ, λ) ES makes more emphasis on exploration than the $(\mu + \lambda)$ ES because it does not allow an individual to remain more than one generation in the population, so it tends to discard good solutions and fails to refine them. On the other hand, the (μ, λ) ES works better than the $(\mu + \lambda)$ ES in noisy and time-variant objective functions since its ability to leave local optimum helps in finding better solutions.

To compare the performance of both algorithms, they have been executed 100 times using the Rastringin function in 30 dimensions with a population of $\mu = 20$, an offspring of $\lambda = 30$, and 500 iterations. The average of the obtained results by the two methods in each iteration is illustrated in Figure 3.16.

As can be seen in Figure 3.16, the algorithm $(\mu + \lambda)$ performs better than the (μ, λ) ES method. This is because the (μ, λ) ES explores excessively the search space and discards good solutions that cannot be refined because they are not allowed to survive more than one generation. In addition, another influencing factor is that the Rastringin function is bounded and presents moderate noise.

From this analysis, it can be concluded that the selection of the best method depends entirely on the problem to be optimized. The non-bounded and noisy target functions that have multiple local optimum require further exploration. Thus, the (μ, λ) ES is recommended in these scenarios. In any other case the $(\mu + \lambda)$ ES is recommended. However, it is not possible to precisely suggest which method to use for each particular problem because normally the surface of the search space is unknown.

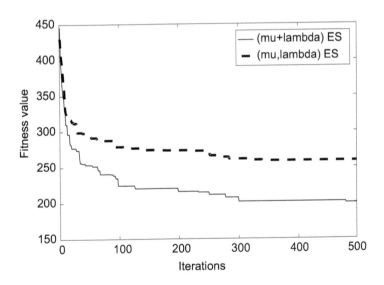

FIGURE 3.16   Convergence analysis of the $(\mu + \lambda)$ ES and the (μ, λ) ES algorithms. Performance comparison of both methods for the Rastringin function in 30 dimensions, considering the average result of 100 independent executions.

3.5.5 $(\mu,\alpha,\lambda,\beta)$ ES

The method $(\mu,\alpha,\lambda,\beta)$ ES is an extension of the methods $(\mu+\lambda)$ ES and (μ,λ) ES since it uses μ parents and λ children, but adds two additional parameters that are α and β. While α determines the number of generations that each individual can remain in the population, β controls the number of parents that will be used for the recombination and generation of each child.

Because the parameter α allows to control the lifetime of each element, if $\alpha=1$, then the $(\mu,\alpha,\lambda,\beta)$ ES method behaves like the (μ,λ) ES since it allows each individual to live only for one generation. On the other hand, if $\alpha=\infty$, then the algorithm behaves like the $(\mu+\lambda)$ ES because there is no restriction regarding the number of generations that an element can remain in the population, as long as this particle belongs to the best individuals. Thus, the control of this parameter can help prevent stagnation in local optimal because those particles that have not improved in a certain number of generations are discarded.

The parameter β allows another type of recombination, such as the global discrete or global intermediate seen in Section 3.5.2. Under this scheme, the information of the offspring is not limited to the recombination of only two parents. Instead, more parents can be considered in the recombination operation with the aim of promoting the diversity in the population.

3.5.6 Adaptive $(\mu+\lambda)$ ES and (μ,λ) ES

Until now, none of the presented methods use any adaptive strategy to modify the standard deviation vector σ, except for the adaptive $(1+1)$ ES that uses the $\dfrac{1}{5}$ rule to automatically modify the sigma values based on the mutation success recorded during a predefined time window. However, this rule cannot be generalized for population methods such as $(\mu+\lambda)$ ES or (μ,λ) ES since the offspring is not only generated from the mutation operator but also from the recombination that involves combining formation from the parents to generate the children. This is why an adaptive strategy is proposed to control the values of σ for the methods that include the recombination operator in their search strategy.

Using a strategy to modify the standard deviations improves the performance of the algorithms because having control over σ implies a better conducted search strategy. Assigning large values to σ at the beginning of iterations would cause further exploration of the search space, and reducing their values as the search progresses would allow refining the best solutions and obtaining greater precision in the results. Hence, just as the offspring is mutated to improve the solutions, it is also possible to mutate the standard deviation vector to optimize its values and control the movement of the particles to manipulate the degree of exploration and exploitation that is required in each generation. Under these considerations, the adaptive strategy consists in modifying the standard deviation vector σ_o associated with the offspring $\mathbf{x}_o$, before the mutation of $\mathbf{x}_o$, using the following definition:

$$\sigma_o = \sigma_o e^{(\tau\varphi+\tau'\varphi')} \tag{3.16}$$

where φ is a constant whose value is randomly chosen from a normal distribution $N(0,1)$. The vector σ' of dimension d is also formed of random constants from the same normal distribution. Regarding τ and τ', these are two constant parameters whose suggested values are defined as

$$\tau = c_1 \left(\frac{1}{\sqrt{2\sqrt{d}}} \right) \tag{3.17}$$

$$\tau' = c_2 \left(\frac{1}{\sqrt{2d}} \right) \tag{3.18}$$

From Eqs. 3.17 and 3.18, c_1 and c_2 are proportional constants whose values are usually $c_1 = 1$ and $c_2 = 1$, but can be adjusted for a better performance depending on the problem to be optimized. According to Eq. 3.16, the term $\tau\varphi$ has a general influence on the mutation of the offspring $\mathbf{x}_o$, while the term $\tau'\varphi'$ particularly affects each of the dimensions of $\mathbf{x}_o$.

The general procedure of the adaptive $(\mu + \lambda)$ ES is presented in Algorithm 3.6, in which discrete sexual recombination has been used. In addition, its implementation in the MATLAB environment can be observed in Program 3.6, where the Rastringin function in two dimensions was used with a population $\mu = 3$, an offspring of $\lambda = 6$, 500 iterations, and the constant parameters $c_1 = 1$ and $c_2 = 1$.

Algorithm 3.6 General Procedure of the Adaptive $(\mu + \lambda)$ ES

Step 1: Parameter configuration

$$\mu, \lambda, d, lb, ub, k \leftarrow 0, k_{max}, c_1, c_2, \tau, \tau'$$

Step 2: Initialize particles and standard deviation
for $i = 1; i \le \mu; i++$

$$\mathbf{x}_{pi}^k \leftarrow \mathbf{r} \cdot (\mathbf{ub} - \mathbf{lb}) + \mathbf{lb}$$
$$\sigma_{pi}^k \leftarrow rand(); \ \sigma_{pi}^k \in \mathbb{R}^d$$

end
Step 3: Evaluate initial particles in the objective function
for $i = 1; i \le \mu; i++$

$$\mathbf{fx}_{pi}^k \leftarrow f\left(\mathbf{x}_{pi}^k\right)$$

end
Step 4: Parents selection

$$\left(\mathbf{x}_{pa}^k, \sigma_{pa}^k\right) \leftarrow rand\left(\mathbf{x}_p^k, \sigma_p^k\right)$$
$$\left(\mathbf{x}_{pb}^k, \sigma_{pb}^k\right) \leftarrow rand\left(\mathbf{x}_p^k, \sigma_p^k\right)$$

Step 5: Recombination

$$\mathbf{x}_{on}^k \leftarrow recombination\left(\mathbf{x}_{pa}^k, \mathbf{x}_{pb}^k\right)$$

$$\boldsymbol{\sigma}_{on}^k \leftarrow recombination\left(\boldsymbol{\sigma}_{pa}^k, \boldsymbol{\sigma}_{pb}^k\right)$$

Step 6: Iterative process

$$\varphi \leftarrow N(0,1)$$

$$\boldsymbol{\varphi}' \leftarrow N(0,1); \ \boldsymbol{\varphi}' \in \mathbb{R}^d$$

$$\boldsymbol{\sigma}_{on}^k \leftarrow \boldsymbol{\sigma}_{on}^k e^{\left(\tau\varphi + \tau'\varphi'\right)}$$

Step 7: Generate mutation vector

$$\Sigma \leftarrow diag\left(\left(\sigma_{on_1}^k\right)^2, \ldots, \left(\sigma_{on_d}^k\right)^2\right) \in \mathbb{R}^{d \times d}$$

$$\rho \leftarrow N(0, \Sigma)$$

Step 8: Mutation

$$\mathbf{x}_{on}^k \leftarrow \mathbf{x}_{on}^k + \rho$$

Step 9: Evaluate the offspring in the objective function

$$\mathbf{fx}_{on}^k \leftarrow f\left(\mathbf{x}_{on}^k\right)$$

Step 10: Verify the number of generated children
if $n == \lambda$
Go to **Step 10**
else

$$n \leftarrow n+1$$

Go to **Step 4**
end
Step 11: Select the best μ individuals

$$\mathbf{x}_p^k \leftarrow best\left(\left\{\mathbf{x}_p^k \bigcup \mathbf{x}_o^k\right\}, \mu\right)$$

Step 12: Verify stop condition
if $k == k_{max}$

$$Best\ solution \leftarrow best\left(\mathbf{x}_p^k\right)$$

End the search process
else

$$k \leftarrow k+1$$

Go to **Step 4**
end

**Program 3.6 MATLAB® Implementation of the Adaptive $(\mu+\lambda)$ ES
Algorithm**

```
%%%%%%%%%%%%%%%%%%%%%%%%%%%%%%%%%%%%%%%%%%%%%%%%%%%%%%%%%%%%%%%%%%%%%
%%%%%%%%%%%%
% Adaptive (μ+λ) ES
% Erik Cuevas, Alma Rodríguez
%%%%%%%%%%%%%%%%%%%%%%%%%%%%%%%%%%%%%%%%%%%%%%%%%%%%%%%%%%%%%%%%%%%%%
%%%%%%%%%%%%

%% Clear memory and close windows
clear all
close all
%% Parameter configuration
mu = 3; % Number of particles
lambda = 6; % Number of children
d = 2; % Dimensions
lb = [-5.12 -5.12]; % Lower bounds
ub = [5.12 5.12]; % Upper bounds
k = 0; % Iteration counter
kmax = 500; % maximum number of iterations
c1 = 1;
c2 = 1;
tau  = c1*(1/(sqrt(2*sqrt(d))));
tau_a = c2*(1/(sqrt(2*d)));
%% Optimization problem (minimization), objective function
definition
f = @(x) 10*d + sum(x.^2 - 10*cos(2*pi.*x));
%% Initialize particles and standard deviation
for i = 1:mu
    Xp(i,:) = rand(1,d).*(ub-lb)+lb;
    sigma_p(i,:) = rand(1,d)*2;
end
%% Evaluate initial particles in the objective function
for i = 1:mu
    fXp(i,1) = f(Xp(i,:));
```

```
end
%% Definition of the search process
xAxis=linspace(min(lb),max(ub),85);
yAxis=xAxis;
zAxis=[];
for i = 1:length(xAxis)
        for j = 1:length(yAxis)
                zAxis(i,j) = f([xAxis(i) yAxis(j)]);
        end
end
[yAxis,xAxis] = meshgrid(xAxis,yAxis);
%% Iterative process
while k<kmax
        for n=1:lambda
                %% Parents selection
                % Parent 1
                a = randi(mu);
                Xpa   = Xp(a,:);
                sigma_pa = sigma_p(a,:);
                % Parent 2
                b = randi(mu);
                Xpb   = Xp(b,:);
                sigma_pb = sigma_p(b,:);
                %% Recombination
                for i=1:d
                        if rand<0.5
                                Xo(n,i) = Xpa(i);
                                sigma_o(n,i) = sigma_pa(i);
                        else
                                Xo(n,i) = Xpb(i);
                                sigma_o(n,i) = sigma_pb(i);
                        end
                end
                %% Adaptative process
                phi = normrnd(0,1);
                phi_prima = normrnd(0,1,1,d);
                sigma_o(n,:) = sigma_o(n,:).*exp(tau*phi +
                tau_a*phi_prima);
                %% Generate mutation vector
                rho = normrnd(0,sigma_o(n,:));
                %% Mutation
                Xo(n,:) = Xo(n,:) + rho;
                %% Verify bounds
                for j=1:d
                        if Xo(n,j) < lb(j)
                                Xo(n,j) = rand*(ub(j)-lb(j))+lb(j);
                        elseif Xo(n,j) > ub(j)
```

```
                          Xo(n,j) = rand*(ub(j)-lb(j))+lb(j);
                end
            end
            %% Evaluate offspring in the objective function
            fXo(n,1) = f(Xo(n,:));
        end
        %% Draw the search space
        figure(1);
        surf(xAxis,yAxis,zAxis)
        hold on
            %% Draw particles Xp y Xo
        plot3(Xp(:,1),Xp(:,2),fXp,'o','MarkerFaceColor','m','Marker
        Size',10)
        plot3(Xo(:,1),Xo(:,2),fXo,'o','MarkerFaceColor','y','Marker
        Size',10)
        pause(0.01)
        hold off
        %% Draw contour
        figure(2)
        contour(xAxis,yAxis,zAxis,20)
        hold on
        %% Draw Xp y Xo in contour
        plot(Xp(:,1),Xp(:,2),'o','MarkerFaceColor','m');
        plot(Xo(:,1),Xo(:,2),'o','MarkerFaceColor','y');
        pause(0.01)
        hold off
        %% Select the best mu individual
        Xpo = [Xp;Xo];
        sigma_po = [sigma_p;sigma_o];
        fXpo = [fXp;fXo];
        [fXpo, ind] = sort(fXpo);
        Xpo = Xpo(ind,:);
        sigma_po = sigma_po(ind,:);
        Xp = Xpo(1:mu,:);
        sigma_p = sigma_po(1:mu,:);
        fXp = fXpo(1:mu);
        k=k+1;
end
%% Show results
display(['Best solution: x1= ',num2str(Xp(1,1)),',',
x2= ',num2str(Xp(1,2))])
display([' f(X)= ',num2str(fXp(1))])
```

The general procedure of adaptive (μ, λ) ES is presented in Algorithm 3.7, in which a discrete sexual recombination has been used. In addition, its implementation in the MATLAB environment can be observed in Program 3.7. Where the Rastrigin function in two dimensions was used, with a population $\mu = 3$, an offspring of $\lambda = 6$, 500 iterations, and the constant parameters $c_1 = 1$ and $c_1 = 2$.

Algorithm 3.7 General Procedure of the Adaptive (μ, λ) ES

Step 1: Parameter configuration

$$\mu, \lambda, d, lb, ub, k \leftarrow 0, k_{max}, c_1, c_2, \tau, \tau'$$

Step 2: Initialize particles and standard deviations
for $i = 1; i \leq \mu; i++$

$$\mathbf{x}_{pi}^k \leftarrow \mathbf{r} \cdot (\mathbf{ub} - \mathbf{lb}) + \mathbf{lb}$$

$$\sigma_{pi}^k \leftarrow rand(); \ \sigma_{pi}^k \in \mathbb{R}^d$$

end
Step 3: Evaluate initial particles in the objective function
for $i = 1; i \leq \mu; i++$

$$\mathbf{fx}_{pi}^k \leftarrow f\left(\mathbf{x}_{pi}^k\right)$$

end
Step 4: Select parents

$$\left(\mathbf{x}_{pa}^k, \sigma_{pa}^k\right) \leftarrow rand\left(\mathbf{x}_{p}^k, \sigma_{p}^k\right)$$

$$\left(\mathbf{x}_{pb}^k, \sigma_{pb}^k\right) \leftarrow rand\left(\mathbf{x}_{p}^k, \sigma_{p}^k\right)$$

Step 5: Recombination

$$\mathbf{x}_{on}^k \leftarrow recombination\left(\mathbf{x}_{pa}^k, \mathbf{x}_{pb}^k\right)$$

$$\sigma_{on}^k \leftarrow recombination\left(\sigma_{pa}^k, \sigma_{pb}^k\right)$$

Step 6: Iterative process

$$\varphi \leftarrow N(0,1)$$

$$\varphi' \leftarrow N(0,1); \ \varphi' \in \mathbb{R}^d$$

$$\sigma_{on}^k \leftarrow \sigma_{on}^k e^{(\tau\varphi + \tau'\varphi')}$$

Step 7: Generate mutation vector

$$\Sigma \leftarrow diag\left(\left(\sigma_{on_1}^k\right)^2, \ldots, \left(\sigma_{on_d}^k\right)^2\right) \in \mathbb{R}^{d \times d}$$

$$\rho \leftarrow N\left(0, \Sigma\right)$$

Step 8: Mutation

$$\mathbf{x}_{on}^k \leftarrow \mathbf{x}_{on}^k + \rho$$

Step 9: Evaluate the offspring in the objective function

$$\mathbf{fx}_{on}^k \leftarrow f\left(\mathbf{x}_{on}^k\right)$$

Step 10: Verify the number of generated children
if $n == \lambda$
Go to **Step 10**
else

$$n \leftarrow n + 1$$

Go to **Step 4**
end
Step 11: Select the best μ individuals

$$\mathbf{x}_p^k \leftarrow best\left(\mathbf{x}_o^k, \mu\right)$$

Step 12: Verify stop condition
if $k == k_{max}$

$$Best\ solution \leftarrow best\left(\mathbf{x}_p^k\right)$$

End the search process
else

$$k \leftarrow k + 1$$

Go to **Step 4**
end

Program 3.7 MATLAB® Implementation of the Adaptive (μ,λ) ES

```
%%%%%%%%%%%%%%%%%%%%%%%%%%%%%%%%%%%%%%%%%%%%%%%%%%%%%%%%%%%%%%%%%%%
%%%%%%%%%%
% Adaptive (μ,λ) ES
% Erik Cuevas, Alma Rodríguez
%%%%%%%%%%%%%%%%%%%%%%%%%%%%%%%%%%%%%%%%%%%%%%%%%%%%%%%%%%%%%%%%%%%
%%%%%%%%%%%
%% Clear memory and close windows
clear all
close all
%% Parameter configuration
mu = 3; % Number of particles
lambda = 6; % Number of children
d = 2; % Dimensions
lb = [-5.2 -5.12]; % Lower bound
ub = [5.12 5.2]; % Upper bound
k = 0; % Iteration counter
kmax = 500; % Maximum number of iterations
c1 = 1;
c2 = 1;
tau  = c1*(1/(sqrt(2*sqrt(d))));
tau_a = c2*(1/(sqrt(2*d)));
%% Optimization problem (minimization), objective function
definition
f = @(x) 10*d + sum(x.^2 - 10*cos(2*pi.*x));
%% Initialize particles and standard deviations
for i = 1:mu
      Xp(i,:) = rand(1,d).*(ub-lb)+lb;
      sigma_p(i,:) = rand(1,d)*2;
end
%% Evaluate initial particles in the objective function
for i = 1:mu
      fXp(i,1) = f(Xp(i,:));
end
%% Definition of the search space
xAxis=linspace(min(lb),max(ub),85);
yAxis=xAxis;
zAxis=[];
for i = 1:length(xAxis)
      for j = 1:length(yAxis)
            zAxis(i,j) = f([xAxis(i) yAxis(j)]);
      end
end
[yAxis,xAxis] = meshgrid(xAxis,yAxis);
%% Iterative process
while k<kmax
    for n=1:lambda
```

```
%% Select parents
% Parent 1
a = randi(mu);
Xpa  = Xp(a,:);
sigma_pa = sigma_p(a,:);
% Parent 2
b = randi(mu);
Xpb  = Xp(b,:);
sigma_pb = sigma_p(b,:);
%% Recombination
for i=1:d
      if rand<0.5
             Xo(n,i) = Xpa(i);
             sigma_o(n,i) = sigma_pa(i);
      else
             Xo(n,i) = Xpb(i);
             sigma_o(n,i) = sigma_pb(i);
      end
end
%% Iterative process
phi = normrnd(0,1);
phi_prima = normrnd(0,1,1,d);
sigma_o(n,:) = sigma_o(n,:).*exp(tau*phi +
tau_a*phi_prima);
%% Generate mutation vector
rho = normrnd(0,sigma_o(n,:));
%% Mutation
Xo(n,:) = Xo(n,:) + rho;
%% Verify bounds
for j=1:d
      if Xo(n,j) < lb(j)
             Xo(n,j) = rand*(ub(j)-lb(j))+lb(j);
      elseif Xo(n,j) > ub(j)
             Xo(n,j) = rand*(ub(j)-lb(j))+lb(j);
      end
end
%% Evaluate the offspring in the objective function
fXo(n,1) = f(Xo(n,:));
end
%% Draw the search space
figure(1);
surf(xAxis,yAxis,zAxis)
hold on
%% Draw particles Xp y Xo
plot3(Xo(:,1),Xo(:,2),fXo,'o','MarkerFaceColor','y','Marker
Size',10)
plot3(Xp(:,1),Xp(:,2),fXp,'o','MarkerFaceColor','m','Marker
Size',10)
```

```
        pause(0.01)
        hold off
        %% Draw contour
        figure(2)
        contour(xAxis,yAxis,zAxis,20)
        hold on
        %% Draw Xp y Xo in contour
        plot(Xo(:,1),Xo(:,2),'o','MarkerFaceColor','y');
        plot(Xp(:,1),Xp(:,2),'o','MarkerFaceColor','m');
        pause(0.01)
        hold off
        %% Select the best mu individuals
        [fXo, ind] = sort(fXo);
        Xo = Xo(ind,:);
        sigma_o = sigma_o(ind,:);
        Xp = Xo(1:mu,:);
        sigma_p = sigma_o(1:mu,:);
        fXp = fXo(1:mu);
        k=k+1;
end
%% Show results
display(['Best solution: x1= ',num2str(Xp(1,1)),',
x2= ',num2str(Xp(1,2))])
display([' f(X)= ',num2str(fXp(1))])
```

From Algorithms 3.4 and 3.5, it can be observed that the only difference regarding to their adaptive versions described in Algorithms 3.6 and 3.7, is the inclusion of the adaptive process, in which the standard deviation vector σ_o associated with the offspring $\mathbf{x}_o$ is modified according to Eq. 3.16 before being used to mutate $\mathbf{x}_o$.

To compare the performance of the algorithms $(\mu+\lambda)$ ES, (μ,λ) ES, and its adaptive versions, several tests have been performed, where the methods have been run 100 times using the Rastrigin function in 30 dimensions with a population of $\mu = 20$, an offspring of $\lambda = 30$, and 500 iterations. In the adaptive methods, the constant parameters $c_1 = 1$ and $c_1 = 2$ have been used. The average of the results obtained in each iteration by the adaptive $(\mu+\lambda)$ ES and $(\mu+\lambda)$ ES is illustrated in Figure 3.17, while Figure 3.18 shows the performance of the (μ,λ) ES algorithm and its adaptive version.

The performance of the adaptive versions is superior than the original methods according to the results illustrated in Figures 3.17 and 3.18. The comparison between adaptive $(\mu+\lambda)$ ES and adaptive (μ,λ) ES method is shown in Figure 3.19, where it is clear that the adaptive $(\mu+\lambda)$ ES algorithm has better performance than the adaptive (μ,λ) ES for the Rastrigin function.

In all variants of the algorithms based on ES that have been studied so far, it is clear that the selection plays an important role in the success of the search. While the (μ,λ) ES and its adaptive version eliminate each generation of solutions to stay only with the best children,

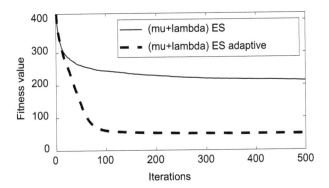

FIGURE 3.17   Convergence analysis of the $(\mu+\lambda)$ ES and the adaptive $(\mu+\lambda)$ ES. Performance comparison of both methods for the Rastringin function in 30 dimensions, considering the average result of 100 independent executions.

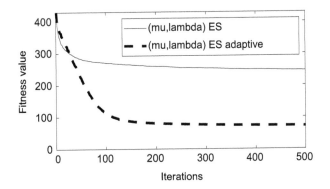

FIGURE 3.18   Convergence analysis of the (μ,λ) ES and the adaptive (μ,λ) ES. Performance comparison of both methods for the Rastringin function in 30 dimensions, considering the average result of 100 independent executions.

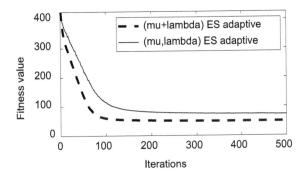

FIGURE 3.19   Convergence analysis of the adaptive $(\mu+\lambda)$ ES and the adaptive (μ,λ) ES. Performance comparison of both methods for the Rastringin function in 30 dimensions, considering the average result of 100 independent executions.

the $(\mu + \lambda)$ ES and its adaptive version retain only the best of the entire population. These mechanisms cause different degrees of exploration and exploitation that favor the search in certain problems. Some other variants include other types of non-elite selection to promote diversity in the population, such as the roulette or tournament method.

In addition to the selection operator, the mutation is also decisive in the search process. In the mutation operator, it is possible to implement covariance matrices where not only the main diagonal is considered, but also the complete covariance information. This change would positively influence the performance of the ES algorithm, but at a higher computational cost. Some more sophisticated variants include this form of mutation. In addition to controlling standard deviations, they also use rotation angles to modify the mutation direction. With these rotations, it is intended to better adjust the distributions to the contour of the search space in such a way that the mutation generates better solutions. More information about the ES methods can be found in Bäck and Schwefel (1993), Beyer (2010), Rechenberg (1994), and Emmerich, Shir, and Wang (2018).

REFERENCES

Bäck, T., & Schwefel, H.-P. (1993). An overview of evolutionary algorithms for parameter optimization. *Evolutionary Computation, 1*(1), 1–23.

Beyer, H.-G. (2010). *The theory of evolution strategies.* Berlin: Springer.

Beyer, H.-G., & Schwefel, H.-P. (2002, March). Evolution strategies—A comprehensive introduction. *Natural Computing, 1*(1), 3–52.

Emmerich, M., Shir, O. M., & Wang, H. (2018). Evolution strategies. In R. Martí, P. M. Pardalos, & M. G. C. (Eds.), *Handbook of heuristics* (pp. 1–31). Basel: Springer International Publishing.

Rechenberg, I. (1965). *Cybernetic solution path of an experimental problem.* Technical Report Library Translation No. 1122, Royal Aircraft Establishment, Farnborough: Ministry of Aviation.

Rechenberg, I. (1973). *Evolutionsstrategie: Optimierung technischer Systeme nach Prinzipien der Biologischen Evolution.* Stuttgart: Frammann-Holzboog Verlag.

Rechenberg, I. (1994). Evolution strategy. In J. M. Zurada, R. Marks II, & C. Robinson (Eds.), *Computational intelligence: Imitating life* (pp. 147–159). New York, NY: IEEE Press.

CHAPTER 4

Moth–Flame Optimization (MFO) Algorithm

4.1 MFO METAPHOR

Moths are insects very similar to butterflies, and their life begins as a larva and evolves into moths in their adulthood. In nature, there is a great variety of moths, approximately 160,000 species (Mirjalili, 2015), of which the majority are nocturnal. Despite the existence of a wide variety of moths, all are characterized by their interesting navigation method, which will be described in detail because it constitutes the main operator of the Moth–Flame Optimization (MFO).

Moths have a particular night navigation in which they use the moonlight to orient themselves. Through this mechanism, called transverse orientation, moths fly at night maintaining a constant angle in relationship with the moon. This form of navigation is very effective for traveling long distances with a straight path. However, when moths are faced with artificial light, their trajectory can change dramatically.

Artificial lights, such as spotlights or bulbs, often confuse moths. These are guided by the light which is closer to them (without matter whether this light is the moon or not). This closeness causes that moths to adjust their angle in terms of artificial light. This adjustment produces a spiral movement around this light source, reducing gradually the distance with regard to the light source. This transversal movement is illustrated in Figure 4.1.

The reason why the path of a moth is a spiral and not in a straight line is due its proximity to the source. When the light source is far enough, as is the moonlight, the angle is almost imperceptible. However, when the moth is in front of an artificial light, it tries to maintain an angle similar to the one it maintains with the moonlight. Under such conditions, the path changes dramatically causing a movement in spiral due to the magnitude of the angle.

The MFO algorithm emulates the navigation moth behavior. Under this scheme, the spiral path of the moths is used as an operator that allows the movement of search agents towards the solution in the search space. In the metaphor, the moth acts as a search agent

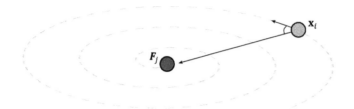

FIGURE 4.1   Spiral path of the moth X_i caused by the artificial light F_j.

or particle, while artificial light (the flame) represents a local solution. Therefore, the search agent (the moth) explores the search space through a spiral movement around the local solution (the flame). Because the MFO algorithm is population-based, a set of moths are used in the search, where each moth performs the same movement.

4.2   MFO SEARCH STRATEGY

The MFO algorithm uses a population $X = \{x_1, x_2, \ldots, x_N\}$ that models the navigation behavior of N moths when they are exposed to artificial light. Each moth is represented by a particle x_i. The objective of the MFO algorithm is the searching of appropriate solutions for an optimization problem within the search space. The particles are considered search agents, and each one corresponds to a possible solution that is improving its quality during the iterative process.

4.2.1   Initialization

In the initialization step, the set of particles X^0, consisting of N search agents such that $X^0 = \{x_1^0, x_2^0, \ldots, x_N^0\}$, is created to produce the initial population. Similar to other meta-heuristic methods, each initial particle $x_i^0 = \left[x_{i,1}^0, x_{i,2}^0, \ldots, x_{i,d}^0 \right]$ is randomly generated with values within the lower lb and upper ub limits of the d-dimensional search space. These limits, which may be different for each dimension, are determined by the problem to be optimized. They represent the limits where possible solutions can be found. Equation 4.1 describes the way in which particles are initialized.

$$x_{ij}^0 = lb_j + r_{ij}\left(ub_j - lb_j\right) \quad i = 1, 2, \ldots, N; j = 1, 2, \ldots, d \tag{4.1}$$

where x_{ij}^0 corresponds to the initial value of the particle i in its dimension j. The limits are defined by lb_j and ub_j, which are the lower and upper limits for the dimension j, respectively. In addition, r_{ij} is a random number that affects the particle i in its dimension j. The value of r_{ij} is within the range [0,1]. In general, the random value of r_{ij} is sampled by using a uniform distribution. However, any other distribution can also be used.

In addition to the initialization of search agents, the general parameters such as the number of particles N, the number of dimensions d, the limits of the search space lb and ub, the maximum number of iterations k_{max} and the restrictions of equality or inequality are also defined. The MFO algorithm described in this chapter considers optimization problems with and without constraints. In the beginning, the use of MFO without constraints is discussed. However, in Section 4.5.2, its implementation is analyzed for constrained optimization problems.

4.2.2 Cross Orientation

In the search strategy, each particle moves in the solution space according to a transversal orientation. This orientation is modeled with a logarithmic spiral $\mathbf{s}_i$ defined as

$$\mathbf{s}_i = \mathbf{D}_i e^{br} \cos(2\pi r) + \mathbf{F}_j \tag{4.2}$$

where $\mathbf{D}_i$ represents the absolute value of the distance between the particle $\mathbf{x}_i$ and the local solution $\mathbf{F}_j$, which is expressed as

$$\mathbf{D}_i = |\mathbf{F}_j - \mathbf{x}_i| \tag{4.3}$$

Furthermore, b is a constant that defines the shape of the logarithmic spiral. In the MFO, b is defined with a value of 1. In the case of r, this is a vector of dimension d with random values within the range $[-2,1]$.

According to Eq. 4.2, the following position of each search agent is defined with respect to a local solution. The parameter r determines how close the new position of a particle will be with respect to a local solution. This value is calculated for each dimension as follows:

$$r = (a-1) \cdot rand + 1 \tag{4.4}$$

where a is a convergence constant used to emphasize exploitation as the iterations progress. The value of a decreases linearly from -1 to -2 to move the particles closer and closer to the local solution to which they are associated. The value of the convergence constant is calculated with the following expression:

$$a = -1 + k\left(\frac{-1}{k_{max}}\right) \tag{4.5}$$

The closest position between a local solution and its associated particle occurs when $r = -2$, while the longest is observed when $r = 1$. Then, a particle can be positioned at any point around the local solution by varying the value of r. The smaller this value, the closer the particle of the local solution will be. Figure 4.2 shows the logarithmic spiral modeled by Eq. 4.2 with $b = 1$. The figure shows some possible positions that a particle $\mathbf{x}_i$ could take around a local solution $\mathbf{F}_j$ considering different values of r.

The spiral movement of the search agents is the main component of the MFO algorithm. This movement determines the way in which the particles update their position around the local solutions. Therefore, local solutions, which represent the best solutions, influence the search process in such a way that they guide the particles towards the best solution through the space of the decision variables.

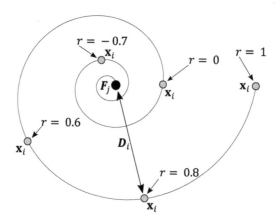

FIGURE 4.2   Logarithmic spiral and the possible positions of the particle x_i around a local solution F_j for different values of r.

4.2.3 Other Mechanisms for the Balance of Exploration–Exploitation

An important aspect to consider in the algorithm is that local solutions are updated in each iteration with the best solutions obtained so far. This means that local solutions are updated in terms of the best particles. In addition, each particle moves with respect to a single local solution to avoid being trapped in local minima. Under these considerations, after updating the local solutions, they are ordered from the best to the worst. Then, each particle is assigned a local solution so that the first particle always moves with respect to the best local solution, while the last particle is positioned around the worst local solution. This procedure is illustrated in Figure 4.3a.

In addition to using the convergence constant as a mechanism that ensures the transition between the exploration and exploitation process, the MFO algorithm uses another interesting mechanism. It avoids the overexploitation that can be generated when each search agent moves around a single local solution. This mechanism regulates the number of local solutions in each iteration, reducing them to only one. From this local solution, all particles move at the end of the iterative process. Under this scheme, the number of local solutions gradually decreases from N to 1.

Figure 4.3 shows the assignment of each x_i particle to a local solution F_j considering two different scenarios. The first scenario occurs when in the first iterations each particle moves around its own local solution, see Figure 4.3a. However, as the iterations progress there is another scheme. In this scenario, the first particles move around their own local solution, while the last particles share the same local solution, so they move around it (see Figure 4.3b). The second scenario arises due to the gradual reduction of the number of local solutions as a mechanism to avoid overexploitation.

The number of local solutions nF for each iteration k is computed considering the integer value resulting from the following expression:

$$nF = entero\left(N - k\frac{N-1}{k_{max}} \right) \tag{4.6}$$

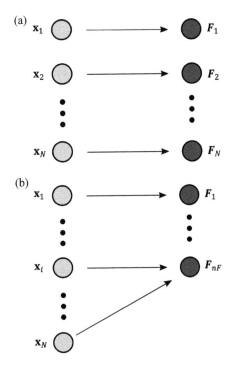

FIGURE 4.3 Particles assignment to a local solution in different scenarios: (a) to local solutions in the first iteration and (b) to local solutions when nF is reduced.

Figure 4.4 shows how the number of local solutions decreases automatically as the iterations progress. The figure illustrates that at the beginning, the number of local solutions is equal to the number of particles, so that each particle is assigned to a different local solution. However, when the iterations advance, the number of local solutions decreases and the last particles are assigned to the same local solution. Therefore, at the end of the iterations, all particles will move around the same local solution. This mechanism prevents the degradation in the exploitation of promising solutions.

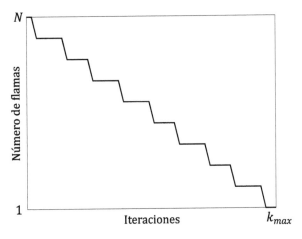

FIGURE 4.4 Gradual decrement in the number of local solutions through iterations.

Like other metaheuristic algorithms, the MFO stores the best global solution **g**, and this solution corresponds to the best particle (best local solution) that has been so far, such that

$$\mathbf{g} = \mathbf{x}_i \in \{\mathbf{X}\} \mid f(\mathbf{x}_i) = \min\{f(\mathbf{x}_1), f(\mathbf{x}_2), \dots, f(\mathbf{x}_N)\} \tag{4.7}$$

4.2.4 MFO Variants

Few variants of the MFO algorithm has been reported in the literature. In general, they use different operators or hybridizations integrated into the original algorithm in order to achieve a better performance. These variants are intended to improve the performance of MFO in more complex scenarios in which the dimensionality of the problem is high or multimodal. Some of these variants are discussed below.

In 2016, a variant of the MFO called Lévy flight MFO (LMFO) (Li, Zhou, Zhang, & Song, 2016) has been proposed. Under this approach, Lévy flight movements are incorporated to increase the diversity of the population with the intention to prevent premature convergence. This mechanism gives it the ability to escape from local optimum more efficiently. With the incorporation of the Lévy flights, the improved algorithm maintains a better balance in the process of exploration and exploitation of the solutions.

Another algorithm was proposed in 2018 called Enhanced MFO (EMFO). In this scheme, the techniques of Cultural Learning and Gaussian Mutation are integrated to increase the exchange of information between particles and to improve the diversity of the population with the intention of avoiding stagnation in a local optimum (Xu et al., 2018).

Another interesting improvement of MFO algorithm is the II-EMFO (Kaur, Singh, & Salgotra, 2018). This method incorporates a Cauchy distribution to improve the exploration capacity of the original MFO. Furthermore, it implements a mechanism to influence the best local solutions with the objective of improving the exploitation process. It also uses an adaptive step size to regulate the movement of particles and divides the iterations for improving the exploration and exploitation control.

In 2019, another variant of the MFO (Xu, Chen, Luo, Zhang, Jiao, & Zhang, 2019) has been introduced in which different mutation types such as Gaussian, Cauchy, and Lévy are combined to improve its general exploration ability. With this inclusion, the random values produced allow a better search of promising solutions.

A new hybrid algorithm has also been proposed in 2019 called Water Cycle-MFO (WCMFO) (Khalilpourazari & Khalilpourazary, 2019). This method is based on the MFO and the Water Cycle algorithm to improve its exploitation process. In addition, the WCMFO incorporates the Lévy flight technique to promote the diversity of the population.

The detailed description of the MFO variants is beyond the scope of this book, so it is suggested to revise the references in order to know the particularities of these methods.

4.3 MFO COMPUTATION PROCEDURE

So far, it has been established that the MFO is an iterative algorithm in which search agents move around local solutions in the search space using cross orientation. In addition, it has been mentioned that the particles are evaluated in each iteration to verify their quality. Then, this information is used to update the local solutions, which will be replaced with the best particles. At the end of the iterations, the best local solution (the best global solution) will be the solution to the optimization problem. This is a general description of the method. However, in this section all the details of the algorithm for its computational implementation will be described in detail.

4.3.1 Algorithm Description

The MFO begins with a set of $\mathbf{X}^0$ particles of size N that are randomly located in the search space by using Eq. 4.1. This set of particles corresponds to the initial population, which is evaluated in terms of the objective function. The quality of the particles is determined from their fitness values. In this evaluation, each particle maintains a fitness value f_i which defines the quality of the particle with regard to the optimization problem. Thus, the best particle in the group is recognized as the best global solution. Equation 4.8 shows the calculation of fitness for each particle $\mathbf{x}_i$.

$$\mathbf{fx}_i = f(\mathbf{x}_i) \tag{4.8}$$

After the evaluation, N local solutions are initialized with the information of the initial population, but ordered from best to worst based on their fitness values. Once ordered, the first local solution F_1 will be initialized with the best particle $\mathbf{x}_{b1}$, the second local solution F_2 with the second-best particle $\mathbf{x}_{b2}$ and so on, as illustrated in Figure 4.5. Then, the particles are assigned to a local solution. For this, the first particle $\mathbf{x}_1$ (regardless of fitness) will be associated to the best local solution F_1, the second particle $\mathbf{x}_2$ to the second-best local solution F_2 and so on, as illustrated in Figure 4.3a. In addition, the best particle $\mathbf{x}_{b1}$ is registered as the best initial global solution $\mathbf{g}^0$.

Then, the iterative process begins. Therefore, the number of local solutions nF in the current iteration is calculated by using Eq. 4.6. Also, the convergence constant a is calculated by using Eq. 4.5. Through transverse orientation, particles are moved around their local solution, placing themselves in new positions in the search space in order to find higher quality solutions. The transverse orientation that the particles use for their movement is determined from the logarithmic spiral defined in Eq. 4.2. The particles that have modified their position with this transverse orientation are evaluated in terms of the objective function to determine their fitness values. Then, the particles and the local solutions

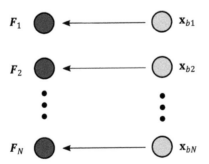

FIGURE 4.5 Initialization of local solutions based on the best particles.

are ordered from lower to higher fitness values to determine the best candidate solutions so far through an elitist selection process.

With this information, the nF local solutions are updated with the nF best solutions. Considering the updated local solutions in terms of number and quality, each particle is assigned a local solution as illustrated in Figure 4.3b. If the number of particles N is greater than the number of local solutions nF, then the last particles will be assigned to the last local solution. The particle with the best fitness so far will be used to update the first local solution F_1 and will also be registered as the current best global particle g^k.

Next, the stop condition is verified, which is generally restricted to a number of iterations. The determination of the number of iterations that the algorithm must execute is adjustable and is associated to the complexity of the problem. If the stop criterion has not been met, the iterative process continues. The flowchart of the MFO algorithm is shown in Figure 4.6. Additionally, to facilitate its implementation, the general procedure of the MFO is also presented as a pseudocode in Algorithm 4.1.

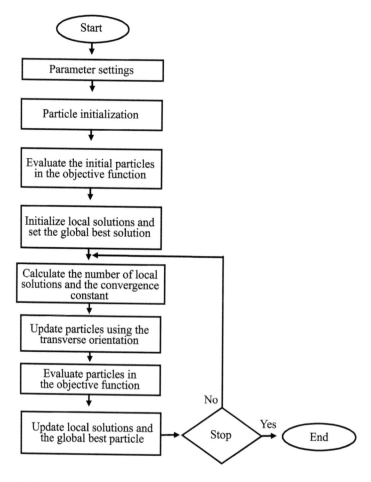

FIGURE 4.6   MFO flowchart.

Algorithm 4.1 General Procedure of the MFO Algorithm

Step 1: Parameter configuration

$$N, d, lb, ub, k = 0, k_{max}, b = 1$$

Step 2: Particle initialization
for $i = 1; i \leq N; i++$

$$\mathbf{x}_i^k = \mathbf{r} \cdot (\mathbf{ub} - \mathbf{lb}) + \mathbf{lb}$$

end
Step 3: Evaluation of the initial particles in the objective function
for $i = 1; i \leq N; i++$

$$\mathbf{fx}_i^k \leftarrow f(\mathbf{x}_i^k)$$

end
Step 4: Sorting particles from best to worst based on their fitness values

$$\mathbf{X}_{sorted}^k = Sort(\mathbf{X}^k)$$

Step 5: Initialize local solutions based on the best elements

$$F^k = \mathbf{X}_{sorted}^k$$

Step 6: Store the best global solution

$$\mathbf{g}^k = \mathbf{x}_i^k \in \{\mathbf{X}^k\} \mid f(\mathbf{x}_i^k) = \min\{f(\mathbf{x}_1^k), f(\mathbf{x}_2^k), \dots, f(\mathbf{x}_N^k)\}$$

$$g_{fit}^k \leftarrow f(\mathbf{x}_i^k)$$

Step 7: Calculation of the number of local solutions

$$nF = Int\left(N - k\frac{N-1}{k_{max}}\right)$$

Step 8: Convergence constant calculation

$$a = -1 + k\left(\frac{-1}{k_{max}}\right)$$

Step 9: Calculation of the new position of the particles by using the transverse orientation
for $i = 1; i \leq N; i++$

$$\mathbf{x}_i^k \leftarrow \boldsymbol{D}_i^k e^{br} \cos(2\pi r) + \boldsymbol{F}_j^k$$

end

Step 10: Evaluation of the new particles in the objective function
for $i = 1; i \leq N; i++$

$$\mathbf{fx}_i^k \leftarrow f\left(\mathbf{x}_i^k\right)$$

end

Step 11: Ordering of local solutions and particles from best to worst nF

$$\mathbf{X}_{sorted}^k = Sort\left(\boldsymbol{F}^k, \mathbf{X}^k\right)$$

Step 12: Update of local solutions based on the best nF particles

$$\boldsymbol{F}^k = \mathbf{X}_{sorted}^k$$

Step 13: Update the best global particle

$$\mathbf{g}^k = \mathbf{x}_i^k \in \left\{\mathbf{X}_{sorted}^k\right\} \bigg| f\left(\mathbf{x}_i^k\right) = \min\left\{f\left(\mathbf{x}_1^k\right), f\left(\mathbf{x}_2^k\right), \dots, f\left(\mathbf{x}_N^k\right)\right\}$$

$$\mathbf{g}_{fit}^k \leftarrow f\left(\mathbf{x}_i^k\right)$$

Step 14: Evaluation of the stop criterion

$$\text{if } k == k_{max}$$

$$Best\ solution \leftarrow \mathbf{g}^k$$

End of the search
else

$$k \leftarrow k + 1$$

Go to **Step 7**
end

4.4 IMPLEMENTATION OF MFO IN MATLAB

The MFO algorithm has been implemented in the MATLAB® environment with the objective of illustrating its search procedure, which can be observed in Program 4.1.

In the example, it is intended to minimize an objective function to find the global minimum. The problem does not represent an engineering problem or a real problem, but is a mathematical test function that generates a surface known as *peaks*. This test function is produced from the translation and weighting of Gaussian functions. This function is defined in two dimensions and is widely used since it represents an interesting optimization challenge. Its shape maintains several minima and maxima (local and global) that allow a quick test of the effectiveness of any metaheuristic algorithm. The function has a global minimum at approximately −6.5 in the coordinates (0.2, −1.6), and its shape is illustrated in Figure 6.1. In order to graphically observe the MFO search process, its implementation has been carried out in two dimensions. Also, comments have been added in the code to explain each operation.

Program 4.1 Implementation of MFO in MATLAB®

```
%%%%%%%%%%%%%%%%%%%%%%%%%%%%%%%%%%%%%%%%%%%%%%%%%%%%%%%%%%%%%%%%%%%%%%%%%%
%%%%%%%%%%%%
% MFO method
% Erik Cuevas, Alma Rodríguez
%%%%%%%%%%%%%%%%%%%%%%%%%%%%%%%%%%%%%%%%%%%%%%%%%%%%%%%%%%%%%%%%%%%%%%%%%%
%%%%%%%%%%%%
%% Clear memory and close MATLAB windows
clear all % Clear memory
close all % close MATLAB windows
%% Problem to optimize (minimize), definition of the objective
function
f = @(xi) 3*(1-xi(1))^2*exp(-(xi(1)^2)-(xi(2)+1)^2)-
10*(xi(1)/5-xi(1)^3 - xi(2)^5)*exp(-xi(1)^2-
xi(2)^2)-1/3*exp(-(xi(1)+1)^2 - xi(2)^2);
%% Parameter configuration
N = 20; % Number of elements
d = 2; % Dimensions
lb = [-3 -3]; % Lower limit of the search space
ub = [3 3]; % Upper limit of the search space
k = 0; % Current iteration
kmax = 100; % Maximum number of iterations
b = 1; % Logarithmic spiral shape constant
%% Particle initialization
for i = 1:N
    X(i,:) = rand(1,d).*(ub-lb)+lb; % Element initialization
end
%% Evaluation of the initial population in the objective function
for i = 1:N
    xi=X(i,:); % Extraction of element xi
```

```matlab
        fx(i,:) = f(xi); % Evaluation of element xi
end
%% Sort the particles from best to worst
[fx_sort,ind]=sort(fx);
X_sort=X(ind,:);
%% Initialize local solutions based on the best particles
F=X_sort;
Ffit=fx_sort;
%% Selection of the best global solution
g=F(1,:);
gfit=Ffit(1);
%% Calculation of the surface
axisx=linspace(min(lb),max(ub),50);
axisy=axisx;
axisz=[];
for i = 1:length(axisx)
        for j = 1:length(axisy)
                axisz(i,j) = f([axisx(i) axisy(j)]);
        end
end
[axisy axisx] = meshgrid(axisx, axisy);
%% Optimization process
while k < kmax % Stop criterion
        k = k + 1; % Iteration increment
        %% Draw the objective function
        figure(1);
        surf(axisx, axisy, axisz)
        hold on
        %% Display particles and local solutions
        % Show the elements in red color
        plot3(X(:,1),X(:,2),fx,'o','MarkerFaceColor','m','Marker
        Size',10)
        % Show local solutions in yellow color
        plot3(F(:,1),F(:,2),Ffit,'o','MarkerFaceColor','y'
        ,'MarkerSize',10)
        % Make a pause to see results
        pause(0.1)
        hold off
        %% Show the contour of the objective function
        figure(2)
        contour(axisx,axisy,axisz,20)
        hold on
        %% Draw particles in contour
        % Show the elements in red color
        plot(X(:,1),X(:,2),'o','MarkerFaceColor','m');
        % Show local solutions in yellow color
        plot(F(:,1),F(:,2),'o','MarkerFaceColor','y');
```

```
% Make a pause to see results
pause(0.1)
hold off
%% Calculation of the number of local solutions
nF = round(N-k*((N-1)/kmax));
%% Convergence constant calculation
a = -1+k*((-1)/kmax);
%% Transverse orientation
for i = 1:N
% Extraction of element xi
xi = X(i,:);
if i <= nF
    % Extraction of local solution Fi
    Fi = F(i,:);
else
    % Extraction of the last local solution
    Fi = F(nF,:);
end
% Calculation of the random value vector r
r = (a-1)*rand(1,d)+1;
% Distance between the local solution and particle
Di = abs(Fi-xi);
% Calculation of the new position of the particle xi
X(i,:) = Di .* exp(b*r) .* cos(2*pi*r) + Fi;
end
%% Verify the limits lb y ub
for i = 1:N
    for j=1:d
        if X(i,j) < lb(j)
            X(i,j) = lb(j);
        elseif X(i,j) > ub(j)
            X(i,j) = ub(j);
        end
    end
end
%% Evaluation of the new particles
for i = 1:N
    xi = X(i,:);
    fx(i,:) = f(xi);
end
%% Combine local solutions with the new particles
X_total = [F;X];
fX_total = [Ffit;fx];
%% Sort particles and local solutions from best to worst
[fX_sort,ind]=sort(fX_total);
X_sort=X_total(ind,:);
%% Update local solutions based on the best nF particles
```

```
        F=X_sort(1:nF,:);
        Ffit=fX_sort(1:nF);
        %% Selection of the best global solution
        g=F(1,:);
        gfit=Ffit(1);
        %% Selection of the best solutions found in each generation
        Evolution(k) = gfit;
end
%% End of the iterative process, display of results
figure
plot(Evolution)
%% Graph of the evolutionary process of the MFO
disp(['The Best solution : ', num2str(g)])
disp(['The best fitness : ', num2str(gfit)])
```

If it is required to apply this method in more dimensions, the reader will have to make some modifications. These changes involve the modification of some algorithm parameters, such as the number of dimensions d, the lower limit lb and upper ub for each dimension.

It is important to point out that the higher the dimensionality of the problem to be optimized, the higher is the difficulty of the search. Having a greater number of search agents and more time to perform the search strategy would certainly help this process. Therefore, a reasonable adjustment in the number of particles and in the number of iterations is also recommended.

In Program 4.1, in addition to the indispensable code to implement the algorithm, the necessary code for to visualize the results has also been included. However, it should be considered that the part of the code responsible for the visualization is not part of the original algorithm.

4.5 APPLICATIONS OF MFO

The MFO algorithm has been used for a wide variety of applications, such as the segmentation of images (El Aziz, Ewees, & Hassanien, 2017), in the detection of the optimal parameters of machines used in the manufacturing process (Yıldız & Yıldız 2017), in the training of the perceptron with network multilayer (Yamany, Fawzy, Tharwat, & Hassanien, 2015), and for selection of features in the area of machine learning (Zawbaa, Emary, Parv, & Sharawi, 2016), to name a few.

The examples presented in this section will allow a better understanding of the MFO capacities and how to use it in real optimization problems. The applications used in this section have been selected for educational purposes. The problems consider one and two dimensions in order to be able to visualize the search process. Because of this, the MFO has been implemented for low dimensions, but it can be easily extended to more dimensions without significant changes.

It should be mentioned that, due to the nature of the problems used, these can be easily solved with other analytical techniques, such as those based on the gradient technique. However, although there are other appropriate methods to address these problems, such problems have been selected as examples of easy interpretation for the operation of the MFO. The solutions to these problems obtained with the MFO will be approximations with respect to the solutions provided by the analytical methods. MFO as any stochastic method, its solutions will not be the same at each execution due to the randomness in its operators.

4.5.1 Application of the MFO to Unconstrained Problems

There are problems in which the solution is only constrained or limited to the boundaries of the search space, so that the entire search area is a feasible area to find solutions. These types of problems are known as unconstrained problems.

Example 4.1

A cylindrical tank with water supply liquid to a well is required (see Figure 4.7). To do this, it is necessary to determine the distance f at which the well must be dug in relation to the tank wall. Furthermore, it is required to determine the distance x at which the tank must be drilled to provide water. Both parameter values should be computed so that the distance f presents its maximum value. The distance f is defined as follows:

$$f = 2\sqrt{x(h-x)} \tag{4.9}$$

where $h = 200$ represents the height (in centimeters) of the tank and x is the distance from the top of the tank to the hole in which water is distributed. The problem then consists in determining what is the distance x at which the tank should be drilled so that the distance f to the well is maximum?

Solution

The solution to this problem is implemented in Program 4.2. It uses a similar implementation as the one shown in Program 4.1, but with some slight changes. The first part that has been modified is the definition of the objective function of the problem. Note that this is a maximization problem. For this reason, the problem must be converted to a minimization problem considering the objective function from $f(x)$ to $-f(x)$. Furthermore, it is necessary to change the values of the parameters of dimension,

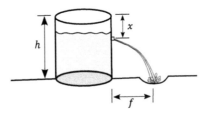

FIGURE 4.7 Tank and well problem.

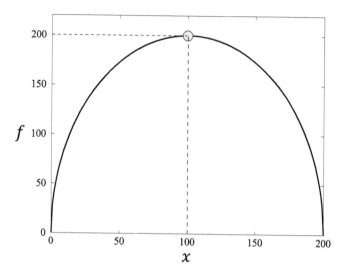

FIGURE 4.8 Graphical solution for the problem of the tank and the well.

number of particles, limits of the search space, and the maximum number of iterations. Therefore, the problem is one-dimensional since it is required to find only the value of x.

Under such conditions, in this problem, 3 particles and 30 iterations have been used. In the case of the limits of the search space, the lower and upper limits of the decision variable must be established. Because x represents the distance from the top of the tank to the output hole, then x must be greater than zero and less than the height of the tank h. Therefore, it is determined that the lower limit must be 0 and the upper be 200.

For visualization, it is necessary to make some changes in Program 4.1, Now, we need to generate graphs in one dimension and not in two. All these changes can be seen directly in Program 4.2. The code has been commented line by line detailing its operation.

Figure 4.8 shows the optimal solution to the problem, which is $x = 100$ and $f(x) = f = 200$. The figure illustrates that the maximum point is when $x = 100$, which means that the optimum distance to which the tank must be drilled is 100 cm and the maximum distance from the tank to the well is 200 cm. After executing Program 4.2, the solution is found. Note that the results may vary slightly when executing the code more than once. This is because stochastic algorithms (such as MFO) do not always converge to the same solution due to the use of random values in its implementation. Since the code includes comments that describe its operation line by line, additional explanation about it is omitted.

Program 4.2 Example 4.1 Application of the MFO to Constrained Problems

```
%%%%%%%%%%%%%%%%%%%%%%%%%%%%%%%%%%%%%%%%%%%%%%%%%%%%%%%%%%%%%%%%%%%%%%%%%%%%
%%%%%%%%%%%%
% Example 4.1
% Erik Cuevas, Alma Rodríguez
```

```
%%%%%%%%%%%%%%%%%%%%%%%%%%%%%%%%%%%%%%%%%%%%%%%%%%%%%%%%%%%%%%%%%%%%%%%%%
%%%%%%%%%%%
%% Clear memory and close MATLAB windows
clear all % Clear memory
close all % close MATLAB windows
%% Problem to optimize (minimize), definition of the objective
function
h = 200; % Tank height
% The objective function is negative because it is a maximization
problem
f = @(xi) -(2*sqrt(xi*(h-xi)));
%% Parameter configuration
N = 3; % Number of elements
d = 1; % Dimensions
lb = 0; % Lower limit of the search space
ub = 200; % Upper limit of the search space
k = 0; % Current iteration
kmax = 30; % Maximum number of iterations
b = 1; % Logarithmic spiral shape constant
%% Particle initialization
for i = 1:N
     X(i,:) = rand(1,d).*(ub-lb)+lb; % Element initialization
end
%% Evaluation of the initial population in the objective function
for i = 1:N
     xi = X(i,:); % Extraction of element xi
     fx(i,:) = f(xi); % Evaluation of element xi
end
%% Sort the particles from best to worst
[fx_sort,ind] = sort(fx);
X_sort = X(ind,:);
%% Initialize local solutions based on the best particles
F = X_sort;
Ffit = fx_sort;
%% Selection of the best global solution
g = F(1,:);
gfit = Ffit(1);
%% Calculation of the surface
axisx = lb:ub; % Solution vector
axisy=[];
for i = 1:length(axisx)
     axisy(i) = f(axisx(i));
end
%% Optimization process
while k < kmax % Stop criterion
     k = k + 1; % Iteration increment
     %% Draw the objective function
```

```
figure(1); % Show figure
plot(axisx,-axisy) % Draw the function
hold on % maintain the figure
%% Display particles and local solutions
% Show the elements in red color
plot(X,-fx,'o','MarkerFaceColor','m','MarkerSize',10)
% Show local solutions in yellow color
plot(F,-Ffit,'o','MarkerFaceColor','y','MarkerSize',10)
% Make a pause to see results
pause(0.3)
hold off
%% Show the contour of the objective function
nF = round(N-k*((N-1)/kmax));
%% Convergence constant calculation
a = -1+k*((-1)/kmax);
%% Transverse orientation
for i = 1:N
      % Extraction of element xi
      xi = X(i,:);
      if i <= nF
            % Extraction of local solution Fi
            Fi = F(i,:);
      else
            % Extraction of the last local solution
            Fi = F(nF,:);
      end
      % Calculation of the random value vector r
      r = (a-1)*rand(1,d)+1;
      % Distance between the local solution and particle
      Di = abs(Fi-xi);
      % Calculation of the new position of the particle xi
      X(i,:) = Di .* exp(b*r) .* cos(2*pi*r) + Fi;
end
%% Verify the limits lb y ub
for i = 1:N
      for j=1:d
            if X(i,j) < lb(j)
                  X(i,j) = lb(j);
            elseif X(i,j) > ub(j)
                  X(i,j) = ub(j);
            end
      end
end
%% Evaluation of the new particles
for i = 1:N
      xi = X(i,:); % Extraction of element xi
      fx(i,:) = f(xi); % Evaluation of element xi
```

```
      end
      %% Combine local solutions with the new particles
      X_total = [F;X];
      fX_total = [Ffit;fx];
      %% Sort particles and local solutions from best to worst
      [fX_sort,ind] = sort(fX_total);
      X_sort = X_total(ind,:);
      %% Update local solutions based on the best nF particles
      F = X_sort(1:nF,:);
      Ffit = fX_sort(1:nF);
      %% Selection of the best global solution
      g = F(1,:);
      gfit = Ffit(1);
      %% Selection of the best solutions found in each generation
      Evolution(k) = -gfit;
end
%% End of the iterative process, display of results
figure
plot(Evolution)
%% Graph of the evolutionary process of the MFO
disp(['Distance x: ', num2str(g)]) % Best solution
disp(['Distance f: ', num2str(-1*gfit)]) % The best fitness value
```

4.5.2 Application of the MFO to Problems with Constrained

In most of the optimization problems, there are restrictions that limit the possible values of the solutions. However, the MFO is an algorithm designed for unconstrained problems. For this reason, it can be adapted to solve these problems. One technique for working with restrictions is to implement a penalty function. These types of functions deteriorate those solutions that do not meet the restrictions of the problem, giving them a high fitness value (if it is a minimization problem) or a low value (if it is a maximization problem). The next example solves a problem with restrictions. This problem corresponds to a minimization formulation with two dimensions and one inequality constraint. Program 4.1 has been used to solve this problem with just a few modifications. Such changes consist of adjusting the values of the parameters and adding the penalty function. In Program 4.3, these modifications have been already implemented.

Example 4.2

In a farm, it is required to delimit a rectangular terrain with a minimum area of $1,500\,m^2$. The land must be fenced and divided into two equal parts, see Figure 4.9. What dimensions should the terrain be in such a way that the least amount of fence is used?

Solution

With just a few modifications, Program 4.1 can be used as a basis for solving this problem. The first part that should be modified is the problem definition corresponding

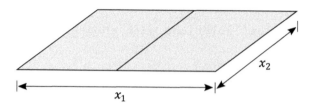

FIGURE 4.9   Fence problem.

to the objective function. Since the problem does not explicitly provide an objective function, it must be modeled based on the information provided by its definition. In the problem, the idea is to minimize the amount of fence used to fence the land area. To calculate the necessary amount of fence z, the perimeter plus the portion of fence that divides the land in two parts must be considered, that is

$$f = 2x_1 + 3x_2 \tag{4.10}$$

The problem has a restriction, which indicates that the fenced area should have a minimal area of 1,500 m², so that

$$x_1 x_2 \geq 1,500 \tag{4.11}$$

Therefore, the problem is to find the values of x_1 and x_2 such that the total fence length f used to limit the land is minimal, but conserving a minimum area of 1,500 m².

To define the limits of the search space, it should be considered that the values of x_1 and x_2 must be higher than zero. Therefore, the lower limit will be greater than zero for both dimensions. To determine the upper limit for each dimension, we can assume an extreme case in which one of the variables is one in Eq. 4.11. Under this consideration, if any of the variables x_1 or x_2 has a value of 1, then the other variable will have the value of 1,500. Consequently, the value of 1,500 represents the upper limit for both variables.

Although the restriction allows that the area of the land maintains a value greater than or equal to 1,500 m², it should be considered that the objective is to minimize the amount of used fence. Under such conditions, it is also considered to minimize the area of the land. Assigning a limit higher than 1,500 means assigning more area to the land. This fact would not make sense because the search area would only be expanding to a region where there are no promising solutions. The algorithm will try to find the solution that minimizes the amount of fence necessary. Therefore, the tendency will be to find a solution that generates an area very close to 1,500 m², since this is the minimum allowed area.

The number of particles and the maximum number of iterations have been modified due to the complexity of the problem. In general, a problem with restrictions represents a greater challenge, as it reduces the area where the feasible solutions can be located. In these cases, a greater number of search agents will be required and probably also a higher number of iterations to perform the search process. In practice, the reader will realize the impact of adjusting these parameters on the quality of the solutions.

The last modification corresponds to the penalty function. This function requires four parameters to initialize, two for equality constraints and two for inequality constraints. Since the problem has only one restriction (this is one of inequality), it is only necessary to initialize two parameters: the penalty constant rg and the penalty multiplier cg. Therefore, the penalty function can be reformulated as follows:

$$P = rg \cdot max(0, g1) \tag{4.12}$$

where $g1$ is the inequality constraint and rg is computed as follows:

$$rg = rg \cdot cg \tag{4.13}$$

Based on the problem information, the restriction considers that the area of the land must be not less than $1{,}500\,m^2$, so that

$$x_1 x_2 \geq 1{,}500$$

$$x_1 x_2 - 1{,}500 \geq 0$$

Then, the restriction would be formulated as follows:

$$g1 = x_1 x_2 - 1{,}500 \tag{4.14}$$

Considering this restriction, a change in Eq. 4.12 is required since the penalized solutions must be those that are less than zero and not upside down. The penalty function of Eq. 4.12 deteriorates those solutions that are greater than zero and the constrain indicates that the solutions must be greater than zero, so this equation should be modified as follows:

$$P = rg \cdot min(0, g1) \tag{4.15}$$

The values of the penalty constant rg and the penalty multiplier cg are adjustable based on the particularity of each problem. The reader can test different values and observe the changes in the performance of the algorithm. The objective is that at the beginning rg maintains a small value. Then it gradually increases as the generations progresses so that the penalty is greater. In the case of cg, its value is constant and is used as a multiplicative factor to modify rg in each iteration.

Due to its linear nature, this problem can be solved by using linear programming techniques. However, this problem is used as an example to illustrate the operation of the MFO. When applying the MFO, it will find values very close to those found with other techniques.

The values that minimize the amount of fence used are $x_1 = 47.43$ and $x_2 = 31.62$. The land area is $x_1 x_2 = (47.43)(31.62) \approx 1{,}500\,\text{m}^2$. The minimum fence length used is $f = 2x_1 + 3x_2 = 2(47.43) + 3(31.62) = 189.72$. The results obtained with the MFO can vary a bit since they are approximations. In addition, due to the randomness of the method, the results may also vary from one execution to another so that the same results are not obtained in independent executions. However, they are very approximate.

Program 4.3 Example 4.2 Application of the MFO to Problems with Constrains

```
%%%%%%%%%%%%%%%%%%%%%%%%%%%%%%%%%%%%%%%%%%%%%%%%%%%%%%%%%%%%%%%%%%%%%%%%%%%
%%%%%%%%%%%%
% Example 4.2
% Erik Cuevas, Alma Rodríguez
%%%%%%%%%%%%%%%%%%%%%%%%%%%%%%%%%%%%%%%%%%%%%%%%%%%%%%%%%%%%%%%%%%%%%%%%%%%
%%%%%%%%%%%%
%% Clear memory and close MATLAB windows
clear all % Clear memory
close all % close MATLAB windows
%% Problem to optimize (minimize), definition of the objective
function
f = @(x) 2*x(1) + 3*x(2);
%% Parameter configuration
N = 150; % Number of elements
d = 2; % Dimensions
lb = [0 0]; % Lower limit of the search space
ub = [1500 1500]; % Upper limit of the search space
k = 0; % Current iteration
kmax = 800; % Maximum number of iterations
b = 1; % Logarithmic spiral shape constant
%% Parameters of the penalization function
rg = 100; % Penalization constant
cg = 1.2; % Penalization multiplier
%% Particle initialization
for i = 1:N
      X(i,:) = rand(1,d).*(ub-lb)+lb; % Element initialization
end
%% Evaluation of the initial population in the objective function
fxp = [];
for i = 1:N
      xi = X(i,:); % Extraction of element xi
      fx(i,:) = f(xi); % Evaluation of element xi
      g1 = xi(1)*xi(2)-1500; % inequality constrain
      P = rg * min(0,g1)^2; % Penalization function
      fxp(i) = fx(i) + P; % Penalized fitness
      rg = rg * cg; % Update the penalization constant
end
```

```matlab
%% Sort the particles from best to worst
[fxp_sort,ind] = sort(fxp);
X_sort = X(ind,:);
%% Initialize local solutions based on the best particles
F = X_sort;
Ffit = fxp_sort;
%% Selection of the best global solution
g = F(1,:);
gfit = Ffit(1);
%% Calculation of the surface
axisx = linspace(min(lb),max(ub),100); % Solution vector for
dimension 1
axisy = axisx; % Solution vector for dimension 2
axisz = []; % Fitness matrix
for i = 1:length(axisx)
      for j = 1:length(axisy)
            axisz(i,j) = f([axisx(i) axisy(j)]);
      end
end
[axisy axisx] = meshgrid(axisx,axisy); % Compute the grid
%% Optimization process
while k < kmax % Stop criterion
      k = k + 1; % Iteration increment
      %% Draw the objective function
      figure(1); % Show figure
      surf(axisx,axisy,axisz) % Draw the function
      hold on % maintain the figure
      %% Display particles and local solutions
      % Show the elements in red color
      plot3(X(:,1),X(:,2),fx,'o','MarkerFaceColor','m','Marker
      Size',10)
      % Show local solutions in yellow color
      plot3(F(:,1),F(:,2),Ffit,'o','MarkerFaceColor','y','Marker
      Size',10)
      % Make a pause to see results
      pause(0.01)
      hold off
      %% Show the contour of the objective function
      figure(2) % Show Figure 2
      contour(axisx,axisy,axisz,20) % Draw the function contour
      hold on
      %% Display particles and local solutions on the contour
      % Show the elements in red color
      plot(X(:,1),X(:,2),'o','MarkerFaceColor','m');
      % Show local solutions in yellow color
      plot(F(:,1),F(:,2),'o','MarkerFaceColor','y');
      % Make a pause to see results
```

```
pause(0.01)
hold off
%% Compute the number of local solutions
nF = round(N-k*((N-1)/kmax));
%% Convergence constant calculation
a = -1+k*((-1)/kmax);
%% Transverse orientation
for i = 1:N
        % Extraction of element xi
        xi = X(i,:);
        if i <= nF
                % Extraction of local solution Fi
                Fi = F(i,:);
        else
                % Extraction of the last local solution
                Fi = F(nF,:);
        end
        % Calculation of the random value vector r
        r = (a-1)*rand(1,d)+1;
        % Distance between the local solution and particle
        Di = abs(Fi-xi);
        % Calculation of the new position of the particle xi
        X(i,:) = Di .* exp(b*r) .* cos(2*pi*r) + Fi;
end
%% Verify the limits lb y ub
for i = 1:N
        for j = 1:d
                if X(i,j) < lb(j)
                        X(i,j) = lb(j);
                elseif X(i,j) > ub(j)
                        X(i,j) = ub(j);
                end
        end
end
%% Evaluation of the new particles
fxp = [];
for i = 1:N
        xi = X(i,:); % Extraction of element xi
        fx(i,:) = f(xi); % Evaluation of element xi
        g1 = xi(1)*xi(2)-1500; % Constrain
        P = rg * min(0,g1)^2; % Penalization function
        fxp(i) = fx(i) + P; % Penalized function
        % Update the constant of penalization
        rg = rg * cg;
end
%% Combine local solutions with the new particles
X_total = [F;X];
```

```
        fX_total = [Ffit,fxp];
        %% Sort particles and local solutions from best to worst
        [fX_sort,ind] = sort(fX_total);
        X_sort = X_total(ind,:);
        %% Update local solutions based on the best nF particles
        F = X_sort(1:nF,:);
        Ffit = fX_sort(1:nF);
        %% Selection of the best global solution
        g = F(1,:);
        gfit = Ffit(1);
        %% Selection of the best solutions found in each generation
        Evolution(k) = gfit;
end
%% End of the iterative process
figure
plot(Evolution)
%% Display of results
disp(['x1 : ', num2str(g(1)),' x2 :',num2str(g(2))])
disp(['Fence length : ', num2str(gfit)])
disp(['Land area : ', num2str(g(1)*g(2))])
```

REFERENCES

El Aziz, M. A., Ewees, A. A., & Hassanien, A. E. (2017). Whale optimization algorithm and moth-flame optimization for multilevel thresholding image segmentation. *Expert Systems with Applications*, 83, 242–256.

Kaur, K., Singh, U., & Salgotra, R. (2018, October). An enhanced moth flame optimization. *Neural Computing and Applications*, 32, 2315–2349.

Khalilpourazari, S., & Khalilpourazary, S. (2019, March). An efficient hybrid algorithm based on water cycle and moth-flame optimization algorithms for solving numerical and constrained engineering optimization problems. *Soft Computing*, 23(5), 1699–1722.

Li, Z., Zhou, Y., Zhang, S., & Song, J. (2016). Lévy-flight moth-flame algorithm for function optimization and engineering design problems. *Mathematical Problems in Engineering*, 2016 1–22.

Mirjalili, S. (2015, November). Moth-flame optimization algorithm: A novel nature-inspired heuristic paradigm. *Knowledge-Based Systems*, 89, 228–249.

Xu, L., Li, Y., Li, K., Beng, G. H., Jiang, Z., Wang, C., & Liu, N. (2018, July). Enhanced moth-flame optimization based on cultural learning and Gaussian mutation. *Journal of Bionic Engineering*, 15(4), 751–763.

Xu, Y., Chen, H., Luo, J., Zhang, Q., Jiao, S., & Zhang, X. (2019). Enhanced moth-flame optimizer with mutation strategy for global optimization. *Information Sciences*, 492, 181–203.

Yamany, W., Fawzy, M., Tharwat, A., & Hassanien, A. E. (2015). *Moth-flame optimization for training multi-layer perceptrons*. In *11th International Computer Engineering Conference (ICENCO)* (pp. 267–272), Cairo. IEEE. https://doi.org/10.1109/ICENCO.2015.7416360

Yıldız, B. S., & Yıldız, A. R. (2017, May). Moth-flame optimization algorithm to determine optimal machining parameters in manufacturing processes. *Materials Testing*, 59(5), 425–429.

Zawbaa, H. M., Emary, E., Parv, B., & Sharawi, M. (2016). *Feature selection approach based on moth-flame optimization algorithm*. In *IEEE Congress on Evolutionary Computation (CEC)* (pp. 4612–4617), Vancouver, Canada: IEEE. https://doi.org/10.1109/CEC.2016.7744378

CHAPTER 5

Differential Evolution (DE)

5.1 INTRODUCTION

In 1995, Rainer Price solved the Chebyshev polynomial adjustment problem (Rozenberg et al., 2005) by using the Genetic Annealing algorithm (Price, 1994). Although he found the solution to this problem, he concludes that this algorithm did not meet the performance requirements of a competitive optimization technique such as strong global search capability, rapid convergence, and easy implementation. Under such circumstances, Price (Storn & Price, 1997) devised a novel scheme based on vector calculus in combination with principles of evolutionary computation. In the proposed method, the generation of parameter vectors is performed by adding the weighted difference between two members of the population with a third member. This operator is known as differential mutation. It has proven to be an efficient proposal showing superior performance to some other metaheuristic schemes for solving optimization problems. Its main characteristics are easy implementation, convergence properties consisting of independent tests, and capacity of parallelization to solve problems of high computational cost. The most important feature of the DE algorithm is the ability of its search strategy to obtain the optimal global solution of multimodal, non-differentiable, and nonlinear functions. DE algorithm has already proven its capabilities in competitions such as the IEEE Congress on Evolutionary Computation (CEC), as well as in various real-world optimization applications. Similar to other metaheuristic methods, the DE algorithm maintains an iterative behavior. Therefore, DE uses a set of exploration–exploitation operators (mutation and crossing), which are used throughout the optimization process to find the best solution to an optimization problem. However, in the area of metaheuristic algorithms, exploration–exploitation operators must present a balance during the search process. Without this balance, the performance of evolutionary optimization techniques decreases by presenting difficulties in certain real-world applications. To avoid this effect, the DE algorithm has mechanisms to avoid falling into local optimal solutions. For this purpose, the mutation operator performs a direct strategy exploring areas of the search space that have not been initially explored. On the other hand, the crossover operator has a mechanism that increases the diversity of the population ensuring that the global optimum can be located.

5.2 DE SEARCH STRATEGY

Similar to other metaheuristic algorithms, DE is a population algorithm where its members are considered as vectors of parameters. The positions of such vectors are modified as the optimization process progresses. The evolutionary process of the DE algorithm can be described by a series of four steps. In the first step, the initialization of a population is generated. In this step, the parameter vectors are stochastically generated by considering random elements over the limits of the search space of the problem to be optimized. In the second phase, the differential mutation is applied to the elements of the population to achieve recombination among individuals. In the third stage, the information between population elements is combined through the crossover operator to increase population diversity. Finally, in the fourth step, an elitist selection mechanism is considered to select the best individuals so that in each generation the promising solutions will prevail.

To illustrate the DE process, Figure 5.1 shows the distribution of nine solutions on a two-dimensional surface. In this figure, the difference between two randomly taken points is calculated. In this case, the vectors x_{r_1} and x_{r_2} corresponding to points 7 and 9, respectively, are considered.

Then, the difference calculated in the previous point is scaled and added to a third vector taken randomly x_{r_3} (corresponding to point 5). A scaling factor F indicates the proportion of the difference between points x_{r_1} and x_{r_2} that will be added to the vector x_{r_3}. All these elements generate a fourth vector known as *mutant* v_1. This procedure is described graphically in Figure 5.2.

Finally, in Figure 5.3, the mutant vector v_1 illustrated a better fitness value than the original point (the point labeled as 1). This implies that in the population the vector v_1 will replace the original vector when it maintains better quality.

The procedure described above will be executed by the DE algorithm until a stop criterion has been reached. It is commonly determined in base on the maximum number of generations that the optimization process requires. At the end of all iterations, the best

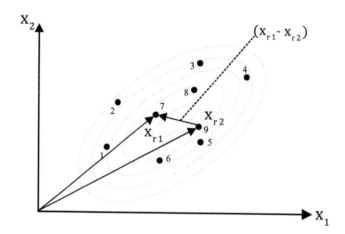

FIGURE 5.1 Graphical description of the difference between two random vectors used by the search process in the DE algorithm.

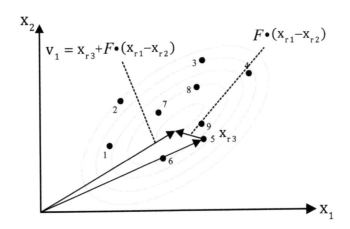

FIGURE 5.2 Graphical representation of the addition between the weighted difference of two vectors with a third random vector used by the search process in the DE algorithm.

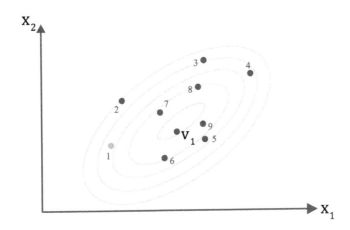

FIGURE 5.3 Graphical representation of the mutant replacement vector.

solution is obtained. This element solves the formulated optimization problem (maximization or minimization).

5.2.1 Population Structure

The population of the DE algorithm maintains a set of N parameter vectors whose positions are defined on a d-dimensional space of real values. The population, symbolized by $\mathbf{X}$, is composed of a set of parameter vectors $\{\mathbf{x}_1^k, \mathbf{x}_2^k, \ldots, \mathbf{x}_N^k\}$, where each element $\mathbf{x}_i^k$ represents a position in a d-dimensional space so that $\{x_1, x_2, \ldots, x_d\}$. These vectors will be manipulated by a set of operators: mutation, crossover, and selection during each generation (iteration) k of the algorithm with the objective of guiding the search strategy towards the global optimum. In each operator of the DE algorithm, the generation of a new candidate solution is carried out in such a way that the balance between exploration and exploitation is maintained. This fact guarantees that the population increases its diversity. Therefore, once the DE algorithm has initialized the positions of each member of the population in a random and uniformly distributed manner, the mutation, crossover, and selection operators are executed iteratively. The mutation operation is the mechanism by which the DE algorithm explores areas within the search space producing a direct search scheme towards the global optimum, while the crossover operation will be responsible for increasing the diversity in the positions of each of the parameter vectors. Finally, the selection operation will be responsible for maintaining the population with the best individuals. For this, in each iteration, the vector generated by the mutation and crossover operations is tested in terms of its fitness value. If it has a better performance than corresponding previous individuals in the population, the new vector will replace it; otherwise, the original vector will remain in the population. This mechanism ensures that only the best solutions will be part of future generations allowing the exchange of information of only promising solutions. Therefore, the algorithm maintains a good convergence to the global optimum of the optimization problem.

5.2.2 Initialization

The initialization is the first step in DE. Initialization is necessary to specify the limits of the search space for the optimization problem to be solved. These vectors represent the lower and upper limits for each of the dimensions of the problem. These constraints are known as box constraints. The lower limit vector is represented by $\mathbf{lb} = [lb_1, lb_2, \ldots, lb_d]$ and the upper limit vector as $\mathbf{ub} = [ub_1, ub_2, \ldots, ub_d]$.

Once the search space limits have been specified, a scheme of random number generation is established. This mechanism follows a uniformly distributed distribution to generate sample data. This scheme will assign a value to every position of each of the members of the population within the range established by the lower and upper limits, as follows:

$$\mathbf{X} = \mathbf{lb} + \mathbf{r}(0,1) \cdot (\mathbf{ub} - \mathbf{lb}) \tag{5.1}$$

where $\mathbf{lb}$ and $\mathbf{ub}$ represent the vectors of lower and upper limits, respectively, while $\mathbf{r}(0,1)$ denotes a vector of random numbers within the uniformly distributed range $(0,1)$.

5.2.3 Mutation

Once the initialization process has been executed, the DE algorithm will use the mutation operator in order to recombine the elements of the population to produce a modified version of each individual. This simple operator allows the DE algorithm to be so popular because of its mathematical simplicity that represents this mutation behavior. Within the specifications of the DE algorithm, the mutation operator is also known as *differential mutation* since it is based on the differences between the different candidate solutions in the population to promote the exchange of information among all elements.

In the published literature referring to the DE algorithm, there are different modifications of the general scheme of operation in the DE algorithm. Many of these improvements involve the modification of the mutation operator. The most commonly used mutation modification in real applications will be described in this section. The mathematical model that defines the differential mutation in its generic form is described below.

The generic model of the differential mutation combines the randomly scaled difference between two vectors belonging to the population, with a third vector of the same population. This fourth vector is known as a mutant vector. Therefore, the differential mutation takes the following mathematical description:

$$\mathbf{v}^k = \left\{ \mathbf{x}_{r_3}^k + F \cdot \left(\mathbf{x}_{r_1}^k - \mathbf{x}_{r_2}^k \right) \right. \tag{5.2}$$

where $\mathbf{x}_{r_1}^k$, $\mathbf{x}_{r_2}^k$, and $\mathbf{x}_{r_3}^k$ $(r_1, r_2, r_3 \in \{1, 2, \ldots, N\}$ and $r_1 \neq r_2 \neq r_3 \neq i)$ represent randomly selected candidate solution among the population, while the scaling value $F \in [0,2]$ corresponds to the so-called differential weight. This factor regulates the magnitude of variation with respect to the difference $\left(\mathbf{x}_{r_1}^k - \mathbf{x}_{r_2}^k \right)$. The scaling factor is a numerical value that controls the magnitude in which the population will evolve. This helps to balance the optimization process. If this value is close to zero, the process will converge faster; otherwise, the process will converge slowly. Under these conditions, this parameter is set with a predefined value. In fact, its value depends on the application at hand.

To illustrate the mutation process, Figure 5.4 graphically represents the differential mutation operator. In the figure, there are three parameter vectors represented by $\mathbf{x}_{r_1}^k$, $\mathbf{x}_{r_2}^k$, and $\mathbf{x}_{r_3}^k$, respectively. The mutation procedure generates a fourth vector (mutant vector) $\mathbf{v}^k$ which is the candidate solution resulting from the addition between the vector $\mathbf{x}_{r_3}^k$ and the scaled difference of the vectors $\mathbf{x}_{r_1}^k$ and $\mathbf{x}_{r_2}^k$. As can be seen in the image, the resulting mutant vector is located in a different area in comparison with the current vectors of the population. Therefore, it is clear that this operator allows to efficiently explore the search space.

Equation 5.2 describes the simplest and most common way of combining three candidate solutions randomly selected from population $\mathbf{X}$ to create a fourth parameter vector. However, the involved vectors with subscript r_1, r_2, r_3 can be selected in a large number of forms. Depending on this selection, several behaviors of the DE algorithm can be expected.

The variants of the DE algorithm are mostly based on modifications made to the mutation operator. These variants have been generated by scientists and engineers who have carefully analyzed the operation of the mutation under different contexts that exhibit

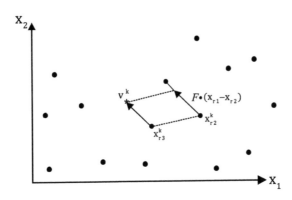

FIGURE 5.4 Graphical representation of the mutation operator used in the search process of the DE algorithm.

complex surfaces to optimize (Qing, 2009). The mutation strategies described below assume that there is a population **X** of solutions, where each of these solutions is initialized uniformly distributed in the search space following the guidelines described in Section 5.2.2. Furthermore, the exposed notation considers the mutation in a certain generation k.

Mutation rand/1

$$\mathbf{v}^k = \left\{ \mathbf{x}_{r_3}^k + F \cdot \left(\mathbf{x}_{r_1}^k - \mathbf{x}_{r_2}^k \right) \right\} \tag{5.3}$$

This mechanism indicates that vectors $\mathbf{x}_{r_1}^k$, $\mathbf{x}_{r_2}^k$, and $\mathbf{x}_{r_3}^k$ are randomly selected from the population, considering that they must be different from each other $\left(r_1, r_2, r_3 \in \{1,2,\ldots,N\} \text{ and } r_1 \neq r_2 \neq r_3 \neq i \right)$. This mutation strategy is the most used among real aplications because it mantains a high level of diversity in the population and low computational cost.

Mutación best/1

$$\mathbf{v}^k = \left\{ \mathbf{x}_{best}^k + F \cdot \left(\mathbf{x}_{r_1}^k - \mathbf{x}_{r_2}^k \right) \right\} \tag{5.4}$$

Under this strategy, individuals $\mathbf{x}_{r_1}^k$ and $\mathbf{x}_{r_2}^k$ (where r_1 and $r_2 \in \{1,2,\ldots,N\}$ and $r_1 \neq r_2 \neq i$) are randomly selected from the population considering that they must be different among them. In turn, the vector $\mathbf{x}_{best}^k$ is the best element of the population in the iteration k. This strategy is the most used, since in most cases it suggests a rapid convergence towards the global optimum. However, this mutation decreases the population diversity causing that candidate solutions are attracted to a local optimum.

Mutation rand/2

$$\mathbf{v}^k = \left\{ \mathbf{x}_{r_5}^k + F \cdot \left(\mathbf{x}_{r_1}^k - \mathbf{x}_{r_2}^k \right) + F \cdot \left(\mathbf{x}_{r_3}^k - \mathbf{x}_{r_4}^k \right) \right\} \tag{5.5}$$

This mutation considers the use of five parameter vectors $\mathbf{x}_{r_1}^k$, $\mathbf{x}_{r_2}^k$, $\mathbf{x}_{r_3}^k$, $\mathbf{x}_{r_4}^k$, and $\mathbf{x}_{r_5}^k$ (where r_1, r_2, r_3, r_4 and $r_5 \in \{1,2,\ldots,N\}$ and $r_1 \neq r_2 \neq r_3 \neq r_4 \neq r_5 \neq i$). They are randomly selected. This strategy is useful in problems that present high dimensionality since they require higher diversity in the population. Since the mutant vector $\mathbf{v}^k$ involves relevant information extracted from the five individuals, the communication channel among individuals becomes more extensive in this model.

Mutation best/2

$$\mathbf{v}^k = \left\{ \mathbf{x}_{best}^k + F \cdot \left(\mathbf{x}_{r_1}^k - \mathbf{x}_{r_2}^k \right) + F \cdot \left(\mathbf{x}_{r_3}^k - \mathbf{x}_{r_4}^k \right) \right\} \tag{5.6}$$

This strategy uses four randomly selected solutions considering that they are different from each other (r_1, r_2, r_3 and $r_4 \in \{1,2,\ldots,N\}$ and $r_1 \neq r_2 \neq r_3 \neq r_4 \neq i$). This strategy is useful when it is faced with multimodal functions that require a rapid convergence towards the global optimum. This variant involves an interesting individual combination that allows also increasing the diversity of the population and improving the exploitation phase of the algorithm.

Mutation current-to-best/1

$$\mathbf{v}^k = \left\{ \mathbf{x}_i^k + F \cdot \left(\mathbf{x}_{best}^k - \mathbf{x}_i^k \right) + F \cdot \left(\mathbf{x}_{r_1}^k - \mathbf{x}_{r_2}^k \right) \right. \tag{5.7}$$

Under this mutation operator, two randomly selected solutions are used, considering that they are different from each other (r_1 and $r_2 \in \{1,2,...,N\}$ and $r_1 \neq r_2 \neq i$). The vector $\mathbf{x}_i^k$ corresponds to the current individual of the population on which the mutation operation is being performed. Also, the vector $\mathbf{x}_{best}^k$ is the best element of the population in the iteration k. Given that in this strategy two random elements of the population are considered, the diversity of the population is maintained at some level. The difference produced between the best individual and the current individual ensures convergence on the best individual. The problem presented in this strategy is when most of the individuals are concentrated in the neighborhoods of the best individual, it consequently decreases the population diversity.

5.2.4 Crossover

The main purpose of crossover is to increase the diversity of each solution vector. This indicates that crossover complements the mutation strategy used causing that the diversity of the population increases. For this operation, the mutant vector $\mathbf{v}^k$ and the individual $\mathbf{x}_i^k$ undergo a recombination process that considers an element-to-element exchange operation between the vectors to generate a test vector $\mathbf{u}^k$. This process is calculated considering the following scheme:

$$\mathbf{u}^k = u_j^k \begin{cases} v_{i,j}^k & \text{if } j = j_{\text{rand}(0,1)} \text{ or } \mathbf{rand}(0,1) \leq CR \\ x_{i,j}^k & \text{otherwise} \end{cases} \tag{5.8}$$

where $j_{\text{rand}(0,1)} \in \{1,2,...,d\}$ represents one of the positions of the i-th solution vector. Also, $\mathbf{rand}(0,1)$ denotes a random value within the uniformly distributed range $(0,1)$. The crossover parameter CR controls the number of parameters that the mutant vector $\mathbf{v}^k$ contributes to the test vector $\mathbf{u}^k$. The crossover parameter is one of the configuration parameters of the DE algorithm and takes a value within the interval $[0,1]$.

The crossover operation randomly exchanges positions between the individual $\mathbf{x}_i^k$ of the population with the mutant vector $\mathbf{v}^k$ calculated in Eq. 5.2. Under crossover, the parameter CR is a probabilistic factor that indicates which positions of the mutant vector will be taken into account for the generation of the test vector $\mathbf{u}^k$, and which positions will be used from the individual $\mathbf{x}_i^k$. If the output of the random number generator $\mathbf{rand}(0,1)$ is less than or equal to the CR value, the parameter for the test vector $\mathbf{u}^k$ is obtained from the mutant vector $\mathbf{v}^k$; if not, then the parameter for the vector test $\mathbf{u}^k$ is extracted from the individual's vector $\mathbf{x}_i^k$.

To illustrate the mutation process described above, Figure 5.5 graphically describes the operation of crossover between the parameter vector $\mathbf{x}_i^k$ with the mutant vector $\mathbf{v}^k$ calculated in Eq. 5.8. In the figure, it can be seen that the vectors $\mathbf{x}_i^k$, $\mathbf{v}^k$, and $\mathbf{u}^k$ are within

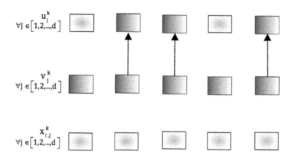

$\forall j \in [1,2,...,d]$ $\mathbf{u}^k_j$

$\forall j \in [1,2,...,d]$ $\mathbf{v}^k_j$

$\forall j \in [1,2,...,d]$ $\mathbf{x}^k_{i,j}$

FIGURE 5.5 Graphical representation of the crossover operator used by the search process in the DE algorithm.

a five-dimensional space ($d=5$). Each of the positions of the vectors is represented by the boxes that appear next to the name corresponding to the vector in question. In the example, the test vector $\mathbf{u}^k$ is generated by considering the first ($j=1$) and fourth ($j=4$) positions of the parameter vector $\mathbf{x}^k_i$, while the mutant vector $\mathbf{v}^k$ contributes to the second ($j=2$), third ($j=3$), and fifth ($j=5$) positions of the vector $\mathbf{u}^k$. In the figure, the arrows represent the test performed in Eq. 5.3. If a random value is less than the CR crossover probability, the parameter value of $\mathbf{u}^k$ is obtained from the corresponding position of the vector $\mathbf{v}^k$. Otherwise, it will be extracted from vector $\mathbf{x}^k_i$.

5.2.5 Selection

The selection operation aims to maintain the best solutions within the population throughout the optimization process. To do this, once the mutation and crossover operations have been executed, the test vector $\mathbf{u}^k$ is a candidate to be part of the population if it meets a quality selection criterion. Under this selection, the test vector will be considered to replace its previous version if and only if it represents a better solution than it.

The selection criterion considers the calculated fitness value of the test vector $\mathbf{u}^k$ and the fitness value of the individual corresponding to it $(\mathbf{x}^k_i)$. The decision is based on the following rule. If the fitness of the test vector $f(\mathbf{u}^k)$ is less than the fitness of the corresponding individual $f(\mathbf{x}^k_i)$, then the test vector $\mathbf{u}^k$ will replace the individual $\mathbf{x}^k_i$ to be part of the population in the next generation Otherwise, $\mathbf{x}^k_i$ will remain in the population for at least one more generation. This selection mechanism is summarized in the following equation:

$$\mathbf{x}^k_i = \begin{cases} \mathbf{u}^k, & \text{if } f(\mathbf{u}^k) \leq f(\mathbf{x}^k_i) \\ \mathbf{x}^k_i, & \text{otherwise} \end{cases} \tag{5.9}$$

where $f()$ represents the objective function to be optimized. This selection operation is repeated in each generation of the algorithm until a stop criterion is reached. The most commonly used stop criterion is the maximum number of generations K_{max} that the user defines at the beginning of the optimization process.

TABLE 5.1   Typical Parameter Setting for the DE Algorithm

Parameters	
F	CR
0.2	0.5

5.3 COMPUTATIONAL PROCESS OF DE

As it is described in the previous section, the DE algorithm conducts a search strategy to find the global optimal value through the addition of the scaled differences of two members of the population to a third member. This mechanism generates a robust search strategy that significantly improves the convergence speed and whose performance is better than other optimization techniques. The DE algorithm is cataloged as a population algorithm since it uses the information of its members to intensify the exploitation to find promising solutions.

The DE algorithm has four basic operations in its operation. Initialization, in this operation a population is created and initialized with values that belong within the limits of the search space. Mutation, this operator is considered the most representative of the DE algorithm, since it uses the weighted difference of the positions of some members of the population and its addition to the position of another vector generating a fast and efficient search strategy. Crossover, this procedure is carried out to increase the diversity of the population. Finally, the selection operation preserves those individuals that are better to be used in later generations.

5.3.1 Implementation of the DE Scheme

For each operator of the DE algorithm, a set of specific steps is required to modify the position of each of the parameter vectors belonging to the population in each iteration. Each of these steps represents a characteristic behavior of individuals on the search surface. Table 5.1 shows the typical parameter setting corresponding to the weighting factor and the crossover factor of the DE. These values have been suggested by works published in the literature of evolutionary computation (Díaz-Cortés, Cuevas, Gálvez, & Camarena, 2017; Gämperle, Müller, & Koumoutsakos, 2002; Rangaiah & Sharma, 2017). The generic DE algorithm can be illustrated by the pseudocode shown in Algorithm 5.1.

Algorithm 5.1 The General Procedure of the DE Algorithm

Step 1: Initialization of the population $\mathbf{X}^k$ (**Section 5.2.2**)

$$\mathbf{X} = \mathbf{lb} + \mathbf{r}(0,1) \cdot (\mathbf{ub} - \mathbf{lb})$$

Step 2: Mutation operator (**Section 5.2.3**)

$$r_1, r_2, r_3 \in \{1, 2, \ldots, N\}, r_1 \neq r_2 \neq r_3 \neq i$$

$$\mathbf{v}^k = \mathbf{x}_{r_3}^k + F \cdot \left(\mathbf{x}_{r_1}^k - \mathbf{x}_{r_2}^k \right)$$

Step 3: Crossover operation (**Section 5.2.4**)
for $(j=1; j<d; j++)$
if $\left(j = j_{\mathbf{rand}(0,1)} \text{ or } \mathbf{rand}(0,1) \leq CR \right)$

$$u_j^k = v_{i,j}^k$$

else

$$u_j^k = x_{i,j}^k$$

end if
end for

$$\mathbf{u}^k = u_j^k$$

Step 4: Selection process (**Section 5.2.5**)
if $\left(f\left(\mathbf{u}^k \right) \leq f\left(\mathbf{x}_i^k \right) \right)$

$$\mathbf{x}_i^k = \mathbf{u}^k$$

else

$$\mathbf{x}_i^k = \mathbf{x}_i^k$$

end if

In general terms, each of the parameter vectors $\mathbf{x}_i^k$ of the population can be subjected to the mutation, crossover, and selection operators described in Section 5.2. Therefore, at the end of this process, a new set of vectors is generated. This process is repeated for each iteration that conforms to the optimization process.

5.3.2 The General Process of DE

Figure 5.6 illustrates the flowchart that describes the entire optimization process that is carried out by the search strategy of the DE algorithm.

As it is shown in the flowchart, the algorithm initializes first considering a set of initial solutions $\mathbf{X}^0 = \left\{ \mathbf{x}_1^0, \mathbf{x}_2^0, \ldots, \mathbf{x}_N^0 \right\}$, generated randomly within the limits of the search space. Then, the algorithm executes the mutation, crossover, and selection operators, implementing for each case the general procedure described by Algorithm 5.1. All operators consider in their operation the parameter configuration values corresponding to those described in Table 5.1. Finally, having elapsed the total number of iterations, the algorithm returns the best solution found by this process.

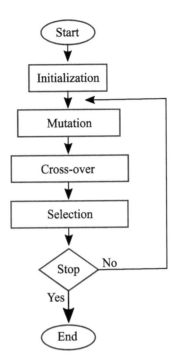

FIGURE 5.6 Computational procedure of the DE in the form of flowchart.

5.4 MATLAB IMPLEMENTATION OF DE

In Program 5.1, the implementation of the Differential Evolution (DE) algorithm in MATLAB® is presented. In the code, the DE algorithm is implemented following the guidelines described in Section 5.2. To present the operation of the DE algorithm, Program 5.1 encodes a test function commonly used to evaluate the performance of optimization methods known as the sphere function. The sphere function exhibits a unimodal, convex, and multidimensional surface. The function has a single global minimum located at position 0 of each of the dimensions used in the generation of the function surface. This multidimensional characteristic is used to test the scaling effect that the operators of a metaheuristic algorithm have when working in high dimensions. On the other hand, the sphere function is continuous and convex, which indicates that almost any optimization technique, whether classical or evolutionary, reaches the global optimum without any problem.

Additionally, in the implementation of the DE algorithm, the numerical values of the configuration parameters are established following the description in Table 5.1. The DE considers the use of a population that contains 50 individuals ($N = 50$) and the iterative process stops when the maximum number of iterations is equal to 1,000 ($k_{max} = 1,000$). Finally, with the objective that the user can see the behavior of the individuals on the surface of the sphere function, in each iteration, the movement of the individuals is plotted. For this reason, it is specified that the DE algorithm is tested using a two-dimensional search space ($d = 2$).

Program 5.1 Implementation in MATLAB® of the DE Algorithm

```
%%%%%%%%%%%%%%%%%%%%%%%%%%%%%%%%%%%%%%%%%%%%%%%%%%%%%%%%%%%%%%%%%%%%%%%%
% DE algorithm
% Erik Cuevas, Alma Rodríguez
%%%%%%%%%%%%%%%%%%%%%%%%%%%%%%%%%%%%%%%%%%%%%%%%%%%%%%%%%%%%%%%%%%%%%%%%
%% Clear memory and MATLAB windows
clear all
close all
% Function definition
fitness = @(xi) (xi(1)^2) + (xi(2)^2);
% Maximum number of iterations
Kmax = 1000;
% Population size
N = 50;
% Scaling factor F
F = 0.2;
% Crossover factor CR
CR = 0.5;
% Number of dimensions
dim = 2;
% Search space limits
lb = -100;
ub = 100;
% Initialization of the population
if size(ub,2)==1
        X=rand(N,dim).*(ub-lb)+lb;
end
if size(ub,2)>1
        for j = 1:N
                for i=1:dim
                        high=ub(i);down=lb(i);
                        X(j,i)=rand(1,1).*(high-down)+down;
                end
        end
end
% The initial population is evaluated
for i = 1:N
        fitnessX(i,1) = fitness(X(i,:));
end
% The best element is selected
[fitnessXbest,ind] = min(fitnessX);
xBest = X(ind,:);
% The values are generated to display the function
if dim<=2
```

```
      range=ub-lb;
      figure(1) % Graph of the current population
      x1=[lb:range/100:ub];
      y1=x1;
      [X1,Y1]=meshgrid(x1,y1);
      [row1,col1]=size(X1);
      for q=1:col1
            for hh=1:row1
                  zz(hh,q)=fitness([X1(hh,q),Y1(hh,q)]);
            end
      end
end
evaluations = 1;
% Iterative process
while (evaluations <= Kmax)
      for i = 1:N
            % Three different individuals from the population are
            selected
            index = randperm(N);
            a = index(1);  % First random element
            b = index(2);  % Second random element
            c = index(3);  % Third random element
            % Mutation operation
            % Mutant vector
            v = X(c,:) + F * (X(a,:) - X(b,:));
            % It is evaluated if the mutant vector v is within the
            search space
            % search defined by upper and lower limits
            if size(ub,2)==1
                  for it = 1:dim
                        if (v(it) < lb)
                              v(it) = lb;
                        end
                        if (v(it) > ub)
                              v(it) = ub;
                        end
                  end
            end
            if size(ub,2) > 1
                  for it = 1:dim
                        high=ub(it);down=lb(it);
                        if (v(it) < down)
                              v(it) = down;
                        end
```

```
                              if (v(it) > high)
                                      v(it) = high;
                              end
                      end
              end
              % Crossover operation
              u=zeros(1,dim);
              j0 = randi([1 dim]);
              for j=1:dim
                      if j==j0 || rand<= CR
                              u(j)=v(j);
                      else
                              u(j)=X(i,j);
                      end
              end
              % The fitness of the vector i is obtained
              fitnessI = fitness(X(i,:));
              % the fitness of the test vector u is evaluated
              fitnessU = fitness(u);
              % Selection operation
              if fitnessU < fitnessI
                      X(i,:) = u;
                      if fitnessU < fitnessXbest
                              fitnessXbest = fitnessU;
                              xBest = u;
                      end
              end
      end
      % Graph of the current population
      if dim <= 2
              surf(X1,Y1,zz);
              hold on
              for iStruct = 1 : N
                      plot(X(iStruct,1),X(iStruct,2),'o','markersize',
                      6,'markerfacecolor','r');
              end
              plot(xBest(1),xBest(2),'o','markersize',10,
              'markerfacecolor','g');
              drawnow;
              hold off
      end
      evaluations = evaluations + 1;
      fprintf('Iteration: %d\n',evaluations);
end
fprintf('Best Solution: (%d,%d)\n',xBest(1),xBest(2));
fprintf('Best fitness: %d\n',fitnessXbest);
```

5.5 SPRING DESIGN USING THE DE ALGORITHM

Optimization problems involve finding an optimal solution within a possible set of solutions. Most of the areas in engineering present optimization problems to obtain the optimal solution in multiple domains such as planning problems, operations research, or even engineering design problems. Under this perspective, the need to develop optimization techniques that solve these problems is of great interest to the scientific and engineering community.

In Section 5.4, the code presented for the implementation of the DE algorithm has been presented considering a function that exhibits a unimodal and convex surface. However, in this case, the operation of the algorithm is tested using a mathematical function that is part of a set of test functions that do not represent a real application. This section analyzes an engineering design problem and describes how the DE algorithm can be used to solve this kind of problem. The issue of designing a simple spring is a complex engineering problem where the goal is to obtain a determined spring that fulfills certain constraints of tension or compression. For this problem, a set of specific design requirements (also called constraints) must be met to include the minimum deflection and frequency, as well as the maximum diameter and shear stress of the spring. The main objective of the design is to minimize the weight of the tension or compression spring. To do this, the mathematical description of the model is formulated as an optimization problem considering the following form:

$$\underset{x_1, x_2, x_3}{\text{Min}} \qquad f(\mathbf{x}) = (x_3 + 2)x_2 x_1^2$$

$$g_1(\mathbf{x}) = 1 - \frac{x_2^3 x_3}{71{,}785 x_1^4} \leq 0$$

$$g_2(\mathbf{x}) = \frac{4x_2^2 - x_1 x_2}{12{,}566\left(x_2 x_1^3 - x_1^4\right)} + \frac{1}{5{,}108 x_1^2} - 1 \leq 0 \qquad (5.10)$$

Subject to:

$$g_3(\mathbf{x}) = 1 - \frac{140.45 x_1}{x_2^2 x_3} \leq 0$$

$$g_4(\mathbf{x}) = \frac{x_1 + x_2}{1.5} - 1 \leq 0$$

where x_1, x_2, and x_3 represent the thickness of the rod (W), the average diameter of the coil (D), and the number of active coils (L), respectively. These values are distributed in a three-dimensional space ($d=3$) and define the decision variables of the problem. The functions $g_1(\mathbf{x}), \ldots, g_4(\mathbf{x})$ correspond to the four nonlinear constraints that must be met to consider the optimal design of the spring. The search space limits corresponding to each dimension of the problem are defined as $0.05 \leq x_1 \leq 2$, $0.25 \leq x_2 \leq 1.3$, and $2 \leq x_3 \leq 15$. In Figure 5.7, the design parameters for the spring problem are illustrated graphically.

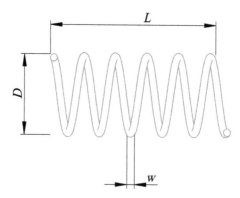

FIGURE 5.7   Design parameters for the spring problem.

In this figure, the parameter D corresponds to the average diameter of the coil, while L indicates the number of active coils and W the thickness of the rod that forms the winding. The simulation of the resolution of this engineering problem using the DE algorithm is shown in Program 5.2.

Program 5.2. Implementation in MATLAB® of DE for Solving the Spring Problem

```
%%%%%%%%%%%%%%%%%%%%%%%%%%%%%%%%%%%%%%%%%%%%%%%%%%%%%%%%%%%%%%%%%%%%%%
% Implementation in MATLAB® of DE for solving the spring problem
% Erik Cuevas, Alma Rodríguez
%%%%%%%%%%%%%%%%%%%%%%%%%%%%%%%%%%%%%%%%%%%%%%%%%%%%%%%%%%%%%%%%%%%%%%
%% Clear memory and MATLAB windows
clear all
close all
% Function definition
fitness = @(xi) (xi(3) + 2) *xi(2)* (xi(1)^2);
% Maximum number of iterations
Kmax = 1000;
% Population size
N = 50;
% Scaling factor F
F = 0.2;
% Crossover factor CR
CR = 0.5;
% Number of dimensions
dim = 3;
% Search space limits
lb = [0.05 0.25 2];
ub = [2 1.3 15];
% Penalization Function definition
rg = 100;
cg = 2;
```

```
% Initialization of the population
if size(ub,2)==1
      X=rand(N,dim).*(ub-lb)+lb;
end
if size(ub,2)>1
      for j = 1:N
            for i=1:dim
                  high=ub(i);down=lb(i);
                  X(j,i)=rand(1,1).*(high-down)+down;
            end
      end
end
% The initial Population is evaluated
for i = 1:N
      fitnessX(i,1) = fitness(X(i,:));
      g1= 1-((X(i,2)^3*X(i,3))/(71785*X(i,1)^4) );
      p1=4*X(i,2)^2-X(i,1)*X(i,2)/12566*(X(i,2)*
      X(i,1)^3-X(i,1)^4);
      p2=1/(5108*X(i,1)^2);
      g2=(p1+p2-1) ;
      g3=(1-( (140.45*X(i,1))/(X(i,2)^2*X(i,3)) ) );
      g4=(((X(i,2)+X(i,1))/1.5)-1);
      P = (rg * min(0,g1)^2) + (rg * min(0,g2)^2) + (rg *
      min(0,g3)^2) + (rg * min(0,g4)^2);
      fitnessX(i,1) = fitnessX(i,1) + P;
      rg = rg * cg;
end
% The best element is selected
[fitnessXbest,ind] = min(fitnessX);
xBest = X(ind,:);
% The values are generated to display the function to optimize
if dim<=2
      range=ub-lb;
      figure(1) % Graph of the current population
      x1=[lb:range/100:ub];
      y1=x1;
      [X1,Y1]=meshgrid(x1,y1);
      [row1,col1]=size(X1);
      for q=1:col1
            for hh=1:row1
                  zz(hh,q)=fitness([X1(hh,q),Y1(hh,q)]);
            end
      end
end
evaluations = 1;
% Iterative process
while (evaluations <= Kmax)
```

```matlab
for i = 1:N
    % Three different individuals from the population are
    selected
    index = randperm(N);
    a = index(1);  % First random element
    b = index(2);  % Second random element
    c = index(3);  % Third random element
    % Mutation operation
    % Mutant vector
    v = X(c,:) + F * (X(a,:) - X(b,:));
    % It is evaluated if the mutant vector v is within the
    search space
    % search defined by upper and lower limits
    if size(ub,2)==1
        for it = 1:dim
            if (v(it) < lb)
                v(it) = lb;
            end
            if (v(it) > ub)
                v(it) = ub;
            end
        end
    end
    if size(ub,2) > 1
        for it = 1:dim
            high=ub(it);down=lb(it);
            if (v(it) < down)
                v(it) = down;
            end
            if (v(it) > high)
                v(it) = high;
            end
        end
    end
    % Crossover operation
    u=zeros(1,dim);
    j0 = randi([1 dim]);
    for j=1:dim
        if j==j0 || rand<= CR
            u(j)=v(j);
        else
            u(j)=X(i,j);
        end
    end
    % The fitness of the vector i is obtained
    fitnessI = fitness(X(i,:));
    % the fitness of the test vector u is evaluated
```

```
            fitnessU = fitness(u);
            g1= 1-((u(2)^3*u(3))/(71785*u(1)^4) );
            p1=4*u(2)^2-u(1)*u(2)/12566*(u(2)*u(1)^3-u(1)^4);
            p2=1/(5108*u(1)^2);
            g2=(p1+p2-1) ;
            g3=(1-( (140.45*u(1))/(u(2)^2*u(3)) ) );
            g4=(((u(2)+u(1))/1.5)-1);
            P = (rg * min(0,g1)^2) + (rg * min(0,g2)^2) + (rg *
            min(0,g3)^2) + (rg * min(0,g4)^2);
            fitnessU = fitnessU + P;
            rg = rg * cg;
            % Selection operation
            if fitnessU < fitnessI
                    X(i,:) = u;
                    if fitnessU < fitnessXbest
                            fitnessXbest = fitnessU;
                            xBest = u;
                    end
            end
    end
    % Graph of the current population
    if dim <= 2
            surf(X1,Y1,zz);
            hold on
            for iStruct = 1 : N
                    plot(X(iStruct,1),X(iStruct,2),'o','markersize',
                    6,'markerfacecolor','r');
            end
            plot(xBest(1),xBest(2),'o','markersize',10,
            'markerfacecolor','g');
            drawnow;
            hold off
    end
    evaluations = evaluations + 1;
    fprintf('Iteration: %d\n',evaluations);
end
fprintf('Best solution: (%d,%d)\n',xBest(1),xBest(2));
fprintf('Best fitness: %d\n',fitnessXbest);
```

REFERENCES

Díaz-Cortés, M. A., Cuevas, E., Gálvez, J., & Camarena, O. (2017). A new metaheuristic optimization methodology based on fuzzy logic. *Applied Soft Computing, 61*, 549–569.

Gämperle, R., Müller, S.D., & Koumoutsakos, P. (2002). A parameter study for differential evolution. *WSEAS Int. Conf. on Advances in Intelligent Systems, Fuzzy Systems, Evolutionary Computation*, 293–298. Press.

Price, K., Storn, R. M., & Lampinen, J. A. 2005. Natural computing series. Differential evolution: A practical approach to global optimization. In G. Rozenberg, Th. Bäck, A.E. Eiben, J.N. Kok, & H.P. Spaink *ACM computing classification* (pp. 13–978). Berlin, Heidelberg: Springer.

Price, K. V. 1994. Genetic annealing. *Dr.Bobb's Journal*, 19(10), 127–132.

Qing, A., 2009. *Differential evolution: Fundamentals and applications in electrical engineering.* Asia: John Wiley & Sons.

Rangaiah, G. P., & Sharma, S. 2017. *Differential evolution in chemical engineering: Developments and applications*, p. 429.

Storn, R., & Price, K. 1997. Differential evolution - A simple and efficient heuristic for global optimization over continuous spaces. *Journal of Global Optimization*, *11*, 341–359.

CHAPTER 6

Particle Swarm Optimization (PSO) Algorithm

6.1 INTRODUCTION

In various natural systems, it is possible to observe collective intelligence. Some clear examples are present in those animals that live in groups. In this context, animal considers the group as a way to facilitate the development of various activities such as protecting themselves from predators, finding food, building shelters, or traveling long distances without risk. In these systems, intelligence does not come from each individual in particular, but it is generated when they interact together in the search for a common goal: survival.

The probability of surviving an attack by a predator is undoubtedly much higher when the animals belong to a group than when they are alone. Therefore, it is more difficult for a predator to concentrate on the hunt of an animal when he is in a group than when he is isolated. This phenomenon is called the effect of a confused predator (Milinski & Heller, 1978).

On the other hand, animals are more successful in the search for food when they remain in a group than when they maintain themselves in an individual way. This could seem a contradiction because in a group it is not possible to be stealthy or unnoticed at the time of the hunt. This fact can cause that the prey is warned of the imminent danger and give it a chance to escape. However, despite these disadvantages, the success of collaborative hunting is largely due to the hypothesis of many eyes (Lima, 1995). This hypothesis is based on the high probability that a group has of finding food because the number of search processes increases with the number of members in the group. The higher the number of members in the group, the greater the number of opportunities in finding food. Another important aspect of the success of collaborative behavior is the possibility of surrounding and cornering prey, an action that would be impossible to achieve individually.

The Particle Swarm Optimization (PSO) algorithm (Kennedy & Eberhart, 1995) is based on the behavior of individuals who collaborate together to improve not only their collective performance in some tasks but also to improve their individual performance. The principles of the PSO can be clearly observed in the behaviors of both animals and humans. To improve the performance in some tasks, humans tend to form collaborative groups that allow them to achieve both a general objective and their particular perspectives. In the search for a common objective, the exchange of information among the members participating in this search is an important factor that favors this task. If an individual performs a search using certain strategies with an unsuccessful result, then its communication with other elements of the group allows correcting the search strategies of all agents according to individual observations of the environment. This mechanism increases the probabilities to get the objective. Under this perspective, humans make improvements in their decisions considering the strategies that have obtained so far good results, those that have obtained good results for their peers (local influence) and those that have obtained good results for the complete group or society (global influence). Local influence and global influence are the basic principles of the PSO.

6.2 PSO SEARCH STRATEGY

The PSO scheme includes a swarm of elements, where each elements corresponds to a potential solution. In analogy with metaheuristic computation, a swarm represents a population, while a particle corresponds to an individual. In general, the particles are "moved" in a multidimensional search space, where the location of each element is modified depending on its own experience and that on its local neighbors.

The PSO algorithm consists of a group of $\mathbf{X}$ particles that model the cooperative behavior of N agents who develop a collective task. Each individual is represented by a particle $\mathbf{x}_i$ and the group of individuals is represented by the group so that $\mathbf{X} = \{\mathbf{x}_1, \mathbf{x}_2, \ldots, \mathbf{x}_N\}$. The objective of the set of particles represents the search for a feasible solution to an optimization problem where the search space is well defined and delimited. Particles are considered search agents, where each particle is a possible solution that evolves during the iterative process. $\mathbf{x}_i$ denote the position of element i in the search space. All element positions are updated considering discrete time steps.

During the evolution, particles exchange information about the spatial information obtained in the search. In addition, the particles have also memory, so they keep track of the best solutions found so far. In this process, each particle moves in the search space with some speed, considering the exchanged information among the agents in the group. Therefore, the movement of the particles is determined by the individual positions obtained in the past (local influence) and by the spatial information of other particles that integrate the swarm (global influence). Under these conditions, the PSO models the particle dynamics produced by the collective behavior of the swarm. This model represents the particle movement considering the local and global influence of the particles. Such mechanisms determine the magnitude of the movement experimented by each agent. With this strategy, the quality of the solutions is refined with the interaction of the particles, since in each iteration (in each generation), the particles undergo a change related to the dynamics produced by local and global mechanisms.

6.2.1 Initialization

In the initialization of the PSO algorithm, a population $\mathbf{X}^0$ of N particles is produced so that $\mathbf{X}^0 = \{\mathbf{x}_1^0, \mathbf{x}_2^0, \ldots, \mathbf{x}_N^0\}$. Each initial particle $\mathbf{x}_i^0 = \left[x_{i,1}^0, x_{i,2}^0, \ldots, x_{i,d}^0\right]$ is randomly generated within values located by the low lb and upper ub bounds considering a d-dimensional search space. These limits that may be different for each dimension j are determined by the problem to be optimized. They limit the position where solutions could be found. Equation 6.1 describes the way in which particles are initialized:

$$x_{ij}^0 = lb_j + r_{ij}\left(ub_j - lb_j\right) \quad i = 1, 2, \ldots, N; j = 1, 2, \ldots, d \tag{6.1}$$

where x_{ij}^0 corresponds to the initial value of the particle i in its dimension j. lb_j and ub_j represent the lower and upper limits for dimension j, respectively. In addition, r_{ij} is a uniformly distributed random value within the range [0,1], corresponding to the particle i in its dimension j.

In addition to the initialization of the population, the parameters of the problem to be optimized are also defined in this phase. They include the number of particles N, the number of dimensions d, the maximum number of iterations k_{max}, and the constraints of equality or inequality required as generic parameters. The definition of the parameters depends on the particular problem to be optimized. In the case of this chapter, the PSO algorithm involves the solution of optimization problems without restrictions. Therefore, the necessary parameters for its initialization correspond to the number of particles, the number of dimensions, the limits of the search space, and the maximum number of iterations. In the case of the optimization of constrained problems, the general scheme of PSO needs to be modified. An example with constrains will be discussed in Section 6.5.2.

6.2.2 Particle Velocity

In the search strategy, each particle moves in the solution space according to a certain velocity $\mathbf{v}_i$. This velocity also requires to have an initial value. In the simplest version of the PSO, the velocity is initialized with zero value for each particle so that

$$\mathbf{v}_i^0 = 0 \tag{6.2}$$

During the evolution process, the velocity is calculated considering the information of the best global particle $\mathbf{g}$ and the best local particle $\mathbf{p}_i$. Where the best global particle represents the best particle in the entire population and corresponds to the best global solution, such that

$$\mathbf{g} = \mathbf{x}_i \in \{\mathbf{X}\} \mid f(\mathbf{x}_i) = \min\{f(\mathbf{x}_1), f(\mathbf{x}_2), \ldots, f(\mathbf{x}_N)\} \tag{6.3}$$

With regard to the best local particle, it refers to the information of its best performance recorded so-far. Thus, it specifies the best solution that cannot be improved yet. In the literature, this local particle is referred to as the best neighboring particle. Therefore, the best so-far particle is determined as follows:

$$\mathbf{p}_i^{k+1} = \mathbf{x}_i^k \in \{\mathbf{X}^k\} \mid \mathbf{x}_i^k = \min\{\mathbf{p}_i^k, \mathbf{x}_i^k\} \tag{6.4}$$

Under such conditions, the best particles, which represent the best solutions, influence the search process so that they guide the population towards the best solutions through the solutions space.

The computation of the velocity is determined based on the global and local influence of the best particles. Both influences are adjusted through different factors known as cognitive and social constants. The cognitive constant affects the local influence while the social constant affects the global influence. Equation 6.2 shows how the speed calculation is performed:

$$\mathbf{v}_i^{k+1} = \mathbf{v}_i^k + c_1 \cdot \left(\mathbf{r}_1^k \cdot \left(\mathbf{p}_i^k - \mathbf{x}_i^k \right) \right) + c_2 \cdot \left(\mathbf{r}_2^k \cdot \left(\mathbf{g}^k - \mathbf{x}_i^k \right) \right) \tag{6.5}$$

where k is the current iteration, $\mathbf{v}_i^{k+1}$ represents the new velocity of the particle, $\mathbf{x}_i^k$ corresponding to the generation $k+1$, $\mathbf{v}_i^k$ is the current velocity of the particle, $\mathbf{g}^k$ symbolizes the best global particle found so far, $\mathbf{p}_i^k$ is the best local value recorded for the particle $\mathbf{x}_i^k$ seen so far (k). Furthermore, $\mathbf{r}_1^k$ and $\mathbf{r}_2^k$ denote two d-dimensional random vectors whose elements are extracted from random values uniformly distributed within the interval [0,1], while parameters c_1 and c_2 represent the cognitive and social constants, respectively.

Due to the success and popularity generated by PSO, several modifications have been generated from the original version. Most of the modifications consider improving the speed calculation. Another aspect that is also modified in the new versions is the initial speed. The new approaches try to refine the speed with which the particles move to reach better performance in the search process.

There are several alternatives to initialize velocity (Helwig & Wanka, 2008). Among them, the most common schemes consider two possibilities. The first one is the random initialization while the second one considers the initialization to zero. For the velocity computation, in the original version, the initial velocity is considered zero. Likewise, the values of the cognitive and social constants are determined as $c_1 = 1$ y $c_2 = 1$. The values of these parameters affect the performance of the algorithm. Therefore, these parameters must be adjusted for each particular problem, so that the values selected for c_1 and c_2 are those that provide the best results.

6.2.3 Particle Movement

The particles move in the search space to explore promising solutions. The movement of each particle is determined by using the speed calculated in Eq. 6.1 so that for every iteration k the position of each particle in the population is updated accordingly with the following expression:

$$\mathbf{x}_i^{k+1} = \mathbf{x}_i^k + \mathbf{v}_i^{k+1} \tag{6.6}$$

where $\mathbf{v}_i^{k+1}$ represents the new velocity of the particle $\mathbf{x}_i^k$ calculated from Eq. 6.2. The particle movement is another of the modifications considered by the variants of PSO. This fact is because the way in which the particles are displaced maintains a high influence on the performance of the algorithm.

Despite the multiple variants of the PSO, in this chapter, a simple version of the algorithm is presented so that the reader can easily understand the main characteristics of PSO.

6.2.4 PSO Analysis

The adjustment of each particle position $\mathbf{x}_i^{k+1}$ in PSO is determined by its vector velocity $\mathbf{v}_i^{k+1}$. The velocity $\mathbf{v}_i^{k+1}$ in PSO is computed considering three terms: the previous velocity $\mathbf{v}_i^k$, a cognitive factor $\mathbf{r}_1^k \cdot \left(\mathbf{p}_i^k - \mathbf{x}_i^k \right)$, and a social term $\mathbf{r}_2^k \cdot \left(\mathbf{g}^k - \mathbf{x}_i^k \right)$.

Previous velocity
It is considered as a memory of the past direction. This factor can also be interpreted as a momentum that avoids drastical changes of direction. With the effect of the previous velocity, particles move towards the current direction.

Cognitive factor
This component involves the performance of particle i during the optimization process. The cognitive factor emulates the individual memory of the position where the particle found its own best location. With the cognitive component, particles are influenced by their own best positions given them the possibility to come back to such positions during the evolution process.

Social term
This factor corresponds to the influence presented by the whole population over the individual. In general, this term conducts the search in direction to the best element found in the population. Therefore, each particle is also drawn towards the best position.

The cognitive and social terms are weighted by random numbers. Under such conditions, their influence is changed during the search strategy.

6.2.5 Inertia Weighting

One of the most simple and effective versions of PSO is the inclusion of the inertia weight ω. Under this incorporation, the adjustment of each particle is determined by the following model:

$$\mathbf{v}_i^{k+1} = \omega \cdot \mathbf{v}_i^k + c_1 \cdot \left(\mathbf{r}_1^k \cdot \left(\mathbf{p}_i^k - \mathbf{x}_i^k \right) \right) + c_2 \cdot \left(\mathbf{r}_2^k \cdot \left(\mathbf{g}^k - \mathbf{x}_i^k \right) \right) \tag{6.7}$$

With its inclusion, it is avoided that the velocity in each iteration can increase without limit. In spite of its stability effects, ω affects the search strategy making its convergence slow. The value of ω is dynamically modified from 0.9 in its first generation to 0.4 in its final iteration.

6.3 COMPUTING PROCEDURE OF PSO

In its simplest version, the PSO uses a population of candidate solutions that are randomly generated to explore the search space. This set of particles represents the initial population which is evaluated in terms of the objective function $f(\mathbf{x}_i)$ that describes the optimization problem. The quality of the solutions is determined from their evaluation in the objective function. In this evaluation, each particle i is associated with an objective function value f_i known as *fitness* that defines its quality as a solution of the particular optimization problem. Therefore, the best particle in the group is recognized as the best global solution and the best individual fitness values (best local solution) are recorded in the memory of each particle. Equation 6.4 shows the calculation of the fitness values.

$$\mathbf{fx}_i = f(\mathbf{x}_i) \qquad (6.8)$$

After the evaluation, the particles are moved to new positions in the search space at a certain speed in order to find solutions that have higher quality. The speed with which the particles move is determined from the influence of the best global particle and the best local particle, in conjunction with a stochastic effect considering also the cognitive and social constant factors. The particles that have modified their position are evaluated in terms of the objective function to determine their fitness values, and then they will move again considering a new speed.

As can be seen, the generation of new particle positions is an iterative process in which particles move in the search space at a certain speed evaluating their quality. At the end of the iterations, the best global particle is considered the solution for the optimization problem.

6.3.1 Algorithm Description

So far, the inspiration of the PSO has been described and the method has been explained in general terms. In this section, all the steps conducted by the algorithm will be described in detail. In the first stage of the PSO search process, the initialization of the particles is carried out by using Eq. 6.1. In this phase, a certain number of particles (which is adjustable depending on the problem to be optimized) is produced considering random positions uniformly distributed. Additionally, the initial velocities of all particles are set to zero. Figure 6.1 shows the initialization of the particles, and it can be seen that the particles and the search space in which they have been uniformly distributed. After initialization, the particles are evaluated in terms of the objective function to determine their quality, which is recorded in the memory of the particles. With this information, the particle with the highest fitness quality in the population is also recorded, that is, the best global particle.

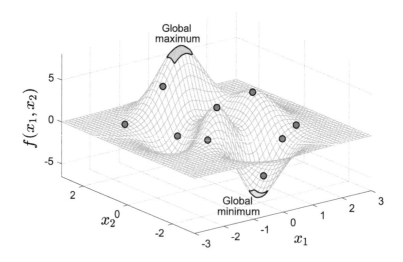

FIGURE 6.1 Initialization of particles in the search space considering the MATLAB® function *peaks*.

Then, the iterative process begins. Therefore, the velocity of each particle is calculated with Eq. 6.2. Once the velocity is calculated, the new position of each particle will be determined using Eq. 6.3. Afterward, the particles are moved to new positions. Then, the candidate solutions are evaluated with the objective function to determine their fitness values. Finally, it is recorded in the memory of the particles the best values obtained during the evolution process. With this information, the particle with the highest fitness quality is also recorded. This solution represents the best global particle. Next, the stop condition is verified, which is generally restricted to a number of iterations. This represents the number of iterations that the algorithm must execute, before finalizing the search process. This parameter is adjustable and is associated with the complexity of the problem to be optimized.

If the stop criterion has not been reached, the iterative process continues. The flow diagram of the PSO algorithm is shown in Figure 6.2. Furthermore, to facilitate the implementation of this optimization method, the general PSO procedure is presented as a pseudocode in Algorithm 6.1.

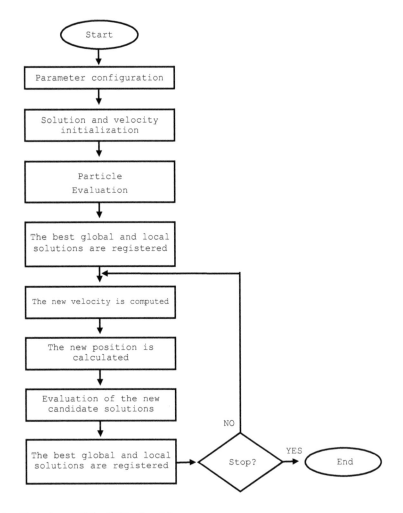

FIGURE 6.2 Flowchart of the PSO algorithm.

Algorithm 6.1 General Implementation of the PSO Algorithm

Step 1: Parameter configuration

$$N, d, lb, ub, k=0, k_{max}, c_1, c_2$$

Step 2: Particle and velocity initialization
for $i=1; i \le N; i++$

$$\mathbf{x}_i^k = \mathbf{r} \cdot (\mathbf{ub} - \mathbf{lb}) + \mathbf{lb}$$

$$\mathbf{v}_i^k = 0$$

end
Step 3: Particle evaluation in terms of the objective function
for $i=1; i \le N; i++$

$$\mathbf{fx}_i^k \leftarrow f(\mathbf{x}_i^k)$$

end
Step 4: The best global and local particles are registered

$$\mathbf{g}^k = \mathbf{x}_i^k \in \{\mathbf{X}^k\} \mid f(\mathbf{x}_i^k) = \min\{f(\mathbf{x}_1^k), f(\mathbf{x}_2^k), \ldots, f(\mathbf{x}_N^k)\}$$

$$g_{fit}^k \leftarrow f(\mathbf{x}_i^k)$$

for $i=1; i \le N; i++$

$$\mathbf{p}_i^k \leftarrow \mathbf{x}_i^k$$

$$\mathbf{fp}_i^k \leftarrow \mathbf{fx}_i^k$$

end
Step 5: The new velocity of each particle is computed
for $i=1; i \le N; i++$

$$\mathbf{v}_i^{k+1} \leftarrow \mathbf{v}_i^k + c_1 \cdot \left(\mathbf{r} \cdot \left(\mathbf{p}_i^k - \mathbf{x}_i^k\right)\right) + c_2 \cdot \left(\mathbf{r} \cdot \left(\mathbf{g}^k - \mathbf{x}_i^k\right)\right)$$

end
Step 6: The new location of each particle is calculated
for $i=1; i \le N; i++$

$$\mathbf{x}_i^{k+1} \leftarrow \mathbf{x}_i^k + \mathbf{v}_i^{k+1}$$

end

Step 7: Particle evaluation in terms of the objective function
for $i = 1; i \leq N; i++$

$$\mathbf{fx}_i^{k+1} \leftarrow f\left(\mathbf{x}_i^{k+1}\right)$$

end
Step 8: The best global and local particles are registered

$$\mathbf{g}^{k+1} = \mathbf{x}_i^{k+1} \in \left\{\mathbf{X}^{k+1}\right\} \,\Big|\, f\left(\mathbf{x}_i^{k+1}\right) = \min\left\{f\left(\mathbf{x}_1^{k+1}\right), f\left(\mathbf{x}_2^{k+1}\right), \ldots, f\left(\mathbf{x}_N^{k+1}\right)\right\}$$

$$g_{fit}^{k+1} \leftarrow f\left(\mathbf{x}_i^{k+1}\right)$$

$$\text{if } \mathbf{g}^{k+1} < \mathbf{g}^k$$

$$\mathbf{g}^k \leftarrow \mathbf{g}^{k+1}$$

$$g_{fit}^k \leftarrow g_{fit}^{k+1}$$

end
for $i = 1; i \leq N; i++$
if $\mathbf{fx}_i^{k+1} < \mathbf{fp}_i^k$

$$\mathbf{p}_i^{k+1} \leftarrow \mathbf{x}_i^{k+1}$$

$$\mathbf{fp}_i^{k+1} \leftarrow \mathbf{fx}_i^{k+1}$$

end
end
Step 9: The stop criterion is tested
if $k == k_{max}$

$$\textit{The best solution} \leftarrow \mathbf{g}^{k+1}$$

End of the process
else

$$k \leftarrow k+1$$

Go to Step **5**
end

6.4 MATLAB IMPLEMENTATION OF THE PSO ALGORITHM

The PSO algorithm has been implemented in the MATLAB® with the objective of illustrating its search procedure. This implementation can be observed in Algorithm 6.1. In the process, the aim is to minimize an objective function to find the global minimum. The optimization problem used in the example does not represent an engineering problem or a real-word application. It is a mathematical formulation known as the peaks function, which is defined as

$$f(x_1, x_2) = 3(1-x_1)^2 e^{-(x_1^2-x_2^2)} - 10\left(\frac{x_1}{5} - x_1^3 - x_2^5\right) e^{(-x_1^2-x_2^2)} - 1/3 e^{(-(x_1+1)^2-x_2^2)} \tag{6.9}$$

The peaks function is defined in two dimensions and is widely used as a consequence of its interesting characteristics. The function has minima and maxima (local and global) that allow a quick test of the effectiveness of any metaheuristic algorithm. The peaks function, shown in Figure 6.1, presents a global minimum of approximately −6.54.

To graphically show the PSO search process, its implementation has been carried out considering the two-dimensional problem of the peaks function. If it is required to apply this method in more dimensions, the reader will have to make appropriate modifications. These changes require the adjustment of some algorithm parameters, such as the number of dimensions d, the lower limit lb and upper ub for each dimension, as well as modifying the number of particles N and the maximum number of iterations k_{max}. The higher the dimensionality of the problem to be optimized, the greater the difficulty it represents for the search. The fact of having a greater number of search agents and more time to perform the search would certainly help the optimization process. Therefore, the adjustment in the number of particles and in the number of iterations is recommended as a way to calibrate the optimization performance. Program 6.1 presents the PSO implementation. Within the code, there are several comments that allow understanding the operation of PSO.

Program 6.1 MATLAB Implementation of the PSO Algorithm

```
%%%%%%%%%%%%%%%%%%%%%%%%%%%%%%%%%%%%%%%%%%%%%%%%%%%%%%%%%%%%%%%%%%
% Particle Swarm Optimization (PSO)
% Erik Cuevas, Alma Rodríguez
%%%%%%%%%%%%%%%%%%%%%%%%%%%%%%%%%%%%%%%%%%%%%%%%%%%%%%%%%%%%%%%%%%
%% Clear memory and close MATLAB Windows
clear all % Clear memory
close all % close MATLAB Windows
%% Problem to optimize (minimize), the definition of the objective
function
funObj = @(xi) 3*(1-xi(1))^2*exp(-(xi(1)^2)-(xi(2)+1)^2)-
10*(xi(1)/5-xi(1)^3 - xi(2)^5)*exp(-xi(1)^2-
xi(2)^2)-1/3*exp(-(xi(1)+1)^2 - xi(2)^2);
%% Parameter configuration
N = 10; % Particle number
```

```matlab
d = 2; % Dimensions
lb = [-3 -3]; % Lower limit of search the space
ub = [3 3]; % Upper limit of search the space
k = 0; % Current iteration
kmax = 100; % Maximum number of iterations
c1 = 2; % Cognitive constant
c2 = 2; % Social constant
%% Initialization of particles and velocity
for i = 1:N
     x(i,:) = rand(1,d).*(ub-lb)+lb; % Initialization of particles
     v(i,:) = zeros(1,d); % Initialization of velocities
end
%% Evaluation of the initial particles in the objective function
for i = 1:N
     xi=x(i,:); % Extraction of the particle xi
     fx(i,:) = funObj(xi); % Evaluation of the particle xi
end
%% Record of the best global particle and the best local particles
[gfit, ind] = min(fx); % Fitness of the best global particle
g = x(ind,:); % Position of the best global particle
fp = fx; % Fitness of the best local particles
p = x; % Position of the best local particles
%% Calculation of the search space for graphical proposes
axisx=linspace(min(lb),max(ub),50); % Solutions for vector d = 1
axisy=axisx; % Solutions for vector d = 2
axisz=[]; % Fitness matrix
for i = 1:length(axisx)
     for j = 1:length(axisy)
          axisz(i,j) = funObj([axisx(i) axisy(j)]);
     end
end
[axisy axisx] = meshgrid(axisx,axisy); % Computation of the
meshgrid
%% Iterative process
while k < kmax % Stop criterion
     k = k + 1; % new iteration
     %% Draw the search space Surface
     figure(1); % Show Figure 1
     surf(axisx,axisy,axisz) % Draw the function surface
     hold on
     %% Draw the particles
     % Draw the particles in red color
     plot3(x(:,1),x(:,2),fx,'o','MarkerFaceColor','m','MarkerS
ize',10)
     % Draw best particles in green color
     plot3(p(:,1),p(:,2),fp,'o','MarkerFaceColor','g','MarkerS
ize',10)
```

```
% Pause to allow viewing the graph
pause(0.3)
hold off
%% Draw the function contour
figure(2)
contour(axisx,axisy,axisz,20)
hold on
%% Draw the particles in the contour
% Draw the particles in red color
plot(x(:,1),x(:,2),'o','MarkerFaceColor','m');
% Draw the particles in green color
plot(p(:,1),p(:,2),'o','MarkerFaceColor','g');
% Pause to allow viewing the graph
pause(0.3)
hold off
%% Computation of the new velocity for each particle
for i= 1:N
        % Extraction of the particle xi
        xi = x(i,:);
        % Extraction of the local particle pi
        pi = p(i,:);
        % Determination of the new velocity for each particle vi
        v(i,:) = v(i,:)+c1*rand(1,d).*(pi-xi)+c2*rand(1,d).*
(g-xi);
    end
    %% Determination of the new position of each particle
    x = x + v;
    %% Verify that the particles do not leave the limits lb and ub
    for i = 1:N % For each particle
        for j=1:d % For each dimension
            if x(i,j) < lb(j) % Check the lower limit
                x(i,j) = lb(j);
            elseif x(i,j) > ub(j) % Check the upper limit
                x(i,j) = ub(j);
            end
        end
    end
    %% Evaluation of new particles with the objective function
    for i = 1:N
        xi = x(i,:); % Extraction of the particle xi
        fx(i,:) = funObj(xi); % Evaluation of the particle xi
    end
    %% Record of the best global particle and the best local
particles
    [gfitkplus1, ind] = min(fx);
    % If a better solution was found, update the global particle
    if gfitkplus1 < gfit
```

```
        % Update the fitness of the best global particle
        gfit = gfitkplus1;
        % Update the position of the best global particle
        g = x(ind,:);
    end
    for i = 1:N
        % If any particle is a better solution than the
previous,
        % update your best local particle
        if fx(i,:) < fp(i,:)
            % Update the fitness of the best local particles
            fp(i,:) = fx(i,:);
            % Update the position of the best local particles
            p(i,:) = x(i,:);
        end
    end
    %% Historical record of the best solutions found in each
generation
    Evolution(k) = gfit;
end
%% End of the iterative process, display of results
figure
% Graph of the evolutionary process of the PSO
plot(Evolution)
%% Results of PSO
disp(['The best solution : ', num2str(g)])
disp(['The best fitness : ', num2str(gfit)])
```

6.5 APPLICATIONS OF THE PSO METHOD

Due to its simplicity and characteristics, the PSO algorithm (as well as its multiple variants) has been extensively studied and applied in a wide variety of areas of science and engineering. As a result, it has become one of the most popular algorithms in swarm intelligence to solve complex optimization problems. The examples shown in this section will allow a better understanding of PSO characteristics and how to use the algorithm to solve real optimization problems. The applications that are used in this section have been considered for didactic purposes. For this reason, they have been structured in one and two dimensions. With few dimensions, it is possible to represent the information graphically; and therefore, the solution can be found and checked by graphical inspection. Therefore, once the method has been developed in low dimensions, it can be easily extended to more dimensions without significant changes.

6.5.1 Application of PSO without Constraints

There are problems in which the solution is only restricted or not by the limits of the search space so that the entire search area is a feasible area to find solutions. The example presented below is an inventory problem (Montufar, 2009) without constraints, considering a single dimension.

Example 6.1

A company has an annual demand of 5,000 units of raw material for its production. The cost per unit is $5.00. The cost per unit is $49.00. The annual percentage storage cost is 20% of the cost per unit. The total cost of an order is determined by the following function:

$$CT = DC + \frac{D}{x}S + \frac{x}{2}M \tag{6.10}$$

where D is the annual demand, C is the cost per unit, S is the cost per order, x is the number of units to be ordered, and M is the storage cost determined as follows:

$$M = PC \tag{6.11}$$

where P represents the percentage storage cost.

What is the optimal number of units to order in such a way that the total cost is the minimum, considering a minimum of 400 units and a maximum of 1,200? What is also the total minimum cost?

Solution

The solution to this problem is shown in Program 6.2. This uses the same implementation shown in Algorithm 6.1 but with some slight changes. The first thing that has been modified is the definition of the objective function of the problem. In addition, it is necessary to change the values of the parameters of dimension, the number of particles, limits of the search space, and the maximum number of iterations. In order to show the results graphically, it is necessary to make some changes to Algorithm 6.1 to include graphs in one dimension and not in two dimensions. All these changes can be seen directly in Program 6.2. The solution to the problem is $x = 700$ and $(x) = CT = 25,700$. Likewise, the optimal number of units to order is 700 and the total minimum cost is $25,700.00.

Program 6.2 Example of Application of PSO

```
%%%%%%%%%%%%%%%%%%%%%%%%%%%%%%%%%%%%%%%%%%%%%%%%%%%%%%%%%%%%%%%%%%%%%%%%
% Example of application of PSO
% Erik Cuevas, Alma Rodríguez
%%%%%%%%%%%%%%%%%%%%%%%%%%%%%%%%%%%%%%%%%%%%%%%%%%%%%%%%%%%%%%%%%%%%%%%%
%% Clear memory and close MATLAB windows
clear all % Clear memory
close all % close MATLAB windows
%% Problem to optimize (minimize), the definition of the objective
function
D = 5000; % Annual demand
C = 5; % Cost per unit
S = 49; % Cost for order
```

```
P = 0.2; % Percent storage cost
M = P*C; % Storage cost
funObj = @(xi) D*C + D/xi*S + xi/2*M; % Objective function
%% Parameter configuration
N = 5; % Particle number
d = 1; % Dimensions
lb = [400]; % Lower limit of search space
ub = [1200]; % Upper limit of search space
k = 0; % Iteration
kmax = 150; % Maximum number of iterations
c1 = 2; % Cognitive constant
c2 = 2; % Social constant
%% Initialization of particles and velocity
for i = 1:N
    x(i,:) = rand(1,d).*(ub-lb)+lb; % Initialization of the
particles
    v(i,:) = zeros(1,d); % Velocity Initialization
end
%% Evaluation of the initial particles with the objective function
for i = 1:N
    xi=x(i,:); % Extraction of the particle xi
    fx(i,:) = funObj(xi); % Evaluation of the particle xi
end
%% Record of the best global particle and the best local particles
[gfit, ind] = min(fx); % Fitness of the best global particle
g = x(ind,:); % Location of the best global particle
fp = fx; % Fitness of the best local particles
p = x; % Position of the best local particle
%% Computation of the surface
axisx= lb:ub; % Solution vector
axisy=[];
for i = 1:length(axisx)
    axisy(i) = funObj(axisx(i));
end
%% Iterative process
while k < kmax % Stop criterion
    k = k + 1; % New generation
    %% The optimization surface is drawn
    figure(1); % Show figure 1
    plot(axisx,axisy) % Drawn figure
    hold on
    %% Draw particles
    % Particles are drawn in red color
    plot(x,fx,'o','MarkerFaceColor','m','MarkerSize',10)
    % Draw the best local particles in green
    plot(p,fp,'o','MarkerFaceColor','g','MarkerSize',10)
```

```
      % Pause to allow visualization
      pause(0.3)
      hold off
      %% Compute the new velocity for each particle
      for i= 1:N
            % Extraction of particle xi
            xi = x(i,:);
            % Extraction of local particle pi
            pi = p(i,:);
            % Determination of the new velocity for each particle vi
            v(i,:) = v(i,:)+c1*rand(1,d).*(pi-xi)+c2*rand(1,d).*
(g-xi);
      end
      %% Determination of the new position of each particle
      x = x + v;
      %% Verify that the particles are within the limits lb and ub
      for i = 1:N % For each particle
            for j=1:d % For each dimension
                  if x(i,j) < lb(j) % Verify the lower limit
                        x(i,j) = lb(j);
                  elseif x(i,j) > ub(j) % Verify the upper limit
                        x(i,j) = ub(j);
                  end
            end
      end
      %% Evaluation of the new particles with the objective function
      for i = 1:N
            xi = x(i,:); % Extraction of the particle xi
            fx(i,:) = funObj(xi); % Evaluation of the particle xi
      end
      %% Record of the best global particle and the best local
particles
      [gfitkplus1, ind] = min(fx);
      % If a better solution is found, update the global particle
      if gfitkplus1 < gfit
            % Update the fitness of the best global particle
            gfit = gfitkplus1;w
            % Update the position of the best global particle
            g = x(ind,:);
      end
      for i = 1:N
            % If any particle is found with a better solution as
previously,
            % update your best local particle
            if fx(i,:) < fp(i,:)
                  % Update the fitness of the best local particles
                  fp(i,:) = fx(i,:);
```

```
                % Update the position of the best local particles
                p(i,:) = x(i,:);
        end
    end
    %% Register the best solutions found in each generation
    Evolution(k) = gfit;
end
%% End of the iterative process, display of results
figure
% Shows graphically the results
plot(Evolution)
disp(['Best Result : ', num2str(g)])
disp(['Best Fitness : ', num2str(gfit)])
```

6.5.2 Application of the PSO to Problems with Constraints

In most of the real optimization problems, there are constraints that limit the possible values of the solutions. The PSO is an algorithm designed for unconstraint problems. However, it can be adapted to solve those problems that contain them. One technique for working with restrictions is to implement a penalty function. These types of functions deteriorate those solutions that do not meet the restrictions of the problem by giving them a high fitness value (if it is a minimization problem) or a low value (if it is a maximization problem). There are several penalty functions that have been proposed, one of which is the External Penalization Function, which has been explained in Chapter 2.

The following example solves an optimization problem with constraints. This problem formulates a minimization case considering two dimensions and a restriction of inequality. Algorithm 6.1 can be used to solve this problem with just a few adjustments that consist of modifying the values of the parameters and adding the penalty function. In Program 6.3 these modifications have been implemented.

Example 6.2

A construction company needs to divide a terrain into equal houses so that they must maintain a determined configuration. In each land area, a house will be built with an area not less than $200\,m^2$. Between the limits of the house and the fence of the land area, there should be a margin of 3 m on the vertical sides and 10 m on the horizontal sides, see Figure 6.3. The land areas must measure a minimum of 5 m on either side. What is the length of the sides r and s that each house should have so that the area of the land area is minimal? What is the minimum area of the land area?

Solution

As mentioned before, Algorithm 6.1 can be used as a basis for solving this problem with just a few modifications. Among them, it is necessary to modify of course the definition of the objective function. In the problem, the idea is to minimize the area

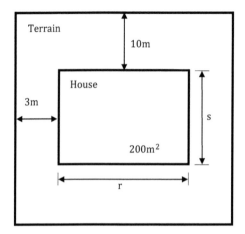

FIGURE 6.3   Optimization problem with constraints.

of the house. For this, it is clear that the horizontal side of the house is assessed horizontally, plus the left and right side margins. This is modeled as follows:

$$r+3+3=r+6$$

and the vertical side of the house must include the vertical measurement, plus the upper and lower margins:

$$s+10+10=s+20$$

Therefore, the area of the house should be

$$A=(r+6)\cdot(s+20) \tag{6.12}$$

Under such conditions, A is the area that should be minimized; therefore, this is the objective function and its dimensions are two: r and s.

Parameter values must also be modified defining new search space limits. According to the problem, the houses must measure a minimum of 5 m on either side, so the lower limit will be 5 for both dimensions. Considering that the lower limits and the construction area of each house should not be less than 200 m², then it is possible to determine that the upper limit for each dimension has a value of 40.

$$5 \times 40 = 200$$

Although the area of the house could be greater than or equal to 200 m², it is considered that the area of the land area should be minimized. Therefore, the area of the house is also minimized. To assume a limit greater than 40 means to give more area, which would not make sense because the search area would only be expanding to a space where there are no promising solutions. The algorithm will try to find a solution that minimizes the areas. Therefore, its tendency will be to select a solution that generates an area very close to 200 m². This value represents the minimum allowed area. With regard to the number of particles and the maximum number of iterations, these values have been modified due to the complexity of the problem. In general terms, a problem with constraints represents a greater challenge as it reduces the area where the feasible solutions are located, but does not reduce the search area. In these cases, a higher number of search agents and probably a greater number of iterations will also be required to perform the search. With more practice, the reader will realize the impact of such parameters in the optimization results. The adjustment of such parameters maintains a clear relationship on the quality of the solutions. The last modification corresponds to the incorporation of a penalty function in the algorithm. This modification requires four parameters to define, two for equality restrictions and two for inequality restrictions. Because the problem has only one restriction and this is one of inequality, it is necessary to initialize two parameters: the penalty constant rg and the penalty multiplier cg. Thus, the penalty function can be formulated as follows:

$$P = rg \cdot max(0, g1) \tag{6.13}$$

where $g1$ is the inequality constraint. Considering the information that provides the problem to be optimized, the restriction is that the area of each house should be not less than $200\,m^2$,

$$r \times s \geq 200$$

$$r \times s - 200 \geq 0$$

Then, the constraint can be formulated as follows:

$$g1 = r \times s - 200 \tag{6.14}$$

However, considering this restriction, a change in Eq. 6.8 is required. Penalized solutions must be those that are less than zero and not vice versa. The penalty function of Eq. 6.8 affects those solutions that are greater than zero, and the constraint indicates which solutions must be greater than zero. Therefore, this equation should be modified as follows:

$$P = rg \cdot min(0, g1) \tag{6.15}$$

The values of the penalty constant rg and the penalty multiplier cg are adjustable based on the characteristics of each problem. The reader can test different values and observe the changes in the performance of the algorithm. It is intended that at the beginning rg be small and gradually increase so that as generations progress, the penalty is greater. In the case of cg, its value is constant and is used as a multiplicative factor to modify rg in each iteration.

Solution

The lengths that minimize the area of the land area are $r = 7.75$ and $s = 25.8$. The minimum area of the plot is $A = 629.75$.

Program 6.3 Application of PSO for Constraint Problems

```
%%%%%%%%%%%%%%%%%%%%%%%%%%%%%%%%%%%%%%%%%%%%%%%%%%%%%%%%%%%%%%%%%%%%%%%%%%%
% PSO for constraint problems
% Erik Cuevas, Alma Rodríguez
%%%%%%%%%%%%%%%%%%%%%%%%%%%%%%%%%%%%%%%%%%%%%%%%%%%%%%%%%%%%%%%%%%%%%%%%%%%
%% Clear memory and close MATLAB windows
clear all % Clear memory
close all % close MATLAB windows
%% Problem to optimize (minimize), the definition of the objective
function
funObj = @(xi) (xi(1)+6) * (xi(2)+20);
%% Parameter configuration
N = 50; % Particle number
d = 2; % Dimensions
lb = [5 5]; % Lower limit of search space
ub = [40 40]; % Upper limit of search space
k = 0; % Iteration
kmax = 500; % Maximum number of iterations
c1 = 2; % Cognitive constant
c2 = 2; % Social constant
%% Parameters of the penalization function
rg=100; % Penalization constant
cg=2; % Penalization multiplier
%% Initialization of particles and velocity
for i = 1:N
    x(i,:) = rand(1,d).*(ub-lb)+lb; % Initialization of the
particles
    v(i,:) = zeros(1,d); % Velocity Initialization
end
%% Evaluation of the initial particles with the objective function
fxp = [];
for i = 1:N
    xi=x(i,:); % Extraction of the particle xi
    fx(i) = funObj(xi); % Evaluation of the particle xi, fitness
of xi
    g1 = xi(1)*xi(2)-200; % Inequality constraint
    P = rg * min(0,g1)^2; % Penalization function
    fxp(i) = fx(i) + P; % Penalized fitness
    rg = rg * cg; % Update of the penalty constant
end
%% Record of the best global particle and the best local particles
[gfit, ind] = min(fxp); % Fitness of the best global particle
g = x(ind,:); % Location of the best global particle
fp = fxp; % Fitness of the best local particles
p = x; % Position of the best local particle
%% Computation of the surface
```

```
axisx=linspace(min(lb),max(ub),100); % Solution vector for
dimension 1
axisy=axisx; % Solution vector for dimension 2
axisz=[]; % Fitness Matrix
for i = 1:length(axisx)
      for j = 1:length(axisy)
            % Evaluation of objective function for the values of
x-axis and y-axis
            axisz(i,j) = funObj([axisx(i) axisy(j)]);
      end
end
[axisy axisx] = meshgrid(axisx,axisy); % Computation of the grid
%% Iterative process
while k < kmax % Stop criterion
      k = k + 1; % New generation
      %% The optimization surface is drawn
      figure(1); % Show figure 1
      surf(axisx,axisy,axisz) % Drawn figure
      hold on
      %% Draw particles
      % Particles are drawn in red color
      plot3(x(:,1),x(:,2),fx,'o','MarkerFaceColor','m','Marker
Size',10)
      % Draw the best local particles in green
      plot3(p(:,1),p(:,2),fp,'o','MarkerFaceColor','g','Marker
Size',10)
      % Pause to allow visualization
      pause(0.3)
      hold off
      %% Draw the contour of the optimization surface
      figure(2) % Show figure 2
      contour(axisx,axisy,axisz,20) % Draw the contour
      hold on
      %% Draw the particles on the contour
      % Particles are drawn in red color
      plot(x(:,1),x(:,2),'o','MarkerFaceColor','m');
      % Draw the best local particles in green
      plot(p(:,1),p(:,2),'o','MarkerFaceColor','g');
      % Pause to allow visualization
      pause(0.3)
      hold off
      %% Determine the new velocity for each particle
      for i= 1:N
            % Extraction of particle xi
            xi = x(i,:);
            % Extraction of local particle pi
```

```
            pi = p(i,:);
            % Determination of the new velocity for each particle vi
            v(i,:) = v(i,:)+c1*rand(1,d).*(pi-xi)+c2*rand(1,d).*
(g-xi);
      end
      %% Determination of the new position of each particle
      x = x + v;
      %% Verify that the particles are within the limits lb and ub
      for i = 1:N % For each particle
            for j=1:d % For each dimension
                  if x(i,j) < lb(j) % Verify the lower limit
                        x(i,j) = lb(j);
                  elseif x(i,j) > ub(j) % Verify the upper limit
                        x(i,j) = ub(j);
                  end
            end
      end
      %% Evaluation of the new particles with the objective
function
      fxp=[];
      for i = 1:N
            xi=x(i,:); % Extraction of the particle xi
            % Evaluation of the particle xi, fitness of xi
            fx(i) = funObj(xi);
            g1 = xi(1)*xi(2)-200; % Inequality constraint
            P = rg * min(0,g1)^2; % Penalization function
            fxp(i) = fx(i) + P; % Penalized fitness
            % Update of the penalty constant
            rg = rg * cg;
      end
      %% Record of the best global particle and the best local
particles
      [gfitkplus1, ind] = min(fxp);
      % If a better solution is found, update the global particle
      if gfitkplus1 < gfit
            % Update the fitness of the best global particle
            gfit = gfitkplus1;
            % Update the position of the best global particle
            g = x(ind,:);
      end
      for i = 1:N
            % If any particle is found with a better solution a
previously,
            % update your best local particle
            if fxp(i) < fp(i)
                  % Update the fitness of the best local particles
                  fp(i) = fxp(i);
```

```
                    % Update the position of the best local particles
                    p(i,:) = x(i,:);
              end
        end
        %% Register the best solutions found in each generation
        Evolution(k) = gfit;
end
%% End of the iterative process, display of results
figure
% Shows graphically the results
plot(Evolution)
disp(['Best Results : ', num2str(g)])
disp(['Best Fitness : ', num2str(gfit)])
```

REFERENCES

Helwig, S., & Wanka, R. (2008). Theoretical analysis of initial particle swarm behavior. In G. Rudolph, T. Jansen, S. Lucas, C. Poloni, & N. Beume, (Eds.), *Parallel problem solving from nature - PPSN X* (pp. 889–898). Springer.

Kennedy, J., & Eberhart, R. (1995). Particle swarm optimization. In Proceedings of ICNN'95 - International Conference on Neural Networks (Vol. 4, pp. 1942–1948). Berlin, Heidelberg: IEEE. doi:10.1109/ICNN.1995.488968

Lima, S. (1995). Back to the basics of anti-predatory vigilance: The group-size effect. *Animal Behaviour, 49*(1), 11–20.

Milinski, H., & Heller, R. (1978). Influence of a predator on the optimal foraging behavior of sticklebacks. *Nature, 275*(5681), 642–644.

Artificial Bee Colony (ABC) Algorithm

7.1 INTRODUCTION

Swarm intelligence is a paradigm in the field of artificial intelligence that is used to solve optimization problems. It is based on the collective behaviors of social insects, flocks of birds, and schools of fish, among others; because these and other animals have shown that they are capable of solving complex problems without centralized control.

Recently, it has experienced a great increase in new algorithm developments inspired by natural phenomena, as well as in the area of research related to animal behavior.

The algorithm of the Artificial Bee Colony (ABC) was proposed by Dervis Karaboga in 2005, and since then, its capabilities have been demonstrated in a wide variety of real-world applications (Karaboga, 2005). This algorithm takes its inspiration from the intelligent search behavior of a bee colony. The method consists of three essential components: positions of food sources, amount of nectar, and different kinds of bees.

Numerical comparisons have shown that the ABC algorithm is competitive in relation to other metaheuristic algorithms, with the advantage that it requires the use of a smaller number of control parameters (Karaboga & Basturk, 2007, 2009).

Due to its simplicity and easy implementation, the ABC algorithm has captured a lot of attention, so it has been applied in solving many practical optimization problems (Sabat, Udgata, & Abraham, 2010; Singh, 2009).

There are three groups of bees according to the operation that they perform. In general, they correspond to positions of candidate solutions that represent positions of food sources under the natural metaphor. Under the ABC algorithm, they are classified as worker, onlooker, and explorer bees.

Half of the colony includes worker bees and the other half involves onlooker bees. The number of worker bees is equal to the number of food sources in the hive, and these bees look for food around the food source stored in their memory, while they pass this information to the onlooker bees. Onlooker bees tend to select the best food sources from those found by the workers. On the other hand, the exploring bees are transferred from a few worker bees, who previously abandoned their food sources in search of new ones.

The ABC algorithm begins with the random production of a uniformly distributed initial population, which will be the candidate solutions. After this initialization, the objective function is evaluated, which determines whether these positions are acceptable solutions to the problem.

The candidate solutions are modified by three different operators of the algorithm, according to the values given by the objective function. Every time that the fitness value cannot be improved after a certain number of cycles, its corresponding food source (position) is abandoned, and it is reinitialized in a new random position until a termination criterion is met.

In this algorithm, while the onlooker and worker bees carry out the exploitation process in the search space, the explorers control the exploration process as the name implies. The main steps of the algorithm are given in the flowchart of Figure 7.1.

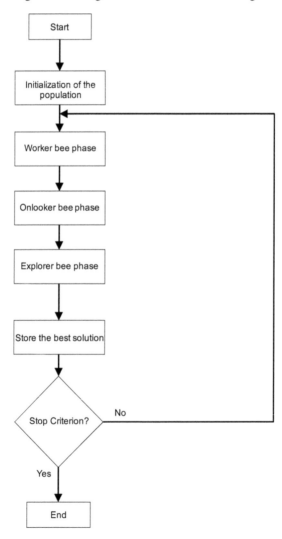

FIGURE 7.1 Flowchart of the ABC.

7.2 ARTIFICIAL BEE COLONY

The general procedure for performing the ABC algorithm is briefly described in the pseudo-code of Figure 7.2. The steps will be detailed in the next sections for each respective operator.

7.2.1 Initialization of the Population

In this process, N_p food sources are initialized. Each food source is a vector that contains the values of the parameters to be optimized, which are distributed randomly and evenly between the lower x_j^{inf} and upper limits x_j^{sup}.

Therefore, the position of each individual is determined by

$$x_{j,i} = x_j^{inf} + rand(0,1) \times \left(x_j^{sup} - x_j^{inf}\right) \quad j=1,2,\ldots,d; i=1,2,\ldots,N_p; \tag{7.1}$$

where j and i represent the parameter and the element, respectively.

7.2.2 Sending Worker Bees

As previously mentioned, the first half of the colony includes worker bees and the second half onlooker bees. For each food source, there is only one worker bee. That worker bee that has exhausted its food source becomes an explorer.

At this stage, each worker bee generates a new food source in the neighborhood of its current position as follows:

$$v_{j,i} = x_{j,i} + \phi_{j,i}\left(x_{j,i} - x_{j,k}\right); \quad k \in \{1,2,\ldots,N_p\}; j \in \{1,2,\ldots,d\}; \tag{7.2}$$

where $x_{j,i}$ corresponds to the j parameter of the i element which is randomly selected. k is one of the food sources so that the condition $i \neq k$ is satisfied. An adjustment factor $\phi_{j,i}$ is a random number between $[-1,1]$.

Send explorer bees to initial food sources (solutions)

REPEAT

        Send worker bees to food sources and determine their amount of nectar

        Calculate the probability value of food sources that have been preferred by onlooker bees

        Send onlooker bees to food sources and determine their amount of nectar

        Stop the process of exploitation of sources depleted by bees

        Send explorer bees to the search area to discover new food sources, randomly

        Memorize the best food source found so-far

UNTIL (a termination criterion has been reached)

FIGURE 7.2 Pseudocode of the ABC.

Each position of a food source represents a candidate solution to the problem under consideration. Likewise, the amount of nectar of a food source corresponds to the quality of this solution in terms of the objective function.

Thus, whenever a new solution $v_{j,i}$ is generated, its fitness value should be evaluated. This value, in the case of a minimization problem, can be assigned by the following expression:

$$fit_i = \begin{cases} \dfrac{1}{1+J_i} & \text{si } J_i \geq 0 \\ 1+abs(J_i) & \text{si } J_i < 0 \end{cases} \tag{7.3}$$

where J_i is the objective function to be minimized. Then, a Greedy criterion for the selection between v_i and x_i is applied. If the amount of nectar in x_i is greater, then the solution is replaced by v_i; otherwise, x_i is preserved.

7.2.3 Selecting Food Sources by Onlooker Bees

According to the fitness value, onlooker bees must select one of the available food sources. The fitness value is determined by the worker bees. The probability of selecting a specific food source is calculated by the following expression:

$$\text{Prob}_i = \frac{fit_i}{\sum_{i=1}^{N_p} fit_i} \tag{7.4}$$

where fit_i is the fitness value for the food source i, which is related to the objective function J_i. The probability that a food source is selected increases according to the value in the fitness value of the food source in question.

7.2.4 Determining the Exploring Bees

The number of attempts to leave a food source is equal to the "limit" value. The refinement of the solutions obtained depends on this parameter and with their quality. In order to verify if a candidate solution has reached the predetermined "limit," a counter A_i is added to each food source i.

Therefore, if a food source i cannot be improved after the number of attempts given by the value of "limit" has elapsed, it is abandoned by its corresponding worker or onlooker bee, which will then become an explorer. For this reason, such a parameter is also called the "abandonment criterion."

7.2.5 Computational Process ABC

Once all the stages and operators of the ABC algorithm have been described in this section, they are combined to produce the complete ABC method. Figure 7.3 shows the complete flowchart of the ABC algorithm. Although a diagram was presented in the Introduction section, it did not contain the complete procedure with the corresponding equations.

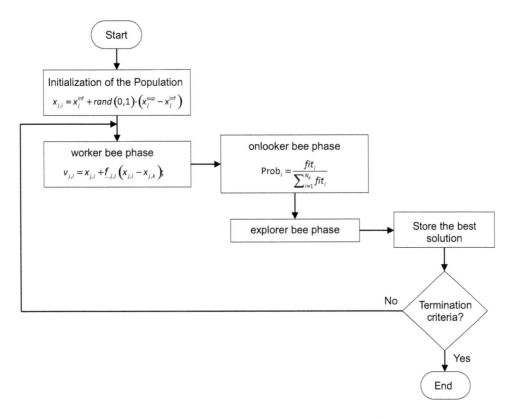

FIGURE 7.3   Flowchart of the ABC with the respective operation at each stage.

7.2.6 Computational Example in MATLAB

In order to exemplify the operation of the ABC algorithm and its practical implementation in MATLAB®, the following minimization problem is considered to be solved:

$$\text{Minimize} \quad -(y+47)\sin\left(\sqrt{\left|y+\frac{x}{2}+47\right|}\right)-x\sin\left(\sqrt{|x-(y+47)|}\right)$$

$$-10\le x_1 \le 10$$

$$\text{Subject to:}$$

$$-10\le x_2 \le 10$$

(7.5)

In this formulation, a two-dimensional function $f(x_1,x_2)$ with a search space defined in the interval $[-10,10]$ for the decision variables x_1 and x_2 is considered. Figure 7.4 shows a representation of the objective function $f(x_1,x_2)$.

As can be seen, the function $f(x_1,x_2)$ has several minima, where one is the global optimum positioned at $x_1=512$ and $x_2=404.2319$ with a value in the objective function of $f(x^*)=-959.6407$, and the rest are considered local optima. Due to the nature of its surface, it is suitable to be minimized using the ABC algorithm, and in Figure 7.5, the two-dimensional contour is shown to visualize the position of the optima elements.

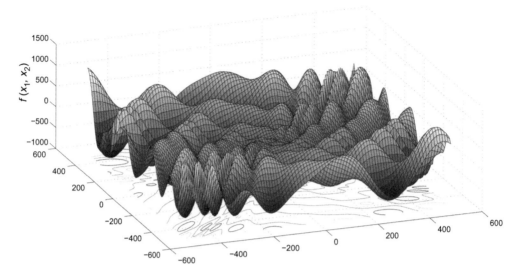

FIGURE 7.4   Graphical representation of the function $-(y+47)\sin\left(\sqrt{\left|y+\dfrac{x}{2}+47\right|}\right)-x\sin\left(\sqrt{|x-(y+47)|}\right)$.

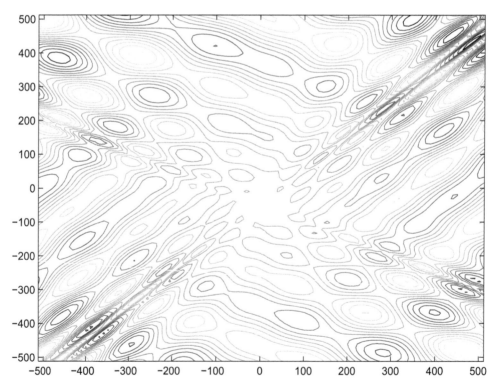

FIGURE 7.5   Contour of the function $-(y+47)\sin\left(\sqrt{\left|y+\dfrac{x}{2}+47\right|}\right)-x\sin\left(\sqrt{|x-(y+47)|}\right)$.

The process to minimize $f(x_1,x_2)$ by means of the ABC algorithm is presented in the form of a pseudocode in Algorithm 7.1. The procedure begins by randomly selecting a decision vector $\mathbf{x}_g$ $(g = 0)$ within the search space defined in the interval $[-10,10]$ for each of the variables x_1 and x_2.

Algorithm 7.1 ABC to Solve Equation 7.5

1. Parameter Initialization $g \leftarrow 0$, limit, Np, gmax, FC: food sources.
2. Initialization of the population within the limits of the function $x_{1,g} \leftarrow$ random $[-10,10]$, $x_{2,g} \leftarrow$ random $[-10,10]$
3. **while** $(g < g_{\max})\,\{$

Worker bee phase

4. for $(i = 0; i = FC; i{+}{+})\,\{$
5. $v_{g,i} \leftarrow x_{g,i} + \phi_{g,i}\left(x_{g,i} - x_{g,k}\right);$
6. Evaluate $f\left(v_{g,i}\right)$
7. if $f\left(v_{g,i}\right) < f\left(x_{g,i}\right)\,\{$
8. $x_{g,i} \leftarrow v_{g,i}; f\left(x_{g,i}\right) \leftarrow f\left(v_{g,i}\right); trials_{g,i} \leftarrow 0\}$
9. else $\{trials_{g,i} \leftarrow trials_{g,i} + 1; \}\,\}$
10. $\text{Prob}_i \leftarrow \dfrac{fit_i}{\displaystyle\sum_{i=1}^{N_p} fit_i};$

Onlooker bee phase

11. $t \leftarrow 0; s \leftarrow 0;$
12. while $(t < FC)\,\{$
13. $r \leftarrow rand(0,1);$
14. if $r < p(s)\,\{$
15. $t \leftarrow t + 1;$
16. $v_{g,s} \leftarrow x_{g,s} + \phi_{g,s}\left(x_{g,s} - x_{g,k}\right);$
17. Evaluate $f\left(v_{g,s}\right)$
18. if $f\left(v_{g,s}\right) < f\left(x_{g,s}\right)\,\{$
19. $x_{g,s} \leftarrow v_{g,s}; f\left(x_{g,s}\right) \leftarrow f\left(v_{g,s}\right); trials_{g,s} \leftarrow 0\}$
20. else $\{trials_{g,s} \leftarrow trials_{g,s} + 1; \}\,\}$
21. $s \leftarrow (s+1)\bmod(FC-1); \}$

Explorer bee phase

22. $mi \leftarrow \{s : trials_{g,s} \leftarrow \max(trials)\};$
23. If $trials_{mi} > limit$
24. $x_{g,s} = x_g^{\inf} + rand(0,1) \cdot \left(x_g^{\sup} - x_g^{\inf}\right);$
25. $f_{mi} \leftarrow f\left(x_{g,s}\right); \}$
26. $g \leftarrow g + 1; \}\}$

TABLE 7.1   Parameters of the ABC
Algorithm Implemented in Program 7.1

Parameter	Value
limit	15
N_p	100
g_{max}	150

In the case of Algorithm 7.1, g_{max} represents the maximum number of generations to complete, and g the generation in question.

In order to provide the reader with aid in the implementation of Algorithm 7.1, Program 7.1 shows the MATLAB code. The algorithm parameters have been configured as shown in Table 7.1.

The code shown in Program 7.1 includes the different three bee phases described in previous sections. The code is explained step by step with the objective that it is possible to compare what is explained with the respective code. We tried to maintain a simple code style to benefit the understanding. It is worth mentioning that the parameter called "limit" corresponds to the value of the food source abandonment criterion.

Program 7.1 ABC Algorithm to Minimize the Optimization Problem Formulated in Equation 7.5

```
%%%%%%%%%%%%%%%%%%%%%%%%%%%%%%%%%%%%%%%%%%%%%%%%%%%%%%%%%%%%%%%%%%%%%%%%%%
%%%%%%%%%%%
% ABC example
% Erik Cuevas, Alma Rodríguez
%%%%%%%%%%%%%%%%%%%%%%%%%%%%%%%%%%%%%%%%%%%%%%%%%%%%%%%%%%%%%%%%%%%%%%%%%%
%%%%%%%%%%%
function ABC()
      % Function to optimize definen in Eq. 7.5
      % Function Eggholder
      func='((-1)*(y+47)*(sin(sqrt(abs(y+(x/2)+47)))))-(x*sin(sqrt
      (abs(x-(y+47)))))'; f=vectorize(inline(func));
      range=[-512 512 -512 512];
      % Initial parameter
      d=2; %Dimensions
      Np=100; %Population size
      food_source=round(Np/2); % Food sources
      gmax=150; % Maximum number of generations
      limit=15; % Abandonment criterion
      Range=range(2)-range(1);
      % Random initial population
      Pop = (rand(food_source,d) * Range) + range(1);
      % The function is drawn
      Ndiv=100;
      dx=Range/Ndiv;
      dy=dx;
```

```
[x,y]=meshgrid(range(1):dx:range(2),range(3):dy:range(4));
z=f(x,y);
figure, surfc(x,y,z);
figure, contour(x,y,z,15);
% Evaluate the fitness values
for ii=1:food_source
      ValFit(ii)=f(Pop(ii,1),Pop(ii,2));
      % Compute the relative fitness
      Fitness(ii)=calculateFitness(ValFit(ii));
end
% The initial population is plotted
figure, contour(x,y,z,15); hold on;
plot(Pop(:,1),Pop(:,2),'b.','markersize',15);
drawnow;
hold on;
% The counters are initialized
test=zeros(1,food_source);
% The best solution is updated
BestInd=find(ValFit==min(ValFit));
BestInd=BestInd(end);
GlobalMin=ValFit(BestInd);
GlobalParams=Pop(BestInd,:);
g=0; % Generation counter
while ((g < gmax))
      % Worker bee phase
      for i=1:(food_source)
            % The parameter to modify is randomly selected
            Param2Change=fix(rand*d)+1;
            % A random solution is used to produce a new
            % mutant solution, both must be different
            neighbor=fix(rand*(food_source))+1;
            while(neighbor==i)
                  neighbor=fix(rand*(food_source))+1;
            end
            solutions=Pop(i,:);
            % It is applied: v_{ij}=x_{ij}+\phi_{ij}*(x_
            {kj}-x_{ij})
            solutions(Param2Change)=Pop(i,Param2Change)+(Pop
            (i,Param2Change)-Pop(neighbor,Param2Change))*(
            rand-0.5)*2;
            % If the value of the generated parameter is
            outside the
            % limits, It is taken to the nearest limit
            ind=find(solutions<range(1));
            solutions(ind)=range(1);
            ind=find(solutions>range(2));
            solutions(ind)=range(2);
```

```matlab
            % The new candidate solution is evaluated
            ValFitSol=f(solutions(1),solutions(2));
            FitnessSol=calculateFitness(ValFitSol);
            % A Greedy selection criterion is applied
            between the
            % current solution and the one produced (mutant),
            and the
            % best among them is preserved
            if (FitnessSol>Fitness(i))
                    Pop(i,:)=solutions;
                    Fitness(i)=FitnessSol;
                    ValFit(i)=ValFitSol;
                    test(i)=0;
            else
                    test(i)=test(i)+1;
            end
    end
    % End of the worker bee phase
    % Probabilities are calculated using normalized
    fitness values
    probab=(0.9.*Fitness./max(Fitness))+0.1;
    % Onlooker bee phase
    i=1;
    t=0;
    while(t<food_source)
            if(rand<probab(i))
                    t=t+1;
                    % The parameter to be modified is randomly
                    selected
                    Param2Change=fix(rand*d)+1;
                    % A random solution is used to produce a new
                    % solution.
                    neighbor=fix(rand*(food_source))+1;
                    while(neighbor==i)
                            neighbor=fix(rand*(food_source))+1;
                    end
                    solutions=Pop(i,:);
                    % applied: v_{ij}=x_{ij}+\phi_{ij}*(x_
                    {kj}-x_{ij})
                    solutions(Param2Change)=Pop(i,Param2Change)+
                    (Pop(i,Param2Change)-
                    Pop(neighbor,Param2Change))*(rand-0.5)*2;
                    % If the value of the generated parameter
                    is outside % the limits,
                    it is taken to the nearest limit
                    ind=find(solutions<range(1));
                    solutions(ind)=range(1);
```

```
            ind=find(solutions>range(2));
            solutions(ind)=range(2);
            % The new solution is evaluated
            ValFitSol=f(solutions(1),solutions(2));
            FitnessSol=calculateFitness(ValFitSol);
            % A Greedy selection criterion is applied
            between the % current solution
            and the candidate solution
            if (FitnessSol>Fitness(i))
                    Pop(i,:)=solutions;
                    Fitness(i)=FitnessSol;
                    ValFit(i)=ValFitSol;
                    test(i)=0;
            else
                    test(i)=test(i)+1;
            end
        end
        i=i+1;
        if (i==(food_source)+1)
                i=1;
        end
    end
% The best food source is stored
ind=find(ValFit==min(ValFit));
ind=ind(end);
if (ValFit(ind)<GlobalMin)
    GlobalMin=ValFit(ind);
    GlobalParams=Pop(ind,:);
end
% End of the onlooker bee phase
% Explorer bee phase
% Food sources whose "limit" value is reached are
determined
ind=find(test==max(test));
ind=ind(end);
if (test(ind)>limit)
    test(ind)=0;
    solutions=(Range).*rand(1,d)+range(1);
    ValFitSol=f(solutions(1),solutions(2));
    FitnessSol=calculateFitness(ValFitSol);
    Pop(ind,:)=solutions;
    Fitness(ind)=FitnessSol;
    ValFit(ind)=ValFitSol;
end
g=g+1; % The iteration is increased
clc
```

```
                % The position and fitness of the best individual are
                displayed
                disp(GlobalMin)
                disp(GlobalParams)
        end
end
% This function allows you to calculate the relative Fitness
function fFitness=calculateFitness(fObjV)
        fFitness=zeros(size(fObjV));
        ind=find(fObjV>=0);
        fFitness(ind)=1./(fObjV(ind)+1);
        ind=find(fObjV<0);
        fFitness(ind)=1+abs(fObjV(ind));
end
```

In order to show the evolution process of the algorithm in different stages, in Figure 7.6, the initial population and its operation at 10, 75, and 150 generations are shown.

As can be seen in Figure 7.6, despite the highly multimodal surface of the function to be optimized, the result obtained with this method in two dimensions is satisfactory. In addition, it is possible to analyze their exploration and exploitation capabilities, since during

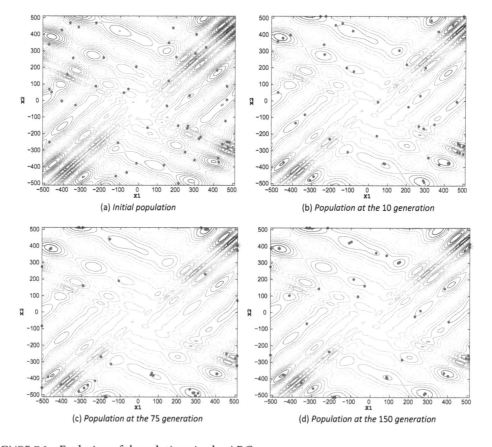

(a) *Initial population*

(b) *Population at the 10 generation*

(c) *Population at the 75 generation*

(d) *Population at the 150 generation*

FIGURE 7.6   Evolution of the solutions in the ABC.

the first generations, the population is distributed over the entire surface of the function to be optimized, and in the latter, only over the global minimum, which is highlighted with a sign * in the images.

7.3 RECENT APPLICATIONS OF THE ABC ALGORITHM IN IMAGE PROCESSING

Next, some of the most recent applications in the area of image processing of the ABC algorithm will be described. They are taken from Bahriye and Karaboga (2015).

7.3.1 Applications in the Area of Image Processing

The ABC algorithm has been applied in many topics belonging to the area of image processing, among which are image enhancement, compression, segmentation, classification, clustering, extraction and features selection, image construction, scene analysis, image recovery, watermarking, fusion, restoration, separation, noise elimination, pattern generation, template comparison, edge detection, pattern recognition, face recognition, remote sensing, and shape detection.

7.3.1.1 Image Enhancement

Image enhancement is important in the preprocessing stage of a computer vision system. This step should improve the histogram of the image as well as the level of contrast, in order to compensate for low lighting conditions. Most of the problems in images are due to climatic conditions or the different acquisition devices.

A common method used for image enhancement is the contrast transform, in which the intensity of each pixel $f(x, y)$, located at the coordinates (x, y) of an image, is transformed into $g(x, y)$ using the function shown in Eq. 7.6:

$$g(x, y) = T(f(x, y)) \tag{7.6}$$

Ye, Mengdi, Zhengbing, and Hongwei (2011) carried out the transformation of the contrast based on the fuzzy set theory and using the ABC algorithm to obtain the fuzzy parameters, to improve the efficiency overtime of the method. In this work, it was concluded that the results obtained from this new method were robust, adaptable, and faster than other schemes.

Yimit, Hagihara, Miyoshi, and Hagihara (2013) presented a method for image improvement based on the ABC algorithm, which uses a grayscale transformation, based on the local distribution of gray levels in the neighborhood of each pixel in an image Dadaist. The intensity of each pixel $f(x, y)$, located in the plane (x, y), is transformed into $g(x, y)$, according to Eq. 7.7:

$$g(x, y) = k \left[\frac{M}{\sigma(x, y) + b} \right] \cdot [f(x, y) - c \cdot m(x, y)] + m(x, y)^a \tag{7.7}$$

In Eq. 7.7, a, b, c, and k are positive real parameters. M is the average value of the intensities of the whole image, $\sigma(x, y)$ and $m(x, y)$ correspond to the standard and average deviations in a neighborhood centered on (x, y), respectively. In this work, it was concluded that the best quality image can be found by obtaining an optimal combination of four parameters a, b, c, and k.

In addition to these conclusions, this method has been also compared with two other techniques for image improvement, one based on genetic algorithms (GAs) and the other based on particle swarm optimization (PSO). From the comparison, it was reported that the method based on the ABC algorithm offered the best results.

7.3.1.2 Image Compression

Recent advances in the generation of high-resolution images, along with strong demand for higher capacities, high-performance devices, and large bandwidths have brought new and better image compression techniques. These methods have reduced the amount of data but without losing quality or producing distortion. Likewise, these techniques have offered the advantage of reducing computational and transmission costs.

In a compression scheme, the color space also called the characteristic space is projected into a new color space but with a smaller amount of tones or features. However, unlike the reduction in color space, decreasing the characteristics present in the image requires a process, in which a portion of them is extracted, but retaining those that are considered the most important. Characteristics can be represented by domain coefficients of a transform (such as discrete Wavelet transform or discrete cosine transform).

In 2011, Akay and Karaboga used the ABC algorithm to find the optimal threshold values corresponding to the coefficients of the Wavelet transform, in order to obtain reconstructed images of better quality, which can be considered as an optimization problem.

The Wavelet transform operates in the first instance dividing an image into different parts in the frequency domain to build a base function located in both the frequency and time domains.

The image (signal) is also divided into four different frequencies: approximation, horizontal details, vertical details, and diagonal details. Such decompositions are repeated using the approximation coefficients until a certain level.

Wavelet decomposition packages are applied recursively to both the approximation coefficients and the detail coefficients with which a binary tree is constituted. In order to obtain a high ratio between quality and compression, the coefficients are thresholded by the values obtained with the ABC algorithm. In the reconstruction stage, the inverse Wavelet transform is used on the compressed image. Therefore, a multiobjective approach was considered that adopts the L2 recovery standard and the value of Peak Signal-to-Noise Ratio (PSNR), which is obtained through Eq. 7.8:

$$PSNR = 20\log_{10}\left(\frac{255}{\sqrt{MSE}}\right) \tag{7.8}$$

where *MSE* corresponds to the minimum square error, and 255 to the maximum gray-level value in an intensity image.

7.3.1.3 Border Detection

The edges in an image represent changes in gray levels (intensity) or discontinuities. The detection of these changes is extensively used in the segmentation of images in order to find a set of connected curves that correspond to the limits of the structures contained in the image so that the amount of redundant information is significantly reduced. Benala, Jampala, Villa, and Konathala (2009), Deng and Duan (2014), Parmaksizoglu and Alci (2011), and Yigitbasi and Baykan (2013) have studied and reported the ABC algorithm in the area of edge detection.

7.3.1.4 Clustering

A Clustering technique, from the image processing point of view, is a segmentation method, which classifies pixels contained in the image into multiple classes, depending on their intensity, distance, or probabilistic distribution. Among the algorithms widely used to implement the Clustering technique are the methods of K-means, fuzzy C-means, and the maximization-expectation algorithm. However, the ABC algorithm has also been used to implement the Clustering technique; such is the case of the work presented by Lin and Wu (2012), where the centers of different clusters were calculated using their membership values using the ABC algorithm and local spatial information of the global pixel intensities.

The approach of Lin and Wu consists of two phases for each iteration. In the first stage, the scanning bees are randomly positioned in the domain of the space of an objective image, and the spatial information is searched by means of an objective function to be minimized by the ABC algorithm. In the second phase, the spatial information produced by phase 1 is evaluated using the cost function of the algorithm fuzzy c-means, presented in Eq. 7.9. Subsequently, the local clustering process is stopped when the maximum difference between two cluster centers is less than a certain threshold. Finally, once convergence is reached, a defuzzification process is applied to assign each pixel in a specific cluster where its membership value is maximum.

$$J_{FCM} = \frac{1}{2}\sum_{x=1}^{2}\sum_{i=1}^{c}\mu_{x,i}^{m}\left\|z_x\bar{\omega}_i\right\| \tag{7.9}$$

where z_x corresponds to the distances between each pixel and the clusters. On the other hand, $\mu_{x,i}^{m}$ refers to the membership value of each pixel in a certain cluster.

7.3.1.5 Image Classification

The classification of images discriminates multiple objects from each other contained in an image. A classification method must assign pixels of the image to specified a priori (supervised) classes or automatic classes of clusters with homogeneous (unsupervised) characteristics, based on the spectral characteristics of the image. In a classification system, (1) classes are defined, (2) characteristics are selected, (3) training data are obtained, (4) pixels are classified, and (5) a verification process is carried out.

In the work presented by George, Karnan and Sivakumar (2013), the ABC algorithm and a classifier based on a vector support machine were used. In the approach, images from Computed Tomography and Magnetic Resonance were segmented using the proposed system, which is divided into four modules: preprocessing, feature extraction, segmentation, and classification. The ABC algorithm was used to segment the input image into two parts, one that contains a tumor and the other that does not, and after this segmentation, the image was classified using the vector support machine.

7.3.1.6 Fusion in Images

The fusion of images combines relevant information from multiple images of a certain scene, into a composite image, which will include a greater amount of information and have a greater visual perception.

Sharma, Bhavya, Navyashree, Sunil, and Pavithra (2012) proposed an image fusion technique based on the ABC algorithm, which is simple to implement and produces an image better than one produced by arithmetic pixel operations. For the evaluation of the objective function, the entropy of the image, as well as information of the spatial frequency, has been used in blocks defined by the specific window size.

Yu and Duan (2013) designed a radial-based neural network based on the ABC algorithm, with granular information for image fusion. The parameters of the radial-based neural network, such as the fuzzification coefficient, the position of the centers, and the values of the amplitudes, are optimized by the ABC algorithm to minimize complexity and maximize accuracy.

7.3.1.7 Scene Analysis

Scene analysis is the process of examining hidden information in an image or another source. This analysis usually begins by reducing the data in a smaller subset, produced by the extraction of characteristics and selection methods.

Mohammadi and Abadeh (2014) proposed a method for the analysis of the hidden scene based on characteristics. The objective of this approach is to detect JPEG scene images with hidden data, using a feature selector based on the ABC algorithm. Thus, the ABC algorithm produces subsets of features. A vector support machine is used as a classifier and evaluates each generated subset. In this work, it is reported that the proposed method based on ABC can be used expeditiously to solve multimodal problems of high dimensionality.

7.3.1.8 Pattern Recognition

Recognizing patterns in an image resulting from a complex scene based on visual information is a challenging task due to the lighting, rotation, and position conditions at the moment of acquisition.

Yu and Ai (2011) used vector support machines for handwriting verification. In this work, the ABC algorithm was used to establish the parameters of these machines. The proposed method was tested in four standard dataset from the University of California, Irving (UCI) repository and compared with methods based on GAs as well as other conventional optimization methods. It was concluded that the proposed method uses the ABC algorithm, overcomes the problem of the local optimum, has greater classification accuracy, and reduces the computational time needed with respect to the other methods.

Li and Li (2012) applied the multiobjective ABC algorithm in a Camellia fruit recognition system, applied in a fruit selector robot. The proposal uses eight characteristic parameters of the color parameter, morphology parameters, and textures to determine preferential recognition regions.

7.3.1.9 Object Detection

The object detection is important in industrial applications to analyze the manufactured products or components that are found in such domains. The Hough transform is widely used for the detection of circles in digital images. However, it has some disadvantages, such as computational complexity, low processing speed, and some degree of sensitivity to noisy conditions. This situation has led researchers to use optimization methods in the recognition of objects.

Cuevas, Sención-Echauri, Zaldivar, and Pérez-Cisneros (2012) presented the multiple detections of circles in images as an optimization problem and proposed a method based on ABC algorithm to solve it. In this proposal, each candidate circle C corresponds to a food source in the ABC algorithm. It is coded as $C = p_{i_1}, p_{i_2}, p_{i_3}$, where i_1, i_2, i_3 are the indexes that represent three border pixel points previously stored in a vector p, so that the candidate circle is marked as a possible solution to the detection problem.

The ABC algorithm searches in the whole border map of the image for candidate circular shapes. Then, an objective function, as described in Eq. 7.10, is used to measure the existence of a candidate circle on the edge map.

$$J(C) = 1 - \frac{\sum_{v=1}^{N_S} E(S_v)}{N_S} \tag{7.10}$$

The objective function $J(C)$ provides the error produced between the pixels S of the candidate circle C and the pixels that exist in the border map. In this function, N_S corresponds to the number of pixels belonging to the perimeter of C, and $E(S_v)$ is defined by Eq. 7.11.

$$E(S_v) = \begin{cases} 1 & \text{if pixel } (x_v, y_v) \text{ is an edge pixel} \\ 0 & \text{otherwise} \end{cases} \tag{7.11}$$

Experimental evidence presented in this work shows the effectiveness of the method to detect circular shapes under different noise conditions.

REFERENCES

Akay, B., & Karaboga, D. (2011, June). *Wavelet packets optimization using artificial bee colony algorithm*. In *IEEE Congress on Evolutionary Computation (CEC)* (pp. 89–94), New Orleans, LA: IEEE.

Bah riye, A., & Karaboga, D. (2015). A survey on the applications of artificial bee colony signal, image and video processing. *Signal Image and Video Processing, 9*, 967–990.

Benala, T., Jampala, S., Villa, S., & Konathala, B. (2009). *A novel approach to image edge enhancement using artificial bee colony optimization algorithm for hybridized smoothening filters*. In NaBIC 2009. *World Congress on Nature Biologically Inspired Computing* (pp. 1071–1076). IEEE.

Cuevas, E., Sención-Echauri, F., Zaldivar, D., & Pérez-Cisneros, M. (2012). Multi-circle detection on images using artificial bee colony (ABC) optimization. *Soft Computing, 16*(2), 281–296.

Deng, Y., & Duan, H. (2014). Biological edge detection for UCAV via improved artificial bee colony and visual attention. *Aircraft Engineering and Aerospace Technology, 86*(2), 138–146.

George, M. M., Karnan, M., & Sivakumar, R. (2013). Supervised artificial bee colony system for tumor segmentation in CT/MRI images. *International Journal of Computer Science and Management Research, 2*(5), 2529–2533.

Karaboga D. (2005). *An idea based on honey bee swarm for numerical optimization.* Technical Report – TR06. Kayseri: Erciyes University.

Karaboga, D., & Basturk, B. (2007). A powerful and efficient algorithm for numerical function optimization: Artificial bee colony (ABC) algorithm. *Journal of Global Optimization, 39*, 171–459.

Karaboga D., & Basturk B. (2009) A comparative study of artificial bee colony algorithm. *Applied Mathematics and Computation, 214*, 108–132.

Li, X., & Li, L. J. (2012). Preference multi-objective artificial bee colony and its application in camellia fruit image recognition. *Application Research of Computers, 29*(12), 4779–4781.

Lin, J., & Wu, S. (2012). Fuzzy artificial bee colony system with cooling schedule for the segmentation of medical images by using of spatial information. *Research Journal of Applied Sciences, Engineering and Technology, 4*(17), 2973–2980.

Ming, Y., & Yue-qiao, A. (2011). SVM parameters optimization based on artificial bee colony algorithm and its application in handwriting verification. In *International Conference on Electrical and Control Engineering (ICECE)* (pp. 5026–5029). Yichang, China: IEEE.

Mohammadi, F. G., & Abadeh, M. S. (2014). Image steganalysis using a bee colony based feature selection algorithm. *Engineering Applications of Artificial Intelligence, 31*(SI), 35–43.

Parmaksizoglu, S., & Alci, M. (2011). A novel cloning template designing method by using an artificial bee colony algorithm for edge detection of CNN based imaging sensors. *Sensors, 11*(5), 5337–5359.

Sabat, S. L., Udgata, S. K., & Abraham, K., (2010). Artificial bee colony algorithm for small signal model parameter extraction of MESFET. *Engineering Applications of Artificial Intelligence, 11*, 1573–2916.

Sharma, P., Bhavya, V., Navyashree, K., Sunil, K. S., & Pavithra, P. (2012). Artificial bee colony and its application for image fusion. *International Journal of Information Technology and Computer Science, 4*(11), 42–49.

Singh, A. (2009). An artificial bee colony algorithm for the leaf-constrained minimum spanning tree problem. *Applied Soft Computing, 9*, 625–631.

Survey Zhiwei, Y., Mengdi, Z., Zhengbing, H., & Hongwei, C., (2011). *Image enhancement based on artificial bee colony algorithm and fuzzy set*. In C. B. Povloviq & C. W. Lu (Eds.), *Proceedings of 3rd International Symposium on Information Engineering and Electronic Commerce (IEEC 2011)*, July 22–24 (pp. 127–130). ASME Press.

Yigitbasi, E., & Baykan, N. (2013). Edge detection using artificial bee colony algorithm (ABC). *International Journal of Information and Electronics Engineering, 3*(6), 634–638.

Yimit, A., Hagihara, Y., Miyoshi, T., & Hagihara, Y. (2013). *Automatic image enhancement by artificial bee colony algorithm*. In Z. Zhu (Ed.), *Proceedings of SPIE International Conference on Graphic and Image Processing (ICGIP 2012) (Vol. 8768), 4th International Conference on Graphic and Image Processing (ICGIP)* (OCT 0607 2012), SPIE: Singapore.

Yu, J., & Duan, H. (2013). Artificial bee colony approach to information granulation-based fuzzy radial basis function neural networks for image fusion. *Optik-International Journal for Light and Electron Optics, 124*(17), 3103–3111.

CHAPTER 8

Cuckoo Search (CS) Algorithm

8.1 INTRODUCTION

Optimization is a field with applications in many areas of science, engineering, economics, and others, where mathematical modeling is used (Pardalos Panos, Romeijn Edwin, & Tuy, 2000). In general, the goal is to find an acceptable solution of an objective function defined over a given search space. Optimization algorithms are usually broadly divided into deterministic and stochastic methods (Floudas, Akrotirianakis, Caratzoulas, Meyer, & Kallrath, 2005). Since deterministic methods only provide a theoretical guarantee of locating a local minimum for the objective function, they often face great difficulties in solving optimization problems (Ying, Ke-Cun, & Shao-Jian, 2007). On the other hand, stochastic methods are usually faster in locating a global optimum (Georgieva & Jordanov, 2009). Moreover, they adapt easily to black-box formulations and extremely ill-behaved functions, whereas deterministic methods usually rest on at least some theoretical assumptions about the problem formulation and its analytical properties (such as Lipschitz continuity) (Lera & Sergeyev, 2010).

Evolutionary algorithms (EA), which are considered as members of the stochastic group, have been developed by a combination of rules and randomness that mimics several natural phenomena. Such phenomena include evolutionary processes such as the EA proposed by Fogel, Owens, and Walsh (1966), De Jong (1975), and Koza (1990); the Genetic Algorithm (GA) proposed by Holland (1975) and Goldberg (1989); the Artificial Immune System (AIS) proposed by De Castro and Von Zuben (1999); and the Differential Evolution (DE) Algorithm proposed by Price and Storn (1995). Some other methods which are based on physical processes include the Simulated Annealing proposed by Kirkpatrick, Gelatt and Vecchi (1983); the Electromagnetism-like Algorithm proposed by İlker, Birbil and Shu-Cherng (2003); and the Gravitational Search Algorithm proposed by Rashedi, Nezamabadi-Poura, and Saryazdi (2011). Also, there are other methods based on the animal-behavior phenomena such as the Particle Swarm Optimization (PSO) algorithm proposed by Kennedy and Eberhart (1995) and the Ant Colony Optimization (ACO) algorithm proposed by Dorigo, Maniezzo, and Colorni (1991).

Most of the research work on EA aims for locating the global optimum (Das, Maity, Qu, & Suganthan, 2011). Despite its best performance, a global optimum may be integrated by parameter values that are considered impractical or prohibitively expensive, limiting their adoption into a real-world application. Therefore, from a practical point of view, it is desirable to have access to not only the global optimum but also as many local optima as possible (ideally all of them). Under such circumstances, a local optimum with acceptable performance quality and modest cost may be preferred over a costly global solution with marginally better performance (Wong, Wu, Mok, Peng, & Zhang, 2012). The process of finding the global optimum and multiple local optima is known as multimodal optimization.

EA performs well for locating a single optimum but fail to provide multiple solutions (Das et al., 2011). Several methods have been introduced into the EA scheme to achieve multimodal optimization, such as fitness sharing (Beasley, Bull, & Matin, 1993; Miller & Shaw, 1996; Thomsen, 2004), deterministic crowding (Mahfoud, 1995), probabilistic crowding (Thomsen, 2004; Mengshoel & Goldberg, 1999), clustering-based niching (Yin & Germay, 1993), clearing procedure (CP) (Petrowski, 1996), species conserving GA (Li, Balazs, Parks, & Glarkson, 2002), and elitist population strategies (Lianga & Kwong-Sak, 2011). However, most of these methods have difficulties that need to be overcome before they can be employed successfully to multimodal applications. Some identified problems include difficulties in tuning some niching parameters, difficulties in maintaining discovered solutions in a run, extra computational overheads, and poor scalability when the dimensionality is high. An additional problem represents the fact that such methods are devised for extending the search capacities of popular EAs such as GA and PSO which fail in finding a balance between exploration and exploitation, mainly for multimodal functions (Chen, Low, & Yang, 2009). Furthermore, they do not explore the whole region effectively and often suffer premature convergence or loss of diversity.

As alternative approaches, other researchers have employed AIS to solve multimodal optimization problems. Some examples are the clonal selection algorithm (CSA) (Castro & Zuben, 2002) and the artificial immune network (AiNet) (Castro & Timmis, 2002; Xu, Lei, & Si, 2010). Both approaches use operators and structures which attempt to find multiple solutions by mimicking the natural immune system's behavior.

Every EA needs to address the issue of exploration–exploitation of the search space (Tan, Chiam, Mamun, & Goh, 2009). Exploration is the process of visiting entirely new points of a search space whilst exploitation is the process of refining those points within the neighborhood of previously visited locations in order to improve their solution quality. Pure exploration degrades the precision of the evolutionary process but increases its capacity to find new potential solutions. On the other hand, pure exploitation allows refining existent solutions but adversely driving the process to local optimal solutions.

Multimodal optimization requires a sufficient amount of exploration of the population agents in hyperspace so that all the local and global attractors can be successfully and quickly detected (Roya, Islama, Das, Ghosha, & Vasilakos, 2013; Yahyaiea & Filizadeh, 2011). However, an efficient multimodal optimization algorithm should exhibit not only a good exploration tendency but also a good exploitative power, especially during the last stages of the search, because it must ensure accurately a distributed convergence to different optima in the landscape. Therefore, the ability of an EA to find multiple solutions depends on its capacity to reach a good balance between the exploitation of found-so-far elements and the exploration of the search space (Yazdani, Nezamabadi, & Kamyab, 2014). So far, the exploration–exploitation dilemma has been an unsolved issue within the framework of EA.

Recently, a novel nature-inspired algorithm called the cuckoo search (CS) algorithm (Yang & Deb, 2010a) has been proposed for solving complex optimization problems. The CS algorithm is based on the obligate brood-parasitic strategy of some cuckoo species. One of the most powerful features of CS is the use of Lévy flights to generate new candidate solutions. Under this approach, candidate solutions are modified by employing many small changes and occasionally large jumps. As a result, CS can substantially improve the relationship between exploration–exploitation, still enhancing its search capabilities (Walton, Hassan, Morgan, & Brown, 2013). Recent studies show that CS is potentially far more efficient than PSO and GA (Yang & Deb, 2010b). Such characteristics have motivated the use of CS to solve different sorts of engineering problems such as mesh generation (Walton, Hassan, Morgan, & Brown, 2011), embedded systems (Kumar & Chakarverty, 2011), steel frame design (Kaveh & Bakhshpoori, 2011), scheduling problems (Tein & Ramli, 2010), thermodynamics (Bhargava, Fateen, & Bonilla-Petriciolet, 2013), and distribution networks (Moravej & Akhlaghi, 2013).

8.2 CS STRATEGY

CS is one of the latest nature-inspired algorithms developed by Xin-She Yang and Suash Deb (2010a). CS is based on the brood parasitism of some cuckoo species. In addition, this algorithm is enhanced by the so-called Lévy flights (Pavlyukevich, 2007), rather than by simple isotropic random walks. Recent studies show that CS is potentially far more efficient than PSO and GA (Yang & Deb, 2010b).

Cuckoo birds lay their eggs in the nests of other host birds (usually other species) with amazing abilities, such as selecting nests containing recently laid eggs and removing existing eggs to increase the hatching probability of their own eggs. Some of the host birds are able to combat this parasitic behavior of cuckoos, and throw out the discovered alien eggs or build a new nest in a distinct location. This cuckoo breeding analogy is used to develop the CS algorithm. Natural systems are complex and therefore they cannot be modeled exactly by a computer algorithm in its basic form. Simplification of natural systems is necessary for successful implementation in computer algorithms. Yang and Deb (2010b) simplified the cuckoo reproduction process into three idealized rules:

1. An egg represents a solution and is stored in a nest. An artificial cuckoo can lay only one egg at a time.

2. The cuckoo bird searches for the most suitable nest to lay eggs in (solution) to maximize their eggs' survival rate. An elitist selection strategy is applied, so that only high-quality eggs (best solutions near to the optimal value) which are more similar

to the host bird's eggs have the opportunity to develop (next generation) and become mature cuckoos.

3. The number of host nests (population) is fixed. The host bird can discover the alien egg (worse solutions away from the optimal value) with a probability $p_a \in [0,1]$, and these eggs are thrown away or the nest is abandoned, and a completely new nest is built in a new location. Otherwise, the egg matures and lives to the next generation. New eggs (solutions) laid by a cuckoo choose the nest by Lévy flights around the current best solutions.

From the implementation point of view, in the CS operation, a population $\mathbf{E}^k \{\mathbf{e}_1^k, \mathbf{e}_2^k, \ldots, \mathbf{e}_N^k\}$ of N eggs (individuals) is evolved from the initial point ($k=0$) to a total *gen* number iterations $(k = 2 \cdot gen)$. Each egg $\mathbf{e}_i^k$ $(i \in [1, \ldots, N])$ represents an n-dimensional vector $\{\mathbf{e}_1^k, \mathbf{e}_2^k, \ldots, \mathbf{e}_N^k\}$, where each dimension corresponds to a decision variable of the optimization problem to be solved. The quality of each egg $\mathbf{e}_i^k$ (candidate solution) is evaluated by using an objective function $f(\mathbf{e}_i^k)$ whose final result represents the fitness value of $\mathbf{e}_i^k$. Three different operators define the evolution process of CS: (A) Lévy flight, (B) replacement of some nests by constructing new solutions, and (C) elitist selection strategy.

8.2.1 Lévy Flight (A)

One of the most powerful features of CS is the use of Lévy flights to generate new candidate solutions (eggs). Under this approach, a new candidate solution $\mathbf{e}_i^{k+1}$ $(i \in [1, \ldots, N])$ is produced by perturbing the current $\mathbf{e}_i^k$ with a change of position $\mathbf{c}_i$. In order to obtain $\mathbf{c}_i$, a random step $\mathbf{s}_i$ is generated by a symmetric Lévy distribution. For producing $\mathbf{s}_i$, the Mantegna's algorithm (Mantegna, 1994) is employed as follows:

$$\mathbf{s}_i = \frac{\mathbf{u}}{|\mathbf{v}|^{1/\beta}} \tag{8.1}$$

where $\mathbf{u}(\{u_1, \ldots, u_2\})$ and $\mathbf{v}(\{v_1, \ldots, v_2\})$ are n-dimensional vectors and $\beta = 3/2$. Each element of $\mathbf{u}$ and $\mathbf{v}$ is calculated by considering the following normal distributions:

$$u \sim N(0, \sigma_u^2) \qquad\qquad v \sim N(0, \sigma_v^2)$$

$$\sigma_u = \left(\frac{\Gamma(1+\beta) \cdot \sin\left(\pi \cdot \frac{\beta}{2}\right)}{\Gamma\left(\frac{1+\beta}{2}\right) \cdot \beta \cdot 2^{(\beta-1)/2}} \right)^{1/\beta} \qquad \sigma_v = 1 \tag{8.2}$$

where $\Gamma(\cdot)$ represents the Gamma distribution. Once $\mathbf{s}_i$ has been calculated, the required change of position $\mathbf{c}_i$ is computed as follows:

$$\mathbf{c}_i = 0.01 \cdot \mathbf{s}_i \oplus \left(\mathbf{e}_i^k - \mathbf{e}^{best}\right) \tag{8.3}$$

where the product $\oplus$ denotes entry-wise multiplications, whereas $\mathbf{e}^{best}$ is the best solution (egg) seen so far in terms of its fitness value. Finally, the new candidate solution $\mathbf{e}_i^{k+1}$ is calculated by using

$$\mathbf{e}_i^{k+1} = \mathbf{e}_i^k + \mathbf{c}_i \qquad (8.4)$$

8.2.2 Replace Some Nests by Constructing New Solutions (B)

Under this operation, a set of individuals (eggs) are probabilistically selected and replaced with a new value. Each individual $\mathbf{e}_i^k$ $\left(i \in [1,...,N]\right)$ can be selected with a probability $p_a \in [0,1]$. In order to implement this operation, a uniform random number r_1 is generated within the range [0,1]. If r_1 is less than p_a, the individual $\mathbf{e}_i^k$ is selected and modified according to Eq. 5. Otherwise, $\mathbf{e}_i^k$ remains without change. This operation can be resumed using the following model:

$$\mathbf{e}_i^{k+1} = \begin{cases} \mathbf{e}_i^k + rand \cdot \left(\mathbf{e}_{d_1}^k - \mathbf{e}_{d_2}^k\right) & \text{with probability } p_a \\ \mathbf{e}_i^k & \text{with probability } \left(1 - p_a\right) \end{cases} \qquad (8.5)$$

where rand is a random number normally distributed, while d_1 and d_2 are random integers from 1 to N.

8.2.3 Elitist Selection Strategy (C)

After producing $\mathbf{e}_i^{k+1}$ either by the operator A or operator B, it must be compared with its past value $\mathbf{e}_i^k$. If the fitness value of $\mathbf{e}_i^{k+1}$ is better than $\mathbf{e}_i^k$, then $\mathbf{e}_i^{k+1}$ is accepted as the final solution. Otherwise, $\mathbf{e}_i^k$ is retained. This procedure can be resumed using the following statement:

$$\mathbf{e}_i^{k+1} = \begin{cases} \mathbf{e}_i^{k+1} & \text{if } f\left(\mathbf{e}_i^{k+1}\right) < f\left(\mathbf{e}_i^k\right) \\ \mathbf{e}_i^k & \text{otherwise} \end{cases} \qquad (8.6)$$

This elitist selection strategy denotes that only high-quality eggs (best solutions near to the optimal value) which are more similar to the host bird's eggs have the opportunity to develop (next generation) and become mature cuckoos.

8.2.4 Complete CS Algorithm

CS is a relatively simple algorithm with only three adjustable parameters: p_a, the population size N, and the number of generations gen. According to Yang and Deb (2010b), the convergence rate of the algorithm is not strongly affected by the value of p_a, and it is suggested to use $p_a = 0.25$. The operation of CS is divided into two parts: initialization and the evolution process. In the initialization $(k=0)$, the first population $\mathbf{E}^0 \left\{\mathbf{e}_1^0, \mathbf{e}_2^0,..., \mathbf{e}_N^0\right\}$ is produced. The values $\left\{e_{i,1}^0, e_{i,2}^0,..., e_{i,n}^0\right\}$ of each individual $\mathbf{e}_i^k$ are randomly and uniformly distributed between the pre-specified lower initial parameter bound b_j^{low} and the upper initial parameter bound b_j^{high}.

$$e_{i,j}^0 = b_j^{low} + rand \cdot \left(b_j^{high} - b_j^{low} \right) \quad i=1,2\ldots,N; j=1,2,\ldots,n \tag{8.7}$$

In the evolution process, the operators A (Lévy flight), B (replace some nests by constructing new solutions), and C (elitist selection strategy) are iteratively applied until the number of iterations $k = 2 \cdot gen$ has been reached. The complete CS procedure is illustrated in Algorithm 8.1.

Algorithm 8.1 CS Algorithm

1. **Input:** p_a, N and *gen*
2. Initialize $\mathbf{E}^0 (k=0)$
3. **until** $(k = 2 \cdot gen)$
5. $\mathbf{E}^{k+1} \leftarrow$ Operator A ($\mathbf{E}^k$) Lévy Flight (8.2.1)
6. $\mathbf{E}^{k+1} \leftarrow$ Operator C ($\mathbf{E}^k$, $\mathbf{E}^{k+1}$) Elitist Selection Strategy (8.2.3)
7. $\mathbf{E}^{k+2} \leftarrow$ Operator B ($\mathbf{E}^{k+1}$) Replace Some Nests by Constructing New Solutions (8.2.2)
8. $\mathbf{E}^{k+1} \leftarrow$ Operator C ($\mathbf{E}^{k+1}$, $\mathbf{E}^{k+2}$) Elitist Selection Strategy (8.2.3)
9. **end until**

From Algorithm 8.1, it is important to remark that the Elitist selection strategy (C) is used two times, just after the operator A or operator B is executed.

8.3 CS COMPUTATIONAL PROCEDURE

In this section, the complete process of the CS algorithm is integrated and implemented. In order to illustrate its construction, it is considered to minimize the sphere function:

$$\text{Minimize} \quad f(\mathbf{x}) = \sum_{i=1}^{n} x_i^2 \tag{8.8}$$

$$\text{Subject to} \quad -5 \leq x \leq 5$$

Program 8.1 shows the complete implementation of the CS scheme. The program also contains several functions considered in order to make its analysis easy. The optimization process can be divided into five functions which correspond to each different part of the optimization process: (1) to obtain the best current value, (2) to move existent solutions by using Lévy flight perturbations, (3) to replace some nests by constructing new solutions, (4) to evaluate each solution in terms of the objective function, and (5) to check if the solution is within the defined search space.

Program 8.1 Implementation of the CS in MATLAB®

```
%%%%%%%%%%%%%%%%%%%%%%%%%%%%%%%%%%%%%%%%%%%%%%%%%%%%%%%%%%%%%%%%%%%%%
% CS implementation
% Erik Cuevas, Alma Rodríguez
%%%%%%%%%%%%%%%%%%%%%%%%%%%%%%%%%%%%%%%%%%%%%%%%%%%%%%%%%%%%%%%%%%%%%
function [bestnest,fmin]=cuckoo_search(n)
    if nargin<1
        % Number of different solutions
        n=25;
    end
    % Discovery rate of solutions
    pa=0.25;
    % Tolerance
    Tol=1.0e-5;
    % Bounds of the search space
    % Lower bounds
    nd=15;
    Lb=-5*ones(1,nd);
    Ub=5*ones(1,nd);
    % Initial positions
    for i=1:n,
        nest(i,:)=Lb+(Ub-Lb).*rand(size(Lb));
    end
    % Get the current best
    fitness=10^10*ones(n,1);
    % Fuction I
    [fmin,bestnest,nest,fitness]=get_best_nest(nest,nest,fitness);
    N_iter=0;
    % Starting the evolution process
    while (fmin>Tol)
        % Generate new solutions
        new_nest=get_cuckoos(nest,bestnest,Lb,Ub); % Function II
        [fnew,best,nest,fitness]=get_best_nest(nest,new_nest,
        fitness);
        % Update the counter
        N_iter=N_iter+n;
        % Discovery and randomization
        new_nest=empty_nests(nest,Lb,Ub,pa); % Function III
        % Evaluate the solutions
        [fnew,best,nest,fitness]=get_best_nest(nest,new_nest,
        fitness);
        % Update the counter again
        N_iter=N_iter+n;
        % Select the best objective solution
        if fnew<fmin
            fmin=fnew;
            bestnest=best;
```

```
            end
    end % End of iterations
    % Display the results
    disp(strcat('Total number of iterations=',num2str(N_iter)));
    fmin
    bestnest
end
```

Program 8.2 Function to Find the Current Best Solution (Function I)

```
function [fmin,best,nest,fitness]=get_best_nest(nest,newnest,
fitness)
    % Evaluation of all candidate solutions
    for j=1:size(nest,1)
        fnew=fobj(newnest(j,:)); % Function IV
        if fnew<=fitness(j),
            fitness(j)=fnew;
            nest(j,:)=newnest(j,:);
        end
    end
    % Select the current best solution
    [fmin,K]=min(fitness);
    best=nest(K,:);
end
```

Program 8.3 Function to Implement Lévy Flight Perturbations (Function II)

```
function nest=get_cuckoos(nest,best,Lb,Ub)
    % Levy flights movements
    n=size(nest,1);
    % Levy exponent and coefficient
    beta=3/2;
    sigma=(gamma(1+beta)*sin(pi*beta/2)/(gamma((1+beta)/2)*beta*
    2^((beta-1)/2)))^(1/beta);
    for j=1:n
        s=nest(j,:);
        % This is a simple way of implementing Levy flights
        u=randn(size(s))*sigma;
        v=randn(size(s));
        step=u./abs(v).^(1/beta);
        stepsize=0.01*step.*(s-best);
        s=s+stepsize.*randn(size(s));
        % Apply simple bounds/limits
        nest(j,:)=simplebounds(s,Lb,Ub);   % Function V
    end
end
```

Program 8.4 Function to Implement the Replacement of Some Solutions by Producing New Elemnts (Function III)

```
function new_nest=empty_nests(nest,Lb,Ub,pa)
    % A fraction of worse nests are discovered with a
    probability pa
    n=size(nest,1);
    % Find or not -- a flag
    K=rand(size(nest))>pa;
    % New solution by random walks
    stepsize=rand*(nest(randperm(n),:)-nest(randperm(n),:));
    new_nest=nest+stepsize.*K;
    for j=1:size(new_nest,1)
        s=new_nest(j,:);
        new_nest(j,:)=simplebounds(s,Lb,Ub);
    end
end
```

Program 8.5 Function to Implement the Objective Function for Minimizing (Function IV)

```
function z=fobj(u)
    % n-dimensional sphere function
    z=sum((u-1).^2);
end
```

Program 8.6 Function to Implement the Objective Function for Minimizing (Function V)

```
function s=simplebounds(s,Lb,Ub)
    % Apply the lower bound
    ns_tmp=s;
    I=ns_tmp<Lb;
    ns_tmp(I)=Lb(I);
    % Apply the upper bounds
    J=ns_tmp>Ub;
    ns_tmp(J)=Ub(J);
    % Update this new move
    s=ns_tmp;
end
```

8.4 THE MULTIMODAL CUCKOO SEARCH (MCS)

In CS, individuals emulate eggs which interact in a biological system by using evolutionary operations based on the breeding behavior of some cuckoo species. One of the most powerful features of CS is the use of Lévy flights to generate new candidate solutions. Under this approach, candidate solutions are modified by employing many small changes and occasionally large jumps. As a result, CS can substantially improve the relationship between exploration–exploitation, still enhancing its search capabilities. Despite such characteristics, the CS method still fails in providing multiple solutions in a single execution. In the proposed multimodal CS (MCS) approach, the original CS is adapted to include multimodal capacities. In particular, this adaptation contemplates: (1) the incorporation of a memory mechanism to efficiently register potential local optima according to their fitness value and the distance to other potential solutions, (2) the modification of the original CS individual selection strategy to accelerate the detection process of new local minima, and (3) the inclusion of a depuration procedure to cyclically eliminate duplicated memory elements.

To implement these modifications, the proposed MCS divides the evolution process into three asymmetric states. The first state $(s=1)$ includes from 0% to 50% of the evolution process. The second state $(s=2)$ involves 50%–75%. Finally, the third state $(s=3)$ lasts from 75% to 100%. The idea of this division is that the algorithm can react in a different manner depending on the current state. Therefore, at the beginning of the evolutionary process, exploration can be privileged, while at the end of the optimization process, exploitation can be favored. Figure 8.1 illustrates the division of the evolution process according to MCS.

The next sections examine the operators suggested by MCS as adaptations of CS to provide multimodal capacities. Such operators are (D) the memory mechanism, (E) new selection strategy, and (F) depuration procedure.

8.4.1 Memory Mechanism (D)

In the MCS evolution process, a population $\mathbf{E}^k\left\{\mathbf{e}_1^k,\mathbf{e}_2^k,\ldots,\mathbf{e}_N^k\right\}$ of N eggs (individuals) is evolved from the initial point $(k=0)$ to a total *gen* number iterations $(k=2\cdot gen)$. Each egg $\mathbf{e}_i^k\ (i\in[1,\ldots,N])$ represents an n-dimensional vector $\left\{e_{i,1}^k,e_{i,2}^k,\ldots,e_{i,n}^k\right\}$, where each dimension corresponds to a decision variable of the optimization problem to be solved. The quality of each egg $\mathbf{e}_i^k$ (candidate solution) is evaluated by using an objective function $f(\mathbf{e}_i^k)$ whose final result represents the fitness value of $\mathbf{e}_i^k$. During the evolution process, MCS also maintains the best $\mathbf{e}_i^{best,k}$ and the worst $\mathbf{e}_i^{worst,k}$ eggs seen so far, such that

$$\mathbf{e}^{best,k} = \underset{i\in\{1,\ldots,N\},\,a\in\{1,\ldots,k\}}{\arg\min}\ f\left(\mathbf{e}_i^a\right) \quad \mathbf{e}^{worst,k} = \underset{i\in\{1,\ldots,N\},\,a\in\{1,\ldots,k\}}{\arg\max}\ f\left(\mathbf{e}_i^a\right) \tag{8.9}$$

Global and local optima possess two important characteristics: (1) they have a significant-good fitness value, and (2) they represent the best fitness value inside a determined neighborhood. Therefore, the memory mechanism allows efficiently registering potential global and local optima during the evolution process, involving a memory array $\mathbf{M}$ and a storage procedure. $\mathbf{M}$ stores the potential global and local optima $\{\mathbf{m}_1,\ldots,\mathbf{m}_T\}$ during the evolution process, T being the number of elements so far that are contained in the memory $\mathbf{M}$.

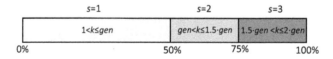

FIGURE 8.1   Division of the evolution process according to MCS.

On the other hand, the storage procedure indicates the rules that the eggs $\{\mathbf{e}_1^k, \mathbf{e}_2^k, \ldots, \mathbf{e}_N^k\}$ must fulfill in order to be captured as memory elements. The memory mechanism operates in two phases: initialization and capture.

8.4.1.1 Initialization Phase

This phase is applied only once within the optimization process. Such an operation is achieved in the null iteration $(k=0)$ of the evolution process. In the Initialization phase, the best egg $\mathbf{e}_B$ of $\mathbf{E}^0$, in terms of its fitness value, is stored in the memory $\mathbf{M}$ ($\mathbf{m}_1 = \mathbf{e}_B$), where $\mathbf{e}_B = \arg\min_{i \in \{1, \ldots, N\}} f(\mathbf{e}_i^0)$, for a minimization problem.

8.4.1.2 Capture Phase

This phase is applied from the first $(k=1)$ iteration to the last iteration $(k=1,2,\ldots,2 \cdot gen)$, at the end of each operator (A and B). At this stage, eggs $\{\mathbf{e}_1^k, \mathbf{e}_2^k, \ldots, \mathbf{e}_N^k\}$ corresponding to potential global and local optima are efficiently registered as memory elements $\{\mathbf{m}_1, \ldots, \mathbf{m}_T\}$ according to their fitness value and the distance to other potential solutions. In the operation, each egg $\mathbf{e}_i^k$ of $\mathbf{E}^k$ is tested in order to evaluate if it must be captured as a memory element. The test considers two rules: (I) significant fitness value rule and (II) non-significant fitness value rule.

8.4.1.3 Significant Fitness Value Rule

Under this rule, the solution quality of $\mathbf{e}_i^k$ is evaluated according to the worst element $\mathbf{m}^{worst}$ that is contained in the memory $\mathbf{M}$, where $\mathbf{m}^{worst} = \arg\max_{i \in \{1, \ldots, T\}} (f(\mathbf{m}_i))$, in case of a minimization problem. If the fitness value of $\mathbf{e}_i^k$ is better than $\mathbf{m}^{worst}$ $(f(\mathbf{e}_i^k) < f(\mathbf{m}^{worst}))$, $\mathbf{e}_i^k$ is considered a potential global and local optimum. The next step is to decide whether $\mathbf{e}_i^k$ represents a new optimum or it is very similar to an existent memory element $\{\mathbf{m}_1, \ldots, \mathbf{m}_T\}$ (if it is already contained in the memory $\mathbf{M}$). Such a decision is specified by an acceptance probability function $\Pr(\delta_{i,u}, s)$ that depends, on one side, over the distance $\delta_{i,u}$ from $\mathbf{e}_i^k$ to the nearest memory element $\mathbf{m}_u$, and on the other side, over the current state s of the evolution process (1, 2, and 3). Under $\Pr(\delta_{i,u}, s)$, the probability that $\mathbf{e}_i^k$ would be part of $\mathbf{M}$ increases as the distance $\delta_{i,u}$ enlarges. Similarly, the probability that $\mathbf{e}_i^k$ would be similar to an existent memory element $\{\mathbf{m}_1, \ldots, \mathbf{m}_T\}$ increases as $\delta_{i,u}$ decreases. On the other hand, the indicator s that relates a numeric value with the state of the evolution process is gradually modified during the algorithm to reduce the likelihood of accepting inferior solutions. The idea is that at the beginning of the evolutionary process (exploration) large distance differences can be considered while only small distance differences are tolerated at the end of the optimization process.

In order to implement this procedure, the normalized distance $\delta_{i,q}$ $(q \in [1, \ldots, T])$ is calculated from $\mathbf{e}_i^k$ to all the elements of the memory $\{\mathbf{m}_1, \ldots, \mathbf{m}_T\}$. $\delta_{i,q}$ is computed as follows:

$$\delta_{i,q} = \sqrt{\left(\frac{e_{i,1}^k - m_{q,1}}{b_1^{high} - b_1^{low}}\right)^2 + \left(\frac{e_{i,2}^k - m_{q,2}}{b_2^{high} - b_2^{low}}\right)^2 + \cdots + \left(\frac{e_{i,n}^k - m_{q,n}}{b_n^{high} - b_n^{low}}\right)^2} \tag{8.10}$$

where $\{m_{q,1}, m_{q,2}, \ldots, m_{q,n}\}$ represent the n components of the memory element $\mathbf{m}_q$, whereas b_j^{high} and b_j^{low} indicate the lower j parameter bound and the upper j parameter bound $(j \in [1, \ldots, n])$, respectively. One important property of the normalized distance $\delta_{i,q}$ is that its values fall into the interval [0,1].

By using the normalized distances $\delta_{i,q}$, the nearest memory element $\mathbf{m}_u$ to $\mathbf{e}_i^k$ is defined, with $\mathbf{m}_u = \underset{j \in \{1, \ldots, T\}}{\arg\min} (\delta_{i,j})$. Then, the acceptance probability function $\Pr(\delta_{i,u}, s)$ is calculated by using the following expression:

$$\Pr(\delta_{i,u}, s) = (\delta_{i,u})^s \tag{8.11}$$

In order to decide whether $\mathbf{e}_i^k$ represents a new optimum or it is very similar to an existent memory element, a uniform random number r_1 is generated within the range [0,1]. If r_1 is less than $\Pr(\delta_{i,u}, s)$, the egg $\mathbf{e}_i^k$ is included in the memory $\mathbf{M}$ as a new optimum. Otherwise, it is considered that $\mathbf{e}_i^k$ is similar to $\mathbf{m}_u$. Under such circumstances, the memory $\mathbf{M}$ is updated by the competition between $\mathbf{e}_i^k$ and $\mathbf{m}_u$, according to their corresponding fitness values. Therefore, $\mathbf{e}_i^k$ would replace $\mathbf{m}_u$ in case $f(\mathbf{e}_i^k)$ is better than $f(\mathbf{m}_u)$. On other hand, if $f(\mathbf{m}_u)$ is better than $f(\mathbf{e}_i^k)$, $\mathbf{m}_u$ remains with no change. The complete procedure of the significant fitness value rule can be resumed using the following statement:

$$\mathbf{M} = \begin{cases} \mathbf{m}_{T+1} = \mathbf{e}_i^k & \text{with probability } \Pr(\delta_{i,u}, s) \\ \mathbf{m}_u = \mathbf{e}_i^k & \text{with probability } 1 - \Pr(\delta_{i,u}, s) \end{cases} \tag{8.12}$$

In order to demonstrate the significant fitness value rule process, Figure 8.2 illustrates a simple minimization problem that involves a two-dimensional function $f(\mathbf{x})(\mathbf{x} = \{x_1, x_2\})$. As an example, it is assumed a population $\mathbf{E}^k$ of two different particles $(\mathbf{e}_1^k, \mathbf{e}_2^k)$, a memory with two memory elements $(\mathbf{m}_1, \mathbf{m}_2)$, and the execution of the first state $(s = 1)$. According to Figure 8.2, both particles $\mathbf{e}_1^k$ and $\mathbf{e}_2^k$ maintain a better fitness value than $\mathbf{m}_1$ which

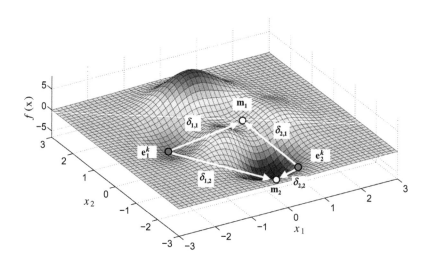

FIGURE 8.2 Graphical illustration of the significant fitness value rule process.

possesses the worst fitness value of the memory elements. Under such conditions, the significant fitness value rule must be applied to both particles. In the case of $\mathbf{e}_1^k$, the first step is to calculate the correspondent distances $\delta_{1,1}$ and $\delta_{1,2}$. $\mathbf{m}_1$ represents the nearest memory element to $\mathbf{e}_1^k$. Then, the acceptance probability function $\mathrm{Pr}(\delta_{1,1},1)$ is calculated by using Eq. 10. Since the value of $\mathrm{Pr}(\delta_{1,1},1)$ has a high value, there exists a great probability that $\mathbf{e}_1^k$ becomes the next memory element $(\mathbf{m}_3 = \mathbf{e}_1)$. On the other hand, for $\mathbf{e}_2^k$, $\mathbf{m}_2$ represents the nearest memory element. As $\mathrm{Pr}(\delta_{1,2},1)$ is very low, there exists a great probability that $\mathbf{e}_2^k$ competes with $\mathbf{m}_2$ for a place within $\mathbf{M}$. In such a case, $\mathbf{m}_2$ remains with no change considering that $f(\mathbf{m}_2) < f(\mathbf{e}_2^k)$.

8.4.1.4 Non-Significant Fitness Value Rule

Different from the significant fitness value rule, the non-significant fitness value rule allows capturing local optima with low fitness values. It operates if the fitness value of $\mathbf{e}_i^k$ is worst than $\mathbf{m}^{worst}$ $\left(f(\mathbf{e}_i^k) \geq f(\mathbf{m}^{worst}) \right)$. Under such conditions, it is necessary, as a first step, to test which particles could represent local optima and which must be ignored as a consequence of their very low fitness value. Then, if the particle represents a possible local optimum, its inclusion inside the memory $\mathbf{M}$ is explored.

The decision on whether represents a new local optimum or not is specified by a probability function P which is based on the relationship between $f(\mathbf{e}_i^k)$ and the so-far valid fitness value interval $\left(f(\mathbf{e}^{worst,k}) - f(\mathbf{e}^{best,k}) \right)$. Therefore, the probability function P is defined as follows:

$$p\left(\mathbf{e}_i^k, \mathbf{e}^{best,k}, \mathbf{e}^{worst,k}\right) = 1 - \frac{f\left(\mathbf{e}_i^k\right) - f\left(\mathbf{e}^{best,k}\right)}{f\left(\mathbf{e}^{worst,k}\right) - f\left(\mathbf{e}^{best,k}\right)}$$

$$(8.13)$$

$$P(p) = \begin{cases} p & 0.5 \leq p \leq 1 \\ 0 & 0 \leq p < 0.5 \end{cases}$$

where $\mathbf{e}^{best,k}$ and $\mathbf{e}^{worst,k}$ represent the best and worst egg seen so far, respectively. In order to decide whether $\mathbf{e}_i^k$ represents a new local optimum or it must be ignored, a uniform random number r_2 is generated within the range [0,1]. If r_2 is less than P, the egg $\mathbf{e}_i^k$ is considered as a new local optimum. Otherwise, it must be ignored. Under P, the so-far valid fitness value interval $\left(f(\mathbf{e}^{worst,k}) - f(\mathbf{e}^{best,k}) \right)$ is divided into two sections: I and II (see Figure 8.3).

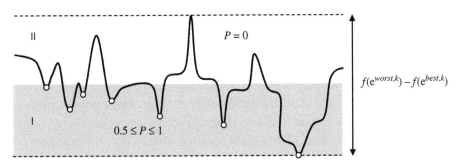

FIGURE 8.3   Effect of the probability function P in a simple example.

Considering this division, the function P assigns a valid probability (greater than zero) only to those eggs that fall into the zone of the best individuals (part I) in terms of their fitness value. Such a probability value increases as the fitness value improves. The complete procedure can be reviewed in Algorithm 8.2.

Algorithm 8.2. Non-Significant Fitness Value Rule Procedure

1. **Input:** $\mathbf{e}_i^k$, $\mathbf{e}^{best,k}$, $\mathbf{e}^{worst,k}$

2. Calculate $p\left(\mathbf{e}_i^k, \mathbf{e}^{best,k}, \mathbf{e}^{worst,k}\right) = 1 - \dfrac{f\left(\mathbf{e}_i^k\right) - f\left(\mathbf{e}^{best,k}\right)}{f\left(\mathbf{e}^{worst,k}\right) - f\left(\mathbf{e}^{best,k}\right)}$

3. Calculate $P(p) = \begin{cases} p & 0.5 \le p \le 1 \\ 0 & 0 \le p < 0.5 \end{cases}$

5. **if** $(\text{rand}(0,1) \le P)$ **then**
6. $\mathbf{e}_i^k$ is considered a local optimum With probability P
7. **Else**
8. $\mathbf{e}_i^k$ is ignored With probability $1 - P$
9. **end if**

If the particle represents a possible local optimum, its inclusion inside the memory $\mathbf{M}$ is explored. In order to consider if $\mathbf{e}_i^k$ could represent a new memory element, another procedure that is similar to the significant fitness value rule process is applied. Therefore, the normalized distance $\delta_{i,q}$ $(q \in [1,\ldots,T])$ from $\mathbf{e}_i^k$ to all the elements of the memory $\mathbf{M}$ $\{\mathbf{m}_1, \mathbf{m}_2, \ldots, \mathbf{m}_T\}$ is calculated, according to Eq. 9. Afterward, the nearest distance $\delta_{i,u}$ to $\mathbf{e}_i^k$ is determined. Then, by using $\text{Pr}(\delta_{i,u}, s)$ (Eq. 10), the following rule can be thus applied:

$$\mathbf{M} = \begin{cases} \mathbf{m}_{T+1} = \mathbf{e}_i^k & \text{with probability } \text{Pr}(\delta_{i,u}, s) \\ \text{no change} & \text{with probability } 1 - \text{Pr}(\delta_{i,u}, s) \end{cases} \tag{8.14}$$

Under this rule, a uniform random number r_3 is generated within the range $[0,1]$. If r_3 is less than $\text{Pr}(\delta_{i,u}, s)$, the egg $\mathbf{e}_i^k$ is included in the memory $\mathbf{M}$ as a new optimum. Otherwise, the memory does not change.

8.4.2 New Selection Strategy (E)

The original CS selection strategy is mainly conducted by an elitist decision where the best individuals in the current population prevail. Such an operation, defined in this paper as operator C (Section 8.2.3), is executed two times, just after the operators A and B in the original CS method. This effect allows incorporating interesting convergence properties to CS when the objective considers only one optimum. However, in the case of multiple-optimum detection, such a strategy is not appropriate. Therefore, in order to accelerate the detection process of potential local minima in our method, the selection strategy is modified to be influenced by the individuals contained in the memory $\mathbf{M}$.

Under the new selection procedure (operator E), the final population $\mathbf{E}^{k+1}$ is built by considering the first N element from the memory $\mathbf{M}$ instead of using the best individuals between the current $\mathbf{E}^{k+1}$ and $\mathbf{E}^{k}$. In case the number of elements in $\mathbf{M}$ is less than N, the rest of the individuals is completed by considering the best elements from the current $\mathbf{E}^{k+1}$.

8.4.3 Depuration Procedure (F)

During the evolution process, the memory $\mathbf{M}$ stores several individuals (eggs). Since such individuals could represent the same local optimum, a depuration procedure is incorporated at the end of each state s (1–3) to eliminate similar memory elements. The inclusion of this procedure allows (1) reducing the computational overhead during each state and (2) improving the search strategy by considering only significant memory elements.

Memory elements tend to concentrate around optimal points (good fitness values), whereas element concentrations are enclosed by areas holding bad fitness values. The main idea in the depuration procedure is to find the distances among concentrations. Such distances, considered as depuration ratios, are later employed to delete all elements inside them, except for the best element in terms of their fitness values.

The method used by the depuration procedure in order to determine the distance between two concentrations is based on the element comparison between the concentration corresponding to the best element and the concentration of the nearest optimum in the memory. In the process, the best element $\mathbf{m}^{best}$ in the memory is compared with a memory element $\mathbf{m}_b$ which belongs to one of both concentrations $\left(\text{Where } \mathbf{m}^{best} = \underset{i \in \{1,\ldots,T\}}{\arg\min} f\left(\mathbf{m}_i\right) \right)$.

If the fitness value of the medium point $f\left(\left(\mathbf{m}^{best} + \mathbf{m}_b\right)/2\right)$ between both is not worse than both $\left(f\left(\mathbf{m}^{best}\right), f\left(\mathbf{m}_b\right)\right)$, the element $\mathbf{m}_b$ is part of the same concentration of $\mathbf{m}^{best}$. However, if $f\left(\left(\mathbf{m}^{best} + \mathbf{m}_b\right)/2\right)$ is worse than both, the element $\mathbf{m}_b$ is considered as part of the nearest concentration. Therefore, if $\mathbf{m}_b$ and $\mathbf{m}^{best}$ belong to different concentrations, the Euclidian distance between $\mathbf{m}_b$ and $\mathbf{m}^{best}$ can be considered as a depuration ratio. In order to avoid the unintentional deletion of elements in the nearest concentration, the depuration ratio D_R is lightly shortened. Thus, the depuration ratio r is defined as follows:

$$D_R = 0.85 \cdot \left\| \mathbf{m}^{best} - \mathbf{m}_b \right\| \tag{8.15}$$

The proposed depuration procedure only considers the depuration ratio r between the concentration of the best element and the nearest concentration. In order to determine all ratios, preprocessing and post-processing methods must be incorporated and iteratively executed.

The preprocessing method must (1) obtain the best element $\mathbf{m}^{best}$ from the memory in terms of its fitness value, (2) calculate the Euclidian distances from the best element to the rest of the elements in the memory, and (3) sort the distances according to their magnitude. This set of tasks allows to identify both concentrations: the one belonging to the best element and that belonging to the nearest optimum, so they must be executed before the depuration ratio D_R calculation. Such concentrations are represented by the elements with the shortest distances to $\mathbf{m}^{best}$. Once D_R has been calculated, it is necessary to remove all the elements belonging to the concentration of the best element. This task is executed as a post-processing method in order to configure the memory for the next step. Therefore, the complete depuration procedure can be represented as an iterative process that at each step determines the distance of the concentration of the best element with regard to the concentration of the nearest optimum.

An especial case can be considered when only one concentration is contained within the memory. This case can happen because the optimization problem has only one optimum or because all the other concentrations have been already detected. Under such circumstances, the condition, where $f\left(\left(\mathbf{m}^{best}+\mathbf{m}_b\right)/2\right)$ is worse than $f\left(\mathbf{m}^{best}\right)$ and $f(\mathbf{m}_b)$, would be never fulfilled.

In order to find the distances among concentrations, the depuration procedure conducts the following procedure:

1. Define two new temporal vectors $\mathbf{Z}$ and $\mathbf{Y}$. The vector $\mathbf{Z}$ will hold the results of the iterative operations, whereas $\mathbf{Y}$ will contain the final memory configuration. The vector $\mathbf{Z}$ is initialized with the elements of $\mathbf{M}$ that have been sorted according to their fitness values so that the first element represents the best one. On the other hand, $\mathbf{Y}$ is initialized as empty.

2. Store the best element $\mathbf{z}_1$ of the current $\mathbf{Z}$ in $\mathbf{Y}$.

3. Calculate the Euclidian distances $\Delta_{1,j}$ between $\mathbf{z}_1$ and the rest of the elements from $\mathbf{Z}\left(j\in\{2,\dots,|\mathbf{Z}|\}\right)$, where $|\mathbf{Z}|$ represents the number of elements in $\mathbf{Z}$.

4. Sort the distances $\Delta_{1,j}$ according to their magnitude. Therefore, a new index a is incorporated to each distance $\Delta_{1,j}^a$, where a indicate the place of $\Delta_{1,j}$ after the sorting operation. ($a=1$ represents the shortest distance).

5. Calculate the depuration ratio D_R:
   for $q=1$ to $|\mathbf{Z}|-1$
   Obtain the element $\mathbf{z}_j$ corresponding to the distance $\Delta_{1,j}^q$

   Compute $f\left(\dfrac{\mathbf{z}_1+\mathbf{z}_j}{2}\right)$

   if $f\left(\dfrac{\mathbf{z}_1+\mathbf{z}_j}{2}\right)>f(\mathbf{z}_1)$ and $f\left(\dfrac{\mathbf{z}_1+\mathbf{z}_j}{2}\right)>f(\mathbf{z}_j)$

   $$D_R=0.85\cdot\left\|\mathbf{m}^{best}-\mathbf{m}_b\right\|$$

   break
   end if
   if $q=|\mathbf{Z}|-1$

There is only one concentration
end if
end for

6. Remove all elements inside D_R from **Z**.

7. Sort the elements of **Z** according to their fitness values.

8. Stop, if there are more concentrations; otherwise, return to step 2.

At the end of the above procedure, the vector **Y** will contain the depurated memory which would be used in the next state or as a final result of the multimodal problem.

In order to illustrate the depuration procedure, Figure 8.4 shows a simple minimization problem that involves two different optimal points (concentrations). As an example, a memory **M** with six memory elements is assumed, whose positions are shown in Figure 8.4a. According to the depuration procedure, the first step is (1) to build the vector **Z** and (2) to calculate the corresponding distances $\Delta_{1,j}^a$ among the elements. Following such operation, the vector **Z** and the set of distances are configured as $\mathbf{Z} = \{\mathbf{m}_5, \mathbf{m}_1, \mathbf{m}_3, \mathbf{m}_4, \mathbf{m}_6, \mathbf{m}_2\}$ and $\{\Delta_{1,2}^1, \Delta_{1,3}^2, \Delta_{1,5}^3, \Delta_{1,4}^4, \Delta_{1,6}^5\}$, respectively. Figure 8.4b shows the configuration of **X**, whereas, for the sake of easiness, only two distances $\Delta_{1,2}^1$ and $\Delta_{1,5}^3$ have been represented. Then, the depuration ratio R is calculated. This process is an iterative computation that begins with the shortest distance $\Delta_{1,2}^1$. The distance $\Delta_{1,2}^1$ (see Figure 8.4c), corresponding to $\mathbf{z}_1$ and $\mathbf{z}_2$, produces the evaluation of their medium point $u\left((\mathbf{z}_1 + \mathbf{z}_2)/2\right)$. Since $f(u)$ is worse than

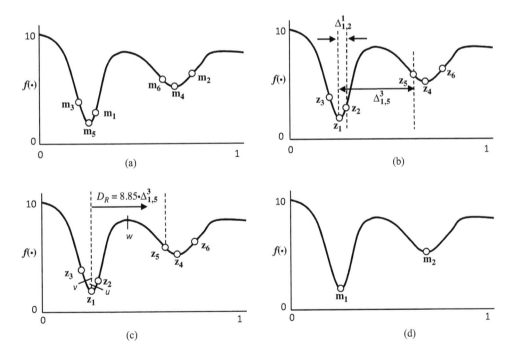

FIGURE 8.4 Depuration procedure: (a) initial memory configuration, (b) vector **Z** and distances $\Delta_{i,j}^a$, (c) the determination of the depuration ratio D_R, and (d) the final memory configuration.

$f(\mathbf{z}_1)$ but not worse than $f(\mathbf{z}_2)$, the element $\mathbf{z}_2$ is considered as part of the same concentration as $\mathbf{z}_1$. The same conclusion is obtained for $\Delta_{1,3}^2$ in case of $\mathbf{z}_3$, after considering the point v. For $\Delta_{1,5}^3$, the point w is produced. Since $f(w)$ is worse than $f(\mathbf{z}_1)$ and $f(\mathbf{z}_5)$, the element $\mathbf{z}_5$ is considered as part of the concentration corresponding to the next optimum. The iterative process ends here, after assuming that the same result is produced with $\Delta_{1,4}^4$ and $\Delta_{1,6}^5$, for $\mathbf{z}_4$ and $\mathbf{z}_6$, respectively. Therefore, the depuration ratio D_R is calculated as 85% of the distance $\Delta_{1,5}^3$. Once the elements inside of D_R have been removed from $\mathbf{Z}$, the same process is applied to the new $\mathbf{Z}$. As a result, the final configuration of the memory is shown in Figure 8.4d.

8.4.4 Complete MCS Algorithm

Once the new operators, namely, (D) the memory mechanism, (E) new selection strategy, and (F) depuration procedure, have been defined, the proposed MCS algorithm can be summarized by Algorithm 8.3. The new algorithm combines operators defined in the original CS with the new ones. Despite these new operators, the MCS maintains the same three adjustable parameters (p_a, N, and gen) than the original CS method.

Algorithm 8.3 MCS Algorithm

1. **Input:** p_a, N and gen
2. Initialize $\mathbf{E}^0$ ($k = 0$)
3. **until** ($k = 2 \cdot gen$)
5. $\mathbf{E}^{k+1} \leftarrow$ Operator A ($\mathbf{E}^k$) Lévy Flight (8.2.1)
6. $\mathbf{M} \leftarrow$ Operator D ($\mathbf{E}^{k+1}$) Memory Mechanism (8.3.1)
7. $\mathbf{E}^{k+1} \leftarrow$ Operator E ($\mathbf{M}$, $\mathbf{E}^{k+1}$) New Selection Strategy (8.3.2)
8. $\mathbf{E}^{k+2} \leftarrow$ Operator B ($\mathbf{E}^{k+1}$) Replace Some Nests by Constructing New Solutions (8.2.2)
9. $\mathbf{M} \leftarrow$ Operator D ($\mathbf{E}^{k+2}$) Memory Mechanism (8.3.1)
10. $\mathbf{E}^{k+2} \leftarrow$ Operator E ($\mathbf{M}$, $\mathbf{E}^{k+2}$) New Selection Strategy (8.3.2)
11. **if** (s has changed)
12. $\mathbf{M} \leftarrow$ Operator F ($\mathbf{M}$) Depuration Procedure (8.3.3)
13. **end if**
14. **end until**

8.5 ANALYSIS OF CS

This section presents the performance of the CS. For the sake of clarity, the analysis is divided into two sections: Sections 8.5.2 and 8.5.3 report the comparison between the MCS experimental results and the outcomes produced by other multimodal metaheuristic algorithms.

8.5.1 Experimental Methodology

This section examines the performance of the proposed MCS by using a test suite of 14 benchmark functions with different complexities. Table 8.1 presents the benchmark functions used in our experimental study. In this table, **NO** indicates the number of optimal

TABLE 8.1   Test Functions Used in the Analysis

$f(\mathbf{x})\left(\mathbf{x}=\{x_1,x_2\}\right)$	S	NO
Bird		
$f_1(\mathbf{x})=\sin(x_1)\cdot e^{\left(1-\cos(x_2)\right)^2}+\cos(x_2)\cdot e^{\left(1-\sin(x_1)\right)^2}+(x_1-x_2)^2$	$[-2\pi,2\pi]$	3
Cross in tray		
$f_2(\mathbf{x})=-0.0001\cdot\left(\left\|\left\|\sin(x_1)\cdot\sin(x_2)\cdot e^{\left\|100-\frac{\sqrt{x_1^2-x_2^2}}{\pi}\right\|}\right\|+1\right\|\right)^{0.1}$	$[-10,10]$	12
DeJongs5		
$f_3(\mathbf{x})=\left\{0.002+\sum_{i=-2}^{2}\sum_{j=-2}^{2}\left[5(i+1)+j+3+\left(x_1-16j\right)^6+\left(x_2-16i\right)^6\right]^{-1}\right\}^{-1}$	$[-40,40]$	25
Eggholder		
$f_4(\mathbf{x})=-(x_2+47)\sin\left(\sqrt{\left\|x_2+\frac{x_1}{2}+47\right\|}\right)-x_1\sin\left(\sqrt{\left\|x_1+\frac{x_2}{2}+47\right\|}\right)$	$[-512,512]$	7
Vincent		
$f_5(\mathbf{x})=-\sum_{i=1}^{n}\sin\left(10\cdot\log(x_i)\right)$	$[0.25,10]$	36
Roots		
$f_6(\mathbf{x})=-\left(1+\left\|(x_1+x_2 i)^6-1\right\|\right)^{-1}$	$[-2,2]$	6
Hilly		
$f_7(\mathbf{x})=10\left[e^{-\frac{\|x_1\|}{50}}\left(1-\cos\left(\frac{6}{100^{\frac{3}{4}}}\pi\|x_1\|^{\frac{3}{4}}\right)\right)+e^{-\frac{\|x_2\|}{250}}\left(1-\cos\left(\frac{6}{100^{\frac{3}{4}}}\pi\|x_2\|^{\frac{3}{4}}\right)\right)+2\left(e^{-\frac{(b-x_1)^2+(b-x_2)^2}{50}}\right)\right]$ with $b=\left(\frac{5}{6}\cdot100^{\frac{3}{4}}\right)^{\frac{4}{3}}$	$[-100,100]$	48
Rastrigin		
$f_8(\mathbf{x})=\sum_{i=1}^{n}x_i^2-10\cos(2\pi x_i)$	$[-5.12,5.12]$	25
Himmemlblau		
$f_9(\mathbf{x})=-\left(x_1^2+x_2-11\right)^2-(x_1+x_2^2-7)^2$	$[-6,6]$	5

(Continued)

TABLE 8.1 (*Continued*) Test Functions Used in the Analysis

Foxholes		
$f_{10}(\mathbf{x}) = -\sum_{i=1}^{30}\left(\sum_{j=1}^{n}\left[(x_j - a_{ij})^2 + c_j\right]\right)^{-1}$	$[0,10]$	8
Guichi_f4		
$f_{11}(\mathbf{x}) = -\left(x_1\sin(4\pi x_1) - x_2\sin(4\pi x_2 + \pi)\right)$	$[-2,2]$	12
Holder Table		
$f_{12}(\mathbf{x}) = -\sin(x_1)\cos(x_2)e^{\left\lvert 1 - \frac{\sqrt{x_1^2 + x_2^2}}{\pi}\right\rvert}$	$[-10,10]$	12
Rastriguin_49m		
$f_{13}(\mathbf{x}) = \sum_{i=1}^{n} x_i^2 - 18\cos(2\pi x_i)$	$[-1,1]$	13
Schwefel		
$f_{14}(\mathbf{x}) = 418.9829 \cdot n + \sum_{i=1}^{n} -x_i\sin\left(\sqrt{\lvert x_i\rvert}\right)$	$[-500,500]$	8

points in the function, and S the search space (a subset of R^2). The experimental suite contains some representative, complicated and multimodal functions with several local optima. Such functions are considered as complex entities to be optimized as they are particularly challenging to the applicability and efficiency of multimodal metaheuristic algorithms. A detailed description of each function is given in Table 8.1.

In the study, three performance indexes are compared: the effective peak number (*EPN*), the maximum peak ratio (*MPR*), the peak accuracy (*PA*), the distance accuracy (*DA*), and the number of function evaluations (*NFE*). The first four indexes assess the accuracy of the solution, whereas the latter measures the computational cost.

The *EPN* expresses the number of detected peaks. An optimum $\mathbf{o}_j$ is considered as detected if the distance between the identified solution $\mathbf{z}_j$ and the optimum $\mathbf{o}_j$ is less than 0.01 $(\mathbf{o}_j - \mathbf{z}_j < 0.01)$. The *MPR* is used to evaluate the quality and number of identified optima. It is defined as follows:

$$MPR = \frac{\sum_{i=1}^{t} f(\mathbf{z}_i)}{\sum_{j=1}^{q} f(\mathbf{o}_j)} \tag{8.16}$$

where t represents the number of identified solutions (identified optima) for the algorithm under testing and q the number of true optima contained in the function. The *PA* specifies the total error produced between the identified solutions and the true optima. Therefore, *PA* is calculated as follows:

$$PA = \sum_{j=1}^{q} \left| f(\mathbf{o}_j) - f(\mathbf{z}_j) \right| \tag{8.17}$$

PA may lead to erroneous results, mainly if the peaks are close to each other or hold an identical height. Under such circumstances, the *DA* is used to avoid such error. *DA* is computed as *PA*, but fitness values are replaced by the Euclidian distance. *DA* is thus defined by the following model:

$$DA = \sum_{j=1}^{q} \left\| \mathbf{o}_j - \mathbf{z}_j \right\| \tag{8.18}$$

The *NFE* indicates the total number of function computations that have been calculated by the algorithm under testing, through the overall optimization process.

The experiments compare the performance of MCS against the Crowding DE (CDE) (Thomsen, 2004), the Fitness Sharing DE (SDE) (Miller & Shaw, 1996; Thomsen, 2004), the CP (Petrowski, 1996), the Adptive Elitist-population Genetic Algorithm (AEGA) (Lianga & Kwong-Sak, 2011), the CSA (Castro & Zuben, 2002), and the AiNet (Castro & Timmis, 2002).

Since the approach solves real-valued multimodal functions and assures a fair comparison, we have used for the GA approaches a consistent real coding variable representation and uniform operators for crossover and mutation. The crossover probability $P_c = 0.8$ and the mutation probability $P_m = 0.1$ have been used. We have employed the standard tournament selection operator with a tournament size = 2 for implementing the Sequential Fitness Sharing, the CP, and the elitist population strategy (AEGA). On the other hand, the parameter values for the AiNet algorithm have been defined as suggested by Castro and Timmis (2002), with the mutation strength $\beta = 100$, the suppression threshold $\sigma_{s(aiNet)} = 0.2$, and the update rate $d = 40\%$. Algorithms based on DE use a scaling factor $F = 0.5$ and a crossover probability $P_c = 0.9$. The CDE employs a crowding factor $CF = 50$ and the SDE considers $\alpha = 1$ with a share radius $\sigma_{share} = 0.1$.

In the case of the MCS algorithm, the parameters are set to $p_a = 0.25$, the population size $N = 50$, and the number of generations $gen = 500$. Once they have been all experimentally determined, they are kept for all the test functions through all experiments.

To avoid relating the optimization results to the choice of a particular initial population and to conduct fair comparisons, we perform each test 50 times, starting from various randomly selected points in the search domain as it is commonly done in the literature.

All algorithms have been tested in MATLAB® over the same Dell Optiplex GX520 computer with a Pentium-4 2.66GHz processor, running Windows XP operating system over 1 Gb of memory. Sections below present experimental results for multimodal optimization problems that have been divided into two groups. The first one considers functions $f_1 - f_7$, while the second gathers functions $f_8 - f_{14}$.

8.5.2 Comparing MCS Performance for Functions $f_1 - f_7$

This section presents a performance comparison for different algorithms solving the multimodal problems $f_1 - f_7$ that are shown in Table 8.1. The aim is to determine whether MCS is more efficient and effective than other existing algorithms for finding all multiple optima of $f_1 - f_7$. All the algorithms employ a population size of 50 individuals using 500 successive generations.

Table 8.2 provides a summarized performance comparison among several algorithms in terms of the *EPN*, the *MPR*, the *PA*, the *DA*, and the *NFE*. The results are averaged by considering 50 different executions.

Considering the *EPN* index, in all functions $f_1 - f_7$, MCS always finds better or equally optimal solutions. Analyzing the results of function f_1, the CDE, AEGA, and the MCS algorithms reach all optima. In case of function f_2, only CSA and AiNet have not been

TABLE 8.2 Performance Comparison among Multimodal Optimization Algorithms for the Test Functions $f_1 - f_7$

Function	Algorithm	EPN	MPR	PA	DA	NFE
f_1	CDE	3 (0)	0.9996 (0.0004)	0.0995 (0.1343)	0.0305 (0.0169)	27,432 (1,432)
	SDE	2.96 (0.18)	0.9863 (0.0523)	1.3053 (0.8843)	0.1343 (0.0483)	31,435 (2,342)
	CP	2.93 (0.25)	0.9725 (0.0894)	1.3776 (1.0120)	0.1432 (0.0445)	34,267 (4,345)
	AEGA	3 (0)	0.9932 (0.0054)	0.0991 (0.2133)	0.1031 (0.0065)	30,323 (2,316)
	CSA	2.91 (0.20)	0.9127 (0.0587)	1.4211 (1.0624)	0.2188 (0.0072)	25,050 (0)
	AiNet	2.94 (0.20)	0.9002 (0.0901)	1.3839 (1.0214)	0.1760 (0.0067)	25,050 (0)
	MCS	3 (0)	1 (0)	0.0005 (0.0001)	0.0007 (0.0002)	25,433 (54)
f_2	CDE	12 (0)	1 (0)	0.0015 (0.0010)	0.2993 (0.0804)	26,321 (1,934)
	SDE	12 (0)	1 (0)	0.0018 (0.0006)	0.3883 (0.0657)	32,563 (1,453)
	CP	12 (0)	1 (0)	0.0009 (0.0003)	0.2694 (0.0506)	30,324 (3,521)
	AEGA	12 (0)	0.9987 (0.0011)	0.0988 (0.0097)	0.3225 (0.0058)	29,954 (1,987)
	CSA	11.92 (0.41)	0.9011 (0.0091)	0.1055 (0.0121)	0.4257 (0.0096)	25,050 (0)
	AiNet	11.96 (0.30)	0.9256 (0.0074)	0.0996 (0.0105)	0.3239 (0.0081)	25,050 (0)
	MCS	12 (0)	1 (0)	0.0001 (0.0001)	0.0073 (0.0002)	25,188 (42)
f_3	CDE	23.03 (1.77)	0.8780 (0.0956)	180.47 (265.54)	9.3611 (6.4667)	28,654 (2,050)
	SDE	20.06 (2.59)	0.6980 (0.1552)	155.52 (184.59)	14.892 (7.5935)	31,432 (1,017)
	CP	21.03 (1.90)	0.7586 (0.1125)	192.32 (146.21)	11.195 (3.1490)	32,843 (2,070)
	AEGA	20.45 (1.21)	0.7128 (0.1493)	134.47 (157.37)	16.176 (8.0751)	30,965 (2,154)
	CSA	18.02 (2.41)	0.5875 (0.1641)	185.64 (104.24)	21.057 (10.105)	25,050 (0)
	AiNet	19.24 (2.01)	0.6123 (0.1247)	179.35 (164.37)	18.180 (9.1112)	25,050 (0)
	MCS	24.66 (1.01)	0.9634 (0.0397)	2.9408 (4.3888)	15.521 (8.0834)	25,211 (37)
f_4	CDE	3.46 (1.00)	0.4929 (0.1419)	395.46 (305.01)	210.940 (72.99)	29,473 (3,021)
	SDE	3.73 (0.86)	0.5301 (0.1268)	544.48 (124.11)	206.65 (160.84)	33,421 (1,342)
	CP	3.26 (0.63)	0.4622 (0.0869)	192.32 (146.21)	199.41 (68.434)	29,342 (1,543)
	AEGA	3.51 (0.52)	0.5031 (0.0754)	188.23 (101.54)	187.21 (33.211)	32,756 (1,759)
	CSA	3.12 (0.11)	0.4187 (0.0464)	257.54 (157.18)	278.14 (47.120)	25,050 (0)
	AiNet	3.20 (0.47)	0.5164 (0.0357)	197.24 (86.21)	178.23 (29.191)	25,050 (0)
	MCS	6.26 (0.82)	0.8919 (0.1214)	41.864 (16,63)	39.938 (12.962)	25,361 (81)

(Continued)

TABLE 8.2 (*Continued*) Performance Comparison among Multimodal Optimization Algorithms for the Test Functions $f_1 - f_7$

Function	Algorithm	*EPN*	*MPR*	*PA*	*DA*	*NFE*
f_5	CDE	22.96 (2.25)	0.4953 (0.0496)	0.2348 (0.0269)	17.83 (7.1214)	28,543 (1,345)
	SDE	31.40 (2.35)	0.6775 (0.0503)	0.7005 (0.0849)	3.9430 (0.9270)	30543 (1576)
	CP	21.33 (2.00)	0.4599 (0.0436)	1.3189 (0.5179)	10.766 (1.9245)	28,743 (2,001)
	AEGA	30.11 (2.01)	0.6557 (0.0127)	0.8674 (0.0296)	2.870 (1.6781)	29,765 (1,911)
	CSA	24.79 (3.14)	0.5107 (0.0308)	0.2121 (0.0187)	8.7451 (3.470)	25,050 (0)
	AiNet	26.57 (2.35)	0.5005 (0.0471)	0.2087 (0.0324)	6.472 (2.4187)	25,050 (0)
	MCS	33.03 (2.07)	0.8535 (0.0251)	0.1617 (0.0283)	4.6012 (1.4206)	25,159 (49)
f_6	CDE	6 (0)	0.9786 (0.0157)	0.1280 (0.0942)	0.1231 (0.0182)	30,234 (2410)
	SDE	5.86 (0.43)	0.9185 (0.0685)	0.3842 (0.1049)	0.1701 (0.0222)	31,453 (1154)
	CP	6 (0)	0.9423 (0.0123)	0.3460 (0.0741)	0.1633 (0.0149)	30,231 (832)
	AEGA	5.11 (0.64)	0.8945 (0.0387)	0.4004 (0.0879)	0.1224 (0,0101)	31,932 (943)
	CSA	4.97 (0.24)	0.8174 (0.0631)	0.4797 (0.0257)	0.1295 (0,0054)	25,050 (0)
	AiNet	5.23 (1)	0.9012 (0.0197)	0.3974 (0.0702)	0.1197 (0,0054)	25,050 (0)
	MCS	6 (0)	0.9993 (0.0002)	0.0037 (0.0014)	0.0006 (0.0002)	25,463 (37)
f_7	CDE	30.36 (2.77)	0.6200 (0.0566)	2.2053 (1.8321)	330.51 (47.531)	33,423 (1021)
	SDE	35.06 (5.15)	0.7162 (0.1051)	1.9537 (0.9290)	243.39 (140.04)	32,832 (995)
	CP	35.06 (3.98)	0.7164 (0.0812)	2.4810 (1.4355)	250.11 (78.194)	31,923 (834)
	AEGA	32.51 (2.59)	0.7004 (0.0692)	2.0751 (0.9561)	278.78 (46.225)	33,821 (1032)
	CSA	31.78 (1.14)	0.6764 (0.4100)	1.9408 (0.9471)	347.21 (38.147)	25,050 (0)
	AiNet	34.42 (1.80)	0.7237 (0.0257)	1.8632 (0.0754)	261.27 (61.217)	25,050 (0)
	MCS	38.86 (1.54)	0.8014 (0.0313)	0.2290 (0.0166)	49.53 (7.1533)	25,643 (97)

For all the parameters, numbers in parentheses are the standard deviations.

able to detect all the optima values each time. Considering function f_3, only MCS can detect all optima at each run. In case of function f_4, most of the algorithms detect only half of the total optima but MCS can recognize most of them. Analyzing the results of the function f_5, CDE, CP, CSA, and AiNet present a similar performance, whereas SDE, AEGA, and MCS obtain the best *EPN* values. In the case of f_6, almost all algorithms present a similar performance; however, only the CDE, CP, and MCS algorithms have been able to detect all optima. Considering function f_7, the MCS algorithm is able to detect most of the optima, whereas the rest of the methods reach different performance levels.

By analyzing the *MPR* index in Table 8.2, MCS has reached the best performance for all the multimodal problems. On the other hand, the rest of the algorithms present different accuracy levels, with CDE and SDE being the most consistent.

Considering the *PA* index, MCS presents the best performance. Since *PA* evaluates the accumulative differences of fitness values, it could drastically change when one or several peaks are not detected (function f_3) or when the function under testing presents peaks with high values (function f_4). For the case of the *DA* index in Table 8.2, it is evident that the MCS algorithm presents the best performance providing the shortest distances among the detected optima.

Analyzing the *NFE* measure in Table 8.2, it is clear that CSA and AiNet need fewer function evaluations than other algorithms considering the same termination criterion. This fact is explained by considering that both algorithms do not implement any additional process in order to detect multiple optima. On the other hand, the MCS method maintains a slightly higher NFE than CSA and AiNet due to the inclusion of the depuration procedure. The rest of the algorithms present a considerable higher *NFE* value.

It can be easily deduced from such results that the MCS algorithm is able to produce better search locations (i.e., a better compromise between exploration and exploitation) in a more efficient and effective way than other multimodal search strategies by using an acceptable NFE.

8.5.3 Comparing MCS Performance for Functions $f_8 - f_{14}$

This section presents a performance comparison for different algorithms solving the multimodal problems $f_8 - f_{14}$ that are shown in Table A. The aim is to determine whether MCS is more efficient and effective than its competitors for finding multiple optima in $f_8 - f_{14}$. All the algorithms employ a population size of 50 individuals using 500 successive generations. Table 8.2 provides a summarized performance comparison among several algorithms in terms of the *EPN*, the *MPR*, the *PA*, the *DA*, and the *NFE*. The results are averaged by considering 50 different executions.

The goal of multimodal optimizers is to find as many as possible global optima and good local optima. The main objective in these experiments is to determine whether MCS is able to find not only optima with prominent fitness value but also optima with low fitness values. Table 8.3 provides a summary of the performance comparison among the different algorithms.

TABLE 8.3 Performance Comparison among Multimodal Optimization Algorithms for the Test Functions $f_8 - f_{14}$

Function	Algorithm	EPN	MPR	PA	DA	NFE
f_8	CDE	24.16 (2.77)	0.9682 (0.0318)	2.4873 (2.4891)	0.8291 (0.8296)	28,453 (2,345)
	SDE	18.56 (2.51)	0.4655 (0.0636)	30.21 (43.132)	2.1162 (0.6697)	31,328 (945)
	CP	8.80 (1.95)	0.2222 (0.0509)	60.52 (56.056)	6.9411 (0.9500)	30,743 (1,032)
	AEGA	15.67 (2.21)	0.3934 (0.0534)	40.56 (10.111)	3.2132 (0.2313)	32,045 (684)
	CSA	14.54 (3.12)	0.3323 (0.0431)	48.34 (8.343)	3.8232 (0.4521)	25,050 (0)
	AiNet	16.78 (2.63)	0.4264 (0.0321)	37.32 (10.432)	2.9832 (0.5493)	25,050 (0)
	MCS	24.73 (0.49)	0.9898 (0.0170)	0.900 (1.4771)	0.2584 (0.1275)	25,582 (74)
f_9	CDE	2.1 (0.20)	0.7833 (0.0211)	23.235 (7.348)	2.9354 (0.3521)	30,074 (1,621)
	SDE	2.3 (0.31)	0.8245 (0.0145)	20.745 (8.012)	2.6731 (0.8621)	31,497 (245)
	CP	2.4 (0.25)	0.8753 (0.0301)	18.563 (5.865)	2.3031 (0.7732)	29,746 (1,114)
	AEGA	2.1 (0.10)	0.7879 (0.0174)	22.349 (6.231)	3.0021 (0.6431)	30,986 (1,027)
	CSA	2 (0)	0.7098 (0.0025)	32.859 (8.659)	3.1432 (0.5431)	25,050 (0)
	AiNet	2 (0)	0.7165 (0.0076)	31.655 (6.087)	3.2265 (0.3467)	25,050 (0)
	MCS	4.74 (0.25)	0.9154 (0.0163)	2.3515 (2.511)	0.0109 (0.0428)	26,043 (112)

(*Continued*)

TABLE 8.3 (*Continued*)   Performance Comparison among Multimodal Optimization Algorithms for the
Test Functions $f_8 - f_{14}$

Function	Algorithm	EPN	MPR	PA	DA	NFE
f_{10}	CDE	4.12 (0.78)	0.7285 (0.0342)	3.546 (1.034)	3.0132 (0.5321)	29,597 (1,034)
	SDE	4.64 (0.54)	0.7893 (0.0532)	3.054 (1.127)	2.864 (0.3271)	32,743 (964)
	CP	4 (0)	0.7092 (0.0298)	3.881 (1.154)	3.3412 (0.4829)	28,463 (1,142)
	AEGA	3.43 (0.33)	0.6734 (0.0745)	4.212 (1.312)	3.9121 (0.8732)	29,172 (1,044)
	CSA	3.76 (0.51)	0.6975 (0.0828)	4.002 (1.197)	3.5821 (0.7498)	25,050 (0)
	AiNet	4 (0)	0.7085 (0.0385)	3.797 (1.002)	3.3002 (0.6496)	25,050 (0)
	MCS	6.82 (0.75)	0.9274 (0.0137)	0.423 (0.064)	0.6842 (0.0598)	25,873 (88)
f_{11}	CDE	10.36 (1.60)	0.8572 (0.1344)	1.859 (0.952)	0.5237 (0.0321)	34,156 (2,321)
	SDE	10.36 (2.04)	0.8573 (0.1702)	1.268 (0.581)	0.6927 (0.0921)	32,132 (975)
	CP	9.16 (1.76)	0.7577 (0.1462)	2.536 (0.890)	0.6550 (0.0440)	30,863 (1,002)
	AEGA	8.34 (1.32)	0.6954 (0.1021)	4.432 (1.232)	0.7021 (0.0231)	31,534 (852)
	CSA	8 (0)	0.6532 (0.1378)	4.892 (1.003)	0.7832 (0.0432)	25,050 (0)
	AiNet	8 (0)	0.6438 (0.2172)	4.921 (1.102)	0.7753 (0.0326)	25,050 (0)
	MCS	12 (0)	0.9998 (0.0003)	0.011 (0.008)	0.0060 (0.0012)	25,789 (121)
f_{12}	CDE	6.21 (1.54)	0.6986 (0.1893)	4.029 (1.401)	5.1514 (1.0351)	31,456 (975)
	SDE	5.34 (2.03)	0.5812 (0.1992)	5.075 (1.071)	6.0117 (1.1517)	32,481 (1,002)
	CP	6.04 (0.61)	0.6312 (0.1771)	4.657 (1.321)	5.3177 (1.7517)	33,123 (563)
	AEGA	4 (0)	0.4112 (0.0343)	6.341 (1.034)	7.8751 (1.652)	32,634 (843)
	CSA	4 (0)	0.3998 (0.0212)	6.151 (1.121)	7.7976 (1.0043)	25,050 (0)
	AiNet	4 (0)	0.4034 (0.0973)	6.003 (1.735)	7.6613 (1.1219)	25,050 (0)
	MCS	9.65 (1.45)	0.9411 (0.0087)	0.015 (0.009)	0.1043 (0.0864)	25,832 (65)
f_{13}	CDE	13 (0)	1 (0)	0.010 (0.003)	0.031 (0.0098)	31,572 (962)
	SDE	13 (0)	1 (0)	0.008 (0.004)	0.021 (0.0065)	33,435 (1,201)
	CP	13 (0)	1 (0)	0.015 (0.002)	0.037 (0.0065)	31,834 (799)
	AEGA	10.66 (1.21)	0.8323 (0.0343)	0.088 (0.033)	0.096 (0.0098)	32,845 (1,182)
	CSA	8.94 (2.34)	0.7998 (0.0564)	0.110 (0.088)	0.113 (0.0104)	25,050 (0)
	AiNet	10.32 (1.52)	0.8297 (0.0206)	0.098 (0.075)	0.087 (0.0086)	25,050 (0)
	MCS	13 (0)	0.9997 (0.0134)	0.011 (0.007)	0.023 (0.0016)	25,740 (101)
f_{14}	CDE	3.04 (1.34)	0.6675 (0.0754)	0.809 (0.101)	176.54 (21.23)	32,273 (1,004)
	SDE	3.55 (0.56)	0.7017 (0.0487)	0.675 (0.079)	115.43 (34.21)	30,372 (965)
	CP	2.87 (1.23)	0.6123 (0.0861)	1.081 (0.201)	202.65 (42.81)	31,534 (1,298)
	AEGA	3 (0)	0.6686 (0.0542)	0.894 (0.076)	150.32 (57.31)	29,985 (1,745)
	CSA	3 (0)	0.6691 (0.0231)	0.897 (0.045)	161.57 (27.92)	25,050 (0)
	AiNet	3.50 (0.25)	0.7001 (0.0765)	0.668 (0.097)	121.43 (43.12)	25,050 (0)
	MCS	7.13 (0.81)	0.9859 (0.0094)	0.023 (0.010)	17.62 (4.13)	25,786 (92)

For all the parameters, numbers in parentheses are the standard deviations.

Considering the *EPN* measure, it is observed that MCS finds more optimal solutions for the multimodal problems $f_8 - f_{14}$ than the other methods. Analyzing function f_8, only MCS can detect all optima, whereas CP, AEGA, CSA, and AiNet exhibit the worst *EPN* performance.

Functions $f_9 - f_{12}$ represent a set of special cases $f_9 - f_{12}$ which contain a few prominent optima (with good fitness value). However, such functions present also several optima with bad fitness values. In these functions, MCS is able to detect the highest number of optimum points. On the contrary, the rest of the algorithms can find only prominent optima.

For function f_{13}, four algorithms (CDE, SDE, CP, and MCS) can recognize all optima for each execution. In case of function f_{14}, it features numerous optima with different fitness values. However, MCS still can detect most of the optima.

In terms of the number of *MPRs*, MCS has obtained the best score for all the multimodal problems. On the other hand, the rest of the algorithms present different accuracy levels.

A close inspection of Table 8.3 also reveals that the proposed MCS approach is able to achieve the smallest *PA* and *DA* values in comparison with all other methods. Similar conclusions to those in Section 8.4.2 can be established regarding the *NFEs*. All results demonstrate that MCS achieves the overall best balance in comparison with the other algorithms, in terms of both, the detection accuracy and the NFEs.

REFERENCES

Beasley, D., Bull, D. R., & Matin, R. R. (1993). A sequential niche technique for multimodal function optimization. *Evolutionary Computation*, 1(2), 101–125.

Bhargava, V., Fateen, S. E. K., & Bonilla-Petriciolet, A. (2013). Cuckoo search: A new nature-inspired optimization method for phase equilibrium calculations. *Fluid Phase Equilibria*, 337, 191–200.

Castro, L. N., & Timmis, J. (2002). An artificial immune network for multimodal function optimization. In *Proceedings of the 2002 IEEE International Conference on Evolutionary Computation*, Honolulu, HI (pp. 699–704). New York, NY: IEEE Press.

Castro, L. N., & Zuben, F. J. (2002). Learning and optimization using the clonal selection principle. *IEEE Transactions on Evolutionary Computation*, 6, 239–251.

Chen, G., Low, C. P., & Yang, Z. (2009). Preserving and exploiting genetic diversity in evolutionary programming algorithms. *IEEE Transactions on Evolutionary Computation*, 13(3), 661–673.

Das, S., Maity, S., Qu, B. -Y., & Suganthan, P. N. (2011). Real-parameter evolutionary multimodal optimization—A survey of the state-of-the-art. *Swarm and Evolutionary Computation*, 1(2), 71–88.

de Castro, L. N., & Von Zuben, F. J. (1999, December). *Artificial immune systems: Part I—Basic theory and applications* (Technical Report No. TR-DCA 01/99).

De Jong, K. (1975). *Analysis of the behavior of a class of genetic adaptive systems* (Ph.D. thesis). Ann Arbor, MI: University of Michigan.

Dorigo, M., Maniezzo, V., & Colorni, A. (1991). *Positive feedback as a search strategy* (Technical Report No. 91-016). Milan: Politecnico di Milano.

Fogel, L. J., Owens, A. J., & Walsh, M. J. (1966). *Artificial intelligence through simulated evolution*. Chichester: John Wiley & Sons.

Floudas, C., Akrotirianakis, I., Caratzoulas, S., Meyer, C., & Kallrath, J. (2005). Global optimization in the 21st century: Advances and challenges. *Computers & Chemical Engineering*, 29(6), 1185–1202.

Georgieva, A., & Jordanov, I. (2009). Global optimization based on novel heuristics, low-discrepancy sequences and genetic algorithms. *European Journal of Operational Research*, 196, 413–422.

Goldberg, D. E. (1989). *genetic algorithms in search, optimization and machine learning*. Boston, MA: Addison Wesley.

Holland, J. H. (1975). *Adaptation in natural and artificial systems*. Ann Arbor, MI: University of Michigan Press.

İlker, B., Birbil, S., & Shu-Cherng, F. (2003) An electromagnetism-like mechanism for global optimization. *Journal of Global Optimization, 25*, 263–282.

Kaveh, A., & Bakhshpoori, T. (2011). Optimum design of steel frames using cuckoo search algorithm with Lévy flights. *Structural Design of Tall and Special Buildings, 21*, In press. 1023–1036

Kennedy, J., & Eberhart, R. (1995, December). *Particle swarm optimization*. In *Proceedings of the 1995 IEEE International Conference on Neural Networks* (Vol. 4, pp. 1942–1948). IEEE.

Kirkpatrick, S., Gelatt, C., & Vecchi, M. (1983). Optimization by simulated annealing. *Science, 220*(4598), 671–680.

Koza, J. R. (1990). *Genetic programming: A paradigm for genetically breeding populations of computer programs to solve problems* (Report No. STAN-CS-90-1314). Stanford, CA: Stanford University.

Kumar, A., & Chakarverty, S. (2011). Design optimization for reliable embedded system using cuckoo search. In *Proceedings of 3rd International Conference on Electronics Computer Technology (ICECT 2011)* (pp. 564–568). IEEE.

Lera, D., & Sergeyev, Y. (2010). Lipschitz and Hölder global optimization using space-filling curves. *Applied Numerical Mathematics, 60*(1–2), 115–129.

Li, J. P., Balazs, M. E., Parks, G. T., & Glarkson, P. J. (2002). A species conserving genetic algorithms for multimodal function optimization. *Evolutionary Computation, 10*(3), 207–234.

Lianga, Y., & Kwong-Sak L. (2011). Genetic algorithm with adaptive elitist-population strategies for multimodal function optimization. *Applied Soft Computing, 11*, 2017–2034.

Mahfoud, S. W. (1995). *Niching methods for genetic algorithms* (Ph.D. dissertation), Urbana: University of Illinois, Illinois Genetic Algorithm Laboratory.

Mantegna, R. (1994). Fast and accurate algorithm for numerical simulation of Lévy stable stochastic process. *Physical Review E, 49*(4), 4677–4683.

Mengshoel, O. J., & Goldberg, D. E. (1999). Probability crowding: Deterministic crowding with probabilistic replacement. In W. Banzhaf (Ed.), *Proceedings of the International Conference GECCO-1999* (pp. 409–416). Orlando, FL.

Miller, B. L., & Shaw, M. J. (1996). Genetic algorithms with dynamic niche sharing for multimodal function optimization. In *Proceedings of the 3rd IEEE Conference on Evolutionary Computation* (pp. 786–791). IEEE.

Moravej, Z., & Akhlaghi, A. (2013). A novel approach based on cuckoo search for DG allocation in distribution network. *International Journal of Electrical Power & Energy Systems, 44*, 672–679.

Pardalos Panos, M., Romeijn Edwin, H., & Tuy, H. (2000). Recent developments and trends in global optimization. *Journal of Computational and Applied Mathematics, 124*, 209–228.

Pavlyukevich, I. (2007). Lévy flights, non-local search and simulated annealing. *Journal of Computational Physics, 226*, 1830–1844.

Petrowski, A. (1996). A clearing procedure as a niching method for genetic algorithms, In *Proceedings of the 1996 IEEE International Conference on Evolutionary Computation* (pp. 798–803). New York, NY: IEEE Press.

Rashedia, E., Nezamabadi-pour, H., & Saryazdi, S. (2011). Filter modeling using gravitational search algorithm. *Engineering Applications of Artificial Intelligence, 24*(1), 117–122.

Roya, S., Islama, S. M., Das, S., Ghosha, S., & Vasilakos, A. V. (2013). A simulated weed colony system with subregional differential evolution for multimodal optimization. *Engineering Optimization, 45*(4), 459–481.

Storn, R., & Price, K. (1995). *Differential evolution-a simple and efficient adaptive scheme for global optimisation over continuous spaces* (Technical Report No. TR-95-012). Berkeley, CA: ICSI.

Tan, K. C., Chiam, S. C., Mamun, A. A., & Goh, C. K. (2009). Balancing exploration and exploitation with adaptive variation for evolutionary multi-objective optimization. *European Journal of Operational Research, 197*, 701–713.

Tein, L. H., & Ramli, R. (2010). Recent advancements of nurse scheduling models and a potential path. In *Proceedings of 6th IMT-GT Conference on Mathematics, Statistics and Its Applications (ICMSA 2010)* (pp. 395–409). Kuala Lumpur, Malaysia: Universiti Tunku Abdul Rahman.

Thomsen, R. (2004). *Multimodal optimization using crowding-based differential evolution, evolutionary computation*. In *Proceedings of the 2004 Congress on Evolutionary Computation (IEEE Cat. No.04TH8753)*, 2, 1382–1389. doi:10.1109/CEC.2004.1331058.

Walton, S., Hassan, O., Morgan, K., & Brown, M. R. (2011). Modified cuckoo search: A new gradient free optimization algorithm. *Chaos Solitons Fractals*, 44(9), 710–718.

Walton, S., Hassan, O., Morgan, K., & Brown, M. R. (2013). A review of the development and applications of the cuckoo search algorithm, swarm intelligence and bio-inspired computation theory and applications (pp. 257–271). In X. -S. Yang, Z. Cui, R. Xiao, A. H. Gandomi, & M. Karamanoglu (Eds.), Swarm intelligence and bio-inspired computation: Theory and applications. Amsterdam: Elsevier. doi:10.1016/B978-0-12-405163-8.00011-9.

Wong, K.-C., Wu, C.-H., Mok, R. K. P., Peng, C., & Zhang, Z. (2012). Evolutionary multimodal optimization using the principle of locality. *Information Sciences*, 194, 138–170.

Xu, Q., Lei, W., & Si, J. (2010). Predication based immune network for multimodal function optimization. *Engineering Applications of Artificial Intelligence*, 23, 495–504.

Yahyaiea, F., & Filizadeh, S. (2011). A surrogate-model based multi-modal optimization algorithm. *Engineering Optimization*, 43(7), 779–799.

Yang, X. S., & Deb, S. (2010a). Cuckoo Search via Levey Flights In 2009 World Congress on Nature and Biologically Inspired Computing, NABIC 2009 – Proceedings (pp. 210–214). IEEE Publications, India. doi:10.1109/NABIC.2009.5393690.

Yang, X. S., & Deb, S. (2010b). Engineering optimisation by cuckoo search. *International Journal of Mathematical Modelling and Numerical Optimisation*, 1, 330–343. doi.: 10.1504/IJMMNO.2010.035430.

Yazdani, S., Nezamabadi, H., & Kamyab, S. (2014). A gravitational search algorithm for multimodal optimization. *Swarm and Evolutionary Computation*, 14, 1–14.

Yin, X., & Germay, N. (1993). A fast genetic algorithm with sharing scheme using cluster analysis methods in multimodal function optimization. In *Proceedings of the 1993 International Conference on Artificial Neural Networks and Genetic Algorithms* (pp. 450–457). Springer.

Ying, J., Ke-Cun, Z., & Shao-Jian, Q. (2007). A deterministic global optimization algorithm. *Applied Mathematics and Computation*, 185(1), 382–387.

CHAPTER 9

Metaheuristic Multimodal Optimization

9.1 INTRODUCTION

As the name suggests, multimodal functions have multiple "good" solutions, many of which can be considered as optimal locations. Multimodal optimization problems hinder the operation of the optimization methods in their efforts to find the global optimum. This fact is a consequence that in this type of problems there are many local minima which can attract the production of solutions during the optimization process. Therefore, the search for the optimum global becomes a challenge for a metaheuristic method.

In this section, we will discuss the optimization process from a general perspective. Therefore, the search strategy is not reduced to find the global optimum. Under these conditions, the objective of multimodal optimization is to find many optima as they might exist in the objective function. Such optima not only refer to optimum global, in the case that there exist several optima, but also to local optima.

Most of the research on metaheuristic computation focuses on the design of algorithms that allow to find only the global optimum function goal. However, although the optimal global represents the best possible solution in the search space, there are conditions under which its application to the problem in question could be impractical or too costly. Under these circumstances, from a practical point of view, it is desirable to have access not only to the optimum global but also as many local minima as possible (ideally all them). In this scenario, a local minimum with an acceptable quality and modest cost of implementation would be preferable that the best solution (global optimum) with a slightly higher quality, but a prohibitive cost of implementation. The process of finding the global optimum and the best local optima is known as multimodal optimization.

Classical optimization methods begin with a single candidate solution and modify it iteratively until the best position has been found at the end of the optimization process. As the goal in multimodal optimization is to find multiple optimal solutions, there are at least two problems related to the classical optimization methods to perform this task:

1. A single solution metaheuristic method must be applied several times recording in each execution the optimal found solution.

2. The multiple execution of single solution methods to find multiple optimal solutions does not guarantee to obtain different solutions. This scenario is particularly valid if initial positions are always chosen in such way that they are close to the influence of the same optimal local.

Metaheuristic methods are able to detect a single optimum through the operation of a set of solutions. These algorithms with some slight modifications can be adapted so that during its operation could register the global optimum and as many local optima as possible. With such modifications, metaheuristic algorithms can perform multimodal optimization maintaining their interesting characteristic as search strategies.

The structure and operation of a metaheuristic process suggest that this type of approaches represent the best options to solve the multimodal optimization problems. In this chapter, we will discuss different mechanisms that incorporated with metaheuristic methods provide multimodal capabilities. In this chapter, several techniques are analyzed. However, since the fitness sharing scheme is the most popular, this procedure will be treated in detail.

9.2 DIVERSITY THROUGH MUTATION

Detecting a population of solutions close to different optima positions and keeping it for several generations are two completely different problems. On a metaheuristic method, initially, solutions are randomly distributed in the search space. Then, because of the processing scheme, solutions near to local optimal positions are attracted to them. Therefore, as the number of generations evolves, groups of individuals are concentrated around these local optimal locations. Under this behavior, it is clear that although it is possible to discover multiple optimal in the first iterations of the metaheuristic algorithm, it is not possible to automatically maintain this information in the final population. In order to keep the information of these multiple solutions, it should be included in the metaheuristic method an operator that explicitly preserves the diversity of solutions, without allowing the elimination of multiple solutions.

The mutation operator is often used as an operation that preserves the diversity in a metaheuristic method. Although the operator mutation is most identified as a part of a genetic algorithm, it has become an effective mechanism to provide diversity (Deb, 2001). The operator, applied correctly, modifies individuals injecting diversity in the population.

Typically, the mutation operator has a constructive and destructive effect. The constructive effect results when a mutated individual becomes a higher quality element. The destructive effect can occur when a very good solution degenerates into a bad solution in terms of its fitness value. Since the mutation operator is not normally used to add diversity in metaheuristic computation, the probability of its application to elements of the population is very low. Hence, the operator is insufficient to provide diversity in the population.

9.3 PRESELECTION

The operator of preselection (Cavicchio, 1970) was the first that was explicitly introduced to maintain the diversity of genetic algorithms. In this operator, an individual is replaced with a similar element, but with better quality. This effect can be achieved in a simple way when a new individual created by the crossing of two parents replaces the worse of the two parents in terms of its quality (fitness value). As the new individual is the result of the information exchange between both parents, it has some similarity with respect to them. Therefore, with the replacement of a parent with the new solution, it is allowed that solutions relatively different coexist.

9.4 CROWDING MODEL

DeJong (1975) proposed the crowding model to introduce diversity between the solutions of a genetic algorithm. Although the original model is rather weak for its direct application in multimodal optimization problems, its concepts motivate the generation of new approaches that are used currently as diversity preservation techniques.

As the name suggests, on the crowding model, diversity is added through the incorporation of a mechanism that tries to avoid the clustering of individuals. In this mechanism DeJong introduced the concept of population segment and a clustering strategy. Such elements were first included in a conventional genetic algorithm. Under the approach, only a portion $\mathbf{G}$ of the population (called generation gap) is used to generate new individuals in each iteration. In the method, when a new individual is generated, its inclusion in the portion $\mathbf{G}$ is performed by the following process. First, a number of CF ("crowding factor") elements are selected randomly from the sub-population $\mathbf{G}$. Then, the new individual is compared with these CF elements, in terms of similarity. Therefore, the new individual will replace the random element with which presents a greater similarity. In this study, DeJong uses as parameters $\mathbf{G} = 0.1$ and CF = 2 or 3.

9.5 SHARING FUNCTION MODEL

Goldberg and Richardson (1987) proposed one of the most important concepts for multimodal optimization and multiobjective applications. In this model, known as sharing function, instead of replacing an individual with similar characteristics, the idea is to degrade the quality of similar solutions. As it had been already discussed previously, individuals tend to be attracted to positions where local optima are located. Several groups can be built around these points during the optimization process. Under the model of sharing function, individuals of the population compete within groups to prevail as long as possible. Since this scheme is used by many metaheuristic algorithms, this model will be discussed in more detail in this chapter.

In order to explain this method, assume that it is required to detect q different optimal solutions of a specific objective function. The only available mechanism of storage to keep these solutions is a population $\mathbf{P}^k\left(\mathbf{x}_1^k, \mathbf{x}_2^k, \ldots, \mathbf{x}_N^k\right)$ of N elements. It is also considered that $q \ll N$, in such a way that the number of stored optimal can operate as a sub-population. Since the population will maintain instances of these q optimal during the optimization process, the remaining elements of the population will contain similar solutions to the q

individuals already present. This means that, for each optimal stored solution i, there are m_i individuals with similar positions. Under these conditions, for all optimal individuals, the following distribution of agent is presented:

$$\sum_{i=1}^{q} m_i = N \qquad (9.1)$$

Therefore, if in a certain generation, an optimal individual i maintains a large number m_i of similar positions, the other optimal elements will not be detected as a consequence of the poor exploration produced by the high number of similar elements to i. Under this scenario, the quality (fitness) of these m_i solutions should be degraded so that with this degradation these elements have more difficulties to be selected for producing new individuals. The magnitude of the degradation is usually based on the number of similar positions. Thus, an optimal solution j that has a small number m_j of solutions with similar positions will not be very degraded. Since the selection probability is proportional to deterioration size, individuals with small degradation can be frequently used to produce new agents.

Under the degradation model, the quality of an individual $\mathbf{x}_i^k$ is reduced depending on the number of solutions m_i with a similar position to $\mathbf{x}_i^k$. With the degradation, the new quality $f'(\mathbf{x}_i^k)$ of $\mathbf{x}_i^k$ is calculated by using the following equation:

$$f'(\mathbf{x}_i^k) = \frac{f(\mathbf{x}_i^k)}{m_i} \qquad (9.2)$$

The principle of degradation quality seems reasonable, as it has been discussed so far. However, the implementation of this mechanism in a metaheuristic algorithm presents an interesting practical problem. This restriction refers to the inability to accurately identify all the solutions m_i that present similarity with a particular individual $\mathbf{x}_i^k$. Considering this problem, Goldberg and Deb (1991) introduced the strategy of sharing function to determine the number of solutions that are related to a specific individual $\mathbf{x}_i^k$. A sharing function refers to a model that establishes the manner in which two different solutions $\mathbf{x}_i^k$ and $\mathbf{x}_j^k$ are related. Although there are several ways to select a sharing function, the most used formulation is defined below:

$$\mathrm{Co}(d_{ij}) = \begin{cases} 1 - \left(\dfrac{d_{ij}}{\sigma_s}\right)^{\alpha} & si\ d_{ij} \le \sigma_s \\ 0 & \text{otherwise} \end{cases} \qquad (9.3)$$

The parameter d_{ij} is the Euclidean distance between two different solutions $\mathbf{x}_i^k$ and $\mathbf{x}_j^k$. σ_s represents the maximum radius of influence. The sharing function produces a value [0,1] depending on the values of d_{ij} and σ_s. It is zero (the two solutions $\mathbf{x}_i^k$ and $\mathbf{x}_j^k$ are identical), $\mathrm{Co}(d_{ij}) = 1$. This means that a solution has a complete shared relationship. On the other hand, if $d_{ij} \ge \sigma_s$ (the two solutions are so far that they do not share anything), $\mathrm{Co}(d_{ij}) = 0$. This condition expresses that the solutions $\mathbf{x}_i^k$ and $\mathbf{x}_j^k$ are so dissimilar that they do not maintain any relationship between them. Any other distance d_{ij} between the two solutions will have an effect of similarity between them.

If $\alpha = 1$ is used, the values of $\mathrm{Co}(\cdot)$ are reduced linearly from 1 to 0. According to the sharing model, a solution $\mathbf{x}_i^k$ may not have any effect on other elements of the population $\mathbf{P}^k$. It can also have a partial effect on a small group or a full effect on itself. Figure 9.1 illustrates the value of sharing function as the normalized distance $\left(d_{ij}/\sigma_s \right)$ is varied assuming different values of α.

Calculating the sharing function values for all elements of the population $\mathbf{P}^k$ (including themselves), it is possible to know the way in which each individual $\mathbf{x}_i^k$ is related with other members of the population. In order to calculate the crowding relationship of an individual $\mathbf{x}_i^k$ with the rest of the solutions of the population, it is computed how this individual share characteristic with these solutions. This operation can be defined in the following way:

$$ra_i = \sum_{j=1}^{N} \mathrm{Co}\left(d_{ij} \right) \tag{9.4}$$

Therefore, the crowding relationship ra_i provides an estimation of the number of solutions concentrated around $\mathbf{x}_i^k$. It is important to consider that the ra_i value is always greater than or equal to 1. This is because the sharing function of $\mathbf{x}_i^k$ evaluated with itself $\left(d_{ii} \right)$ is equal to 1.

The final step of the method is to calculate the degradation of $f\left(\mathbf{x}_i^k \right)$ as a result of the concentration of solutions around a local optimum. This effect of degradation is known in this context as a sharing fitness. This sharing fitness is calculated by the following model:

$$f'\left(\mathbf{x}_i^k \right) = \frac{f\left(\mathbf{x}_i^k \right)}{ra_i} \tag{9.5}$$

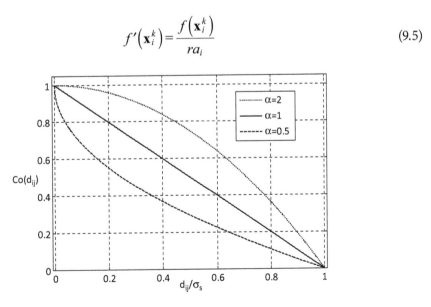

FIGURE 9.1   Sharing function values $\mathrm{Co}(\cdot)$ as the normalized distance $\left(d_{ij}/\sigma_s \right)$ is varied, assuming different values of α.

Under the effect of the sharing fitness, an individual x_i^k surrounded by many solutions would have a high crowding value ra_i and consequently a strong degradation. Therefore, it results in a low value of $f'(x_i^k)$. On the other hand, if the individual x_i^k is surrounded by very few number of solutions, its crowding value ra_i is low producing a moderated degradation of $f(x_i^k)$.

The computing process for the model of sharing function can be summarized in the following steps:

1. Compute the sharing function $Co(\cdot)$ with all elements of the population $\mathbf{P}^k$ (Eq. 9.3).

2. Calculate the crowding value ra_i for each element x_i^k of the population $\mathbf{P}^k$ (Eq. 9.4).

3. Degrade the original fitness value $f(x_i^k)$ through the use of the sharing fitness concept (Eq. 9.5).

Once conducted this process, several members of the population have degraded its quality according to the number of solutions that are around them. With these new qualities, the process of individual selection for the crossover or mutation tend to choose the members whose quality has been less affected.

9.5.1 Numerical Example for Sharing Function Calculation

To illustrate the computation under the sharing function technique, it is considered to solve the following maximization problem:

$$\begin{aligned} \text{Maximize} \quad & f(x)=|\sin(\pi x)| \\ \text{Subject to:} \quad & 0 \le x \le 2 \end{aligned} \tag{9.6}$$

In the example, a population $\mathbf{P}^k$ of six individuals $\left(x_1^k, x_2^k, \ldots, x_6^k\right)$ which are represented in Table 9.1 is considered. Figure 9.2 illustrates the objective function graphically. As it can be seen, the objective function has two global maxima, one at $x^*=0.5$ and another at $x^*=1.5$. From Figure 9.2, it is clear that the distribution of the individuals is very different. At first maximum ($x^*=0.5$), there are practically only two individuals while most of the solutions are grouped in the second mode ($x^*=1.5$). If sharing function model were not used in the solution of this optimization problem, all elements would tend to be distributed around the maximum at $x^*=1.5$.

In the calculation, it is considered as influence factor $\sigma_s=0.5$ and as a function shape $\alpha=1$. Under this configuration, only a linear relationship among the elements is produced. For the sake of space, we will show only the calculation for the first element x_1^k.

Step 1. Assuming x_1^k, calculate the distance with all other elements of $\mathbf{P}^k$.

$d_{11}=0$	$d_{12}=0.254$	$d_{13}=0.731$	$d_{14}=1.302$	$d_{15}=0.127$	$d_{16}=0.191$

TABLE 9.1   Characteristics of the Solutions Used in
the Numerical Example for the Calculation of the
Sharing Function

Solution	Position	$f\left(x_i^k\right)$	ra_i	$f'\left(x_i^k\right)$
x_1^k	1.651	0.890	2.857	0.312
x_2^k	1.397	0.948	3.160	0.300
x_3^k	0.921	0.246	1.048	0.235
x_4^k	0.349	0.890	1.000	0.890
x_5^k	1.524	0.997	3.364	0.296
x_6^k	1.460	0.992	3.364	0.295

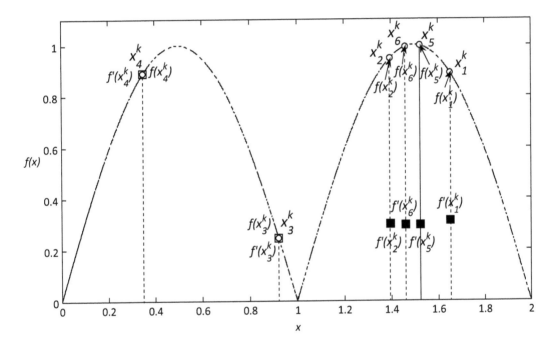

FIGURE 9.2   Individual distribution of the population $\mathbf{P}^k\left(x_1^k,x_2^k,\ldots,x_6^k\right)$. The circles symbolize the individual position in the original objective function, while the squares indicate the produced degradation $f'(\cdot)$.

With the use of Eq. 9.3, compute the sharing function $Co(\cdot)$ for the case of x_1^k.

$Co(d_{11})=1$	$Co(d_{12})=0.492$	$Co(d_{13})=0$	$Co(d_{14})=0$	$Co(d_{15})=0.746$	$Co(d_{16})=0.618$

Note that the solutions x_3^k and x_4^k are located in a distance longer than 0.5 with respect to x_1^k. Therefore, they have no effect on it.

Step 2. The crowding relationship ra_i with respect to the first individual x_1^k is calculated as the sum of the sharing functions already calculated.

$$ra_1 = 1 + 0.492 + 0 + 0 + 0.746 + 0.618 = 2.856$$

Step 3. The degradation of the original objective function $f(x_1^k)$ is calculated by using the value of the sharing fitness:

$$f'(x_1^k) = \frac{f(x_1^k)}{ra_1} = \frac{0.890}{2.856} = 0.312$$

In Figure 9.2, squares show the degradation of the original objective function for all elements of the population $\mathbf{P}^k$.

9.5.2 Computational Example in MATLAB

To illustrate the operation of the sharing function strategy, solving the following maximization problem is considered:

$$\text{Maximizar} \qquad f(x) = 2^{-2\left(\frac{x-0.1}{x-0.8}\right)^2} \cdot \text{sen}^6(5 \cdot \pi \cdot x) \tag{9.7}$$
$$\text{considerando} \qquad 0 \le x \le 1$$

This problem considers a multimodal function with five different maxima and a search space defined on the interval [0,1]. Figure 9.3 shows a representation of the objective function $f(x)$.

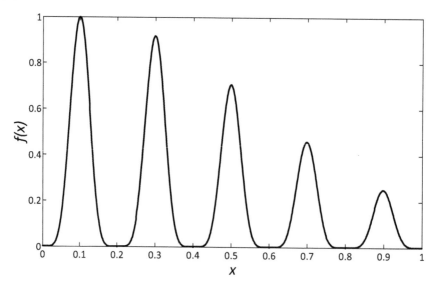

FIGURE 9.3   Graphical representation of the multimodal function $f(x)$ formulated in Eq. 9.7.

The algorithm used for multimodal optimization is a genetic algorithm (Chapter 2) with the most simple operation characteristics. For the convenience of the reader, the employed genetic algorithm is exposed briefly.

The genetic algorithm performs the following procedure:

1. Initialize the configuration parameters such as crossover probability p_c, mutation probability p_m, population size N, and maximal number of generations *niter*.

2. Generate a random population of N individuals

3. Produce a population of parents $\mathbf{M}^k$. This population is produced by selecting n individuals of $\mathbf{P}^k$ through the probabilistic selection method (Section 1.5.2).

4. Select from $\mathbf{M}^k$ two individuals m_1^k and m_2^k randomly

5. Perform crossover with a probability p_c to generate two new individuals c_1^k and c_2^k.

6. Apply mutation to each individual c_1^k and c_2^k with probability p_m. If the operation has been verified, two new elements n_1^k and n_2^k have been produced.

7. If neither crossover nor mutation operations are not applied, the original individuals m_1^k and m_2^k are included in the new population. If the crossover operation is applied, but not mutation, the individuals c_1^k and c_2^k are added to the new population. If only mutation has been performed, the elements n_1^k and n_2^k are considered in the new population.

8. The steps 4–7 are repeated until n individuals have been included in the new population $\mathbf{P}^{k+1}$.

9. Once the new population $\mathbf{P}^{k+1}$ is produced, the complete process is repeated until a number of iterations *niter* has been reached.

The procedure described above represents the normal process of optimization where the idea is to detect a single maximum contained in the objective function. However, in multimodal optimization, the goal is to find as many local maxima as possible. With the objective of illustrating the contrast between these two different processes, both programs are exposed in MATLAB®. One program presents the optimization considering a single optimum while the other includes multimodal capacities (through sharing function).

9.5.3 Genetic Algorithm without Multimodal Capacities

This section implements the genetic algorithm without multimodal capabilities. The main structure of the genetic algorithm is shown in Program 9.1. The algorithm includes five different functions: initialization of the random population (Program 9.2), conversion from binary to decimal (Program 9.3), probabilistic selection (Program 9.4), crossover operation (Program 9.5), and mutation operation (Program 9.6).

Program 9.1 Main Structure of the Genetic Algorithm to Optimize the Problem Formulated in Eq. 9.7

```
%%%%%%%%%%%%%%%%%%%%%%%%%%%%%%%%%%%%%%%%%%%%%%%%%%%%%%%%%%%%%%%
% Genetic algorithm without multimodal capacities
% Erik Cuevas, Alma Rodríguez
%%%%%%%%%%%%%%%%%%%%%%%%%%%%%%%%%%%%%%%%%%%%%%%%%%%%%%%%%%%%%%%
% Clear memory
clear all
global solnew sol pop popnew fitness fitold f range;
% Definition of the objective function
funstr='(2^(-2*(((x-0.1)/0.8)^2)))*(sin(5*pi*x)^6)';
% Definition of the search space
range=[0 1];
f=vectorize(inline(funstr));
% Parameter initialization
popsize=100;      % Population size N
MaxGen=30;        % Maximal number of iterations niter
nsite=3;          % Number of mutations
pc=0.95;          % Crossover probability
pm=0.01;          % Mutation Probability
nsbit=16;         % Binary length
% Initial population
popnew=init_genA(popsize,nsbit); % Program 9.2
fitness=zeros(1,popsize); % Define memory
%Conversion of binary chains into decimal numbers
for i=1:popsize
      solnew(i)=bintodecA(popnew(i,:)); % Program 9.3
      fitness(i)=f(solnew(i));
end
%The optimization process is initialized
for i=1:MaxGen
      fitold=fitness; pop=popnew; sol=solnew;
      % A set of M elements is chosen through probabilistic
      selection
      for z=1:popsize
            % Probabilistic selection
            e=selectionA(fitold); % Program 9.4
            MP(z,:)=pop(e,:);
      end
      % A new generation P(k+1) is produced
      for z1=1:2:popsize
            % The individuals m1 and m2 are obtained
            p1=floor(popsize*rand)+1;
            p2=floor(popsize*rand)+1;
            % Crossover operation
            if pc>rand
                  % The individuals c1 and c2 are obtained
```

```
            [NP(z1,:),NP(z1+1,:)]=crossoverA(MP(p1,:),M
            P(p2,:));
    else
            % If m1 and m2 are not considered
            NP(z1,:)=MP(p1,:);
            NP(z1+1,:)=MP(p2,:);
    end
    % Mutation operation
    if pm>rand
            % If mutation is applied, then n1 y n2 are
            generated
            mu1=NP(z1,:);
            mu2=NP(z1+1,:);
            NP(z1,:)=mutate(mu1,nsite);
            NP(z1+1,:)=mutate(mu2,nsite);
    end
end
% Conversion of binary chains into decimal numbers and
evaluation
for i=1:popsize
        solnew(i)=bintodecA(NP(i,:));
        fitness(i)=f(solnew(i));
end
popnew=NP;
end
% The set of N individuals is drawn
x=range(1):0.001:range(2);
plot(x,f(x));
hold on
plot(solnew,fitness,'or');
```

Program 9.2 Function That Initializes the Population

```
%%%%%%%%%%%%%%%%%%%%%%%%%%%%%%%%%%%%%%%%%%%%%%%%%%%%%%%%%%%%%%
% Function that initializes the population
% Erik Cuevas, Alma Rodríguez
%%%%%%%%%%%%%%%%%%%%%%%%%%%%%%%%%%%%%%%%%%%%%%%%%%%%%%%%%%%%%%
function pop=init_genA(np,nsbit)
        % np individuals of nsbits number of bits is generated
        pop=rand(np,nsbit)>0.5;
end
```

Program 9.3 Function That Converts from Binary into Decimal

```
%%%%%%%%%%%%%%%%%%%%%%%%%%%%%%%%%%%%%%%%%%%%%%%%%%%%%%%%%%%%%%
% Function that converts from binary into decimal
% Erik Cuevas, Alma Rodríguez
%%%%%%%%%%%%%%%%%%%%%%%%%%%%%%%%%%%%%%%%%%%%%%%%%%%%%%%%%%%%%%
```

```
function [dec]=bintodecA(bin)
      global range;
      % It is obtained the size of the binary chain
      nn=length(bin);
      num=bin; % get the binary
      % The accumulator is initialized
      dec=0;
      % According to the search space, it is defined the binary size
      dp=floor(log2(max(abs(range))));
      %I t is converted from binary into decimal
      for i=1:nn
            dec=dec+num(i)*2^(dp-i);
      end
end
```

Program 9.4 Function of Probabilistic Selection

```
%%%%%%%%%%%%%%%%%%%%%%%%%%%%%%%%%%%%%%%%%%%%%%%%%%%%%%%%%%%%%%%%%%%
% Function of probabilistic selection
% Erik Cuevas, Alma Rodríguez
%%%%%%%%%%%%%%%%%%%%%%%%%%%%%%%%%%%%%%%%%%%%%%%%%%%%%%%%%%%%%%%%%%%
function [iE] = selectionA(fP)
      % The population size is obtained
      Ps=length(fP);
      % The accumulator is initialized
      accum=0;
      % The probability of selection of each individual P(k) is
      obtained
      % and also the accumulative A(k)
      for k=1:Ps
            P(k)=fP(k)/(sum(fP));
            accum=accum+P(k);
            A(k)=accum;
      end
      R=rand;
      for u=1:Ps
            if (A(u)>=R)
                  break
            end
      end
      % The element u is selected
      iE=u;
end
```

Program 9.5 Function of Crossover

```
%%%%%%%%%%%%%%%%%%%%%%%%%%%%%%%%%%%%%%%%%%%%%%%%%%%%%%%%%%%%%%%%%%%
% Function of crossover
% Erik Cuevas, Alma Rodríguez
%%%%%%%%%%%%%%%%%%%%%%%%%%%%%%%%%%%%%%%%%%%%%%%%%%%%%%%%%%%%%%%%%%%
```

```
function [c,d]=crossoverA(a,b)
      nn=length(a);
      % Two new individuals c1 y c2 are generated from crossover
      cpoint=floor(nn*rand)+1;
      c=[a(1:cpoint) b(cpoint+1:end)];
      d=[b(1:cpoint) a(cpoint+1:end)];
end
```

Program 9.6 Function of Mutation

```
%%%%%%%%%%%%%%%%%%%%%%%%%%%%%%%%%%%%%%%%%%%%%%%%%%%%%%%%%%%%%%
% Function of mutation
% Erik Cuevas, Alma Rodríguez
%%%%%%%%%%%%%%%%%%%%%%%%%%%%%%%%%%%%%%%%%%%%%%%%%%%%%%%%%%%%%%
function anew=mutate(a,nsite)
      nn=length(a); anew=a;
      % A new individual is through mutation
      for i=1:nsite
             j=floor(rand*nn)+1;
             anew(j)=mod(a(j)+1,2);
      end
end
```

According to Program 9.1, the genetic algorithm is executed with the following configuration $p_c = 0.95$, $p_m = 0.05$, $N = 100$, and *niter* = 30. Each candidate solution with a length of 16 bits is encoded in the algorithm. Once Program 9.1 is executed, the solutions would be distributed as shown in Figure 9.4.

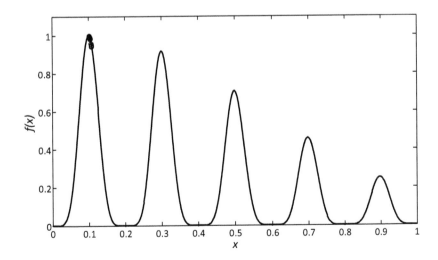

FIGURE 9.4 Solution distribution as a result of the execution of the genetic algorithm without multimodal capabilities. The solutions tend to concentrate around the global maximum as a result of privileging the quality of solutions as a criterion for individual selection.

From Figure 9.4, it is clear that solutions are concentrated around the global maximum. This behavior occurs because the selection criteria to produce a new population $\mathbf{M}^k$ is the quality of each individual. Under these conditions, individuals with a significant fitness value will have more chances to be included, while low-quality elements have a very low probability to be used. Therefore, such solutions will not be considered for the generation of new candidate solutions through the use of crossover and mutation operators.

9.5.4 Genetic Algorithm with Multimodal Capacities

A specific method that considers to solve a multimodal optimization problem needs to register as many optimal as possible. So, instead of focusing on the global optimal, it should implement a mechanism that allows to distribute existing solutions in all local optimal positions. Such a mechanism is the technique of sharing function. Therefore, in order to provide multimodal capabilities, a metaheuristic scheme must incorporate in its structure the sharing function technique.

With the addition of the sharing function method, the distribution of individuals is promoted, while their concentration is penalized. Such actions are implemented by the degradation of the quality of the elements. Under this scenario, individuals which are located in areas scarcely populated will maintain their fitness (quality) values. On the other hand, individuals which are located in crowded regions will decrease their quality.

To incorporate the technique of sharing function in a genetic algorithm, such as the one described in Program 9.1, it is necessary to calculate the sharing function and degrade the fitness values of the involved elements. The idea is to use the degraded fitness values for the selection of individuals that integrate the population of parents. Therefore, highly concentrated individuals will have a very low probability to be selected while well-distributed individuals maintain a high probability of being considered as parents.

Under these conditions, individuals generated through the application of crossover and mutation will tend to be better distributed in the search space. Consequently, this fact increases the ability of the algorithm to register more optimal positions.

Program 9.7 shows the modified genetic algorithm. The program incorporates squares that highlight the changes made with respect to the original version presented in Program 9.1. From this program, it can be seen that the changes include the addition of two functions: sharing function computation (Program 9.8) and degradation of the original fitness values (Program 9.9). Another important modification considers the use of degraded fitness instead of the original for the individual selection. In the calculation of the sharing function, the following configuration $\alpha = 1$ and $\sigma_s = 0.1$ is assumed.

Program 9.7 Main Structure of the Genetic Algorithm with Multimodal Capacities to Optimize the Problem Formulated in Eq. 9.7. The Squares in the Code Express the Differences with Respect to the Genetic Algorithm without Multimodal Capabilities

```
%%%%%%%%%%%%%%%%%%%%%%%%%%%%%%%%%%%%%%%%%%%%%%%%%%%%%%%%%%%%%%%%%%%
% Genetic algorithm without multimodal capacities
% Erik Cuevas, Alma Rodríguez
%%%%%%%%%%%%%%%%%%%%%%%%%%%%%%%%%%%%%%%%%%%%%%%%%%%%%%%%%%%%%%%%%%%
```

```
% Clear memory
clear all
global solnew sol pop popnew fitness fitold f range;
% Objective function definition
funstr='(2^(-2*(((x-0.1)/0.8)^2)))*(sin(5*pi*x)^6)';
% Search space definition
range=[0 1];
f=vectorize(inline(funstr));
% Parameter initialization
popsize=100;     % Population size N
MaxGen=30;       % Number of iterations niter
nsite=3;         % Mutation number
pc=0.95;         % Crossover probability
pm=0.05;         % Mutation probability
nsbit=16;        % Binary length (bits)
% Initial population
popnew=init_genA(popsize,nsbit);
fitness=zeros(1,popsize); % Define memory
% Conversion of binary chains into decimal numbers
for i=1:popsize
      solnew(i)=bintodecA(popnew(i,:));
      fitness(i)=f(solnew(i));
end
% The optimization process is initialized
for i=1:MaxGen
      fitold=fitness; pop=popnew; sol=solnew;
```

```
  % Computation of the sharing function
  ra = functionCo(sol,1,0.1);
  % Degradation of the original fitness
  Dfitness = Degradaf(fitold,ra);
```

```
      % A new set of elements are chosen by probabilistic selection
      % considering the degraded fitness instead of the originals
      for z=1:popsize
```

```
  e=selectionA(Dfitness);
```

```
          MP(z,:)=pop(e,:);
      end
      % A new parent population P(k+1) is produced
      for z1=1:2:popsize
      % Two individual m1 y m2 are selected for crossover
            p1=floor(popsize*rand)+1;
            p2=floor(popsize*rand)+1;
            % Crossover operation
            if pc>rand
```

```
                    % Elements c1 and c2 are obtained
                    [NP(z1,:),NP(z1+1,:)]=crossoverA(MP(p1,:),M
                    P(p2,:));
            else
                    %If crossover is not applied, m1 and m2 remain
                    NP(z1,:)=MP(p1,:);
                    NP(z1+1,:)=MP(p2,:);
            end
            % Mutation operation
            if pm>rand
                    % Elements n1 are n2 obtained
                    mu1=NP(z1,:);
                    mu2=NP(z1+1,:);
                    NP(z1,:)=mutate(mu1,nsite);
                    NP(z1+1,:)=mutate(mu2,nsite);
            end
    end
    % Conversion of binary chains into decimal numbers and
    evaluation
    for i=1:popsize
            solnew(i)=bintodecA(NP(i,:));
            fitness(i)=f(solnew(i));
    end
    popnew=NP;
end
% The set of N individuals are drawn
x=range(1):0.001:range(2);
plot(x,f(x));
hold on
plot(solnew,fitness,'or');
```

Program 9.8 Function that Calculates the Sharing Function

```
%%%%%%%%%%%%%%%%%%%%%%%%%%%%%%%%%%%%%%%%%%%%%%%%%%%%%%%%%%%%%%%%
% Function for sharing function calculation
% Erik Cuevas, Alma Rodríguez
%%%%%%%%%%%%%%%%%%%%%%%%%%%%%%%%%%%%%%%%%%%%%%%%%%%%%%%%%%%%%%%%
function [ra] = functionCo(Vs,alfa,sigma)
    % Population size
    in=length(Vs);
    % Computation of sharing function for all elements
    for s=1:in
            accum=0;
            for d=1:in
                    % Distance computation
                    dis=abs(Vs(s)-Vs(d));
                    % If an element is within the distance sigma
                    % It is calculated Co
```

```
                    if (dis<=sigma)
                         Co=1-((dis/sigma)^alfa); %Eq. 9.3
                    else
                         % If not, there is no influence
                         Co=0;
                    end
                    % The crowding value is computed
                    ra(s)=Co+accum; %Eq. 9.4
                    accum=ra(s);
             end
      end
end
```

Program 9.9 Function That Degrades the Original Fitness Values

```
%%%%%%%%%%%%%%%%%%%%%%%%%%%%%%%%%%%%%%%%%%%%%%%%%%%%%%%%%%%%%%%%%%%
% Function of fitness degradation
% Erik Cuevas, Alma Rodríguez
%%%%%%%%%%%%%%%%%%%%%%%%%%%%%%%%%%%%%%%%%%%%%%%%%%%%%%%%%%%%%%%%%%%
function [Dfitness] = Degradaf(Fo,Ar)
      % Population size
      in=length(Fo);
      % Degradation according to the crowding value
      for n=1:in
             Dfitness(n)=Fo(n)/Ar(n); %Eq. 9.5
      end
end
```

With these modifications, instead of concentrating solutions in the global maximum, the algorithm will distribute the candidate solutions in local optima. Figure 9.5 shows this behavior as a result of having executed the modified genetic algorithm.

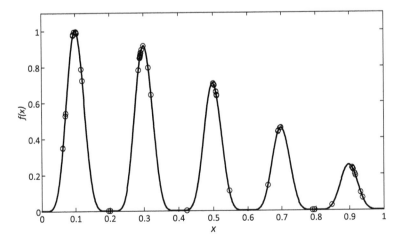

FIGURE 9.5 Result of the implementation of the genetic algorithm with multimodal capabilities. The solutions tend to be distributed in the search space as a result of the sharing function effect.

9.6 FIREFLY ALGORITHM

So far, we have discussed mechanisms which combined with the methods of metaheuristic computation allow to provide multimodal capabilities. These mechanisms are adapted to operate together with the operations defined by the metaheuristic method in question so that its candidate solutions avoid the concentration around optima. This section discusses a metaheuristic scheme known as the firefly method. This approach is designed explicitly to solve multimodal problems considering its original metaheuristic without artificially adding any other multimodal mechanism (such sharing function).

Who has not been witness to the impressive phenomenon of the twinkling lights of fireflies in the summer evenings? It is said that there are around 2,000 different species of fireflies which produce a particular pattern of blinking flashes. The flash produced by these insects is generated by a process of bioluminescence that has two basic functions: attract other fireflies for mating or attract other insects as potential prey. This mechanism from some level of abstraction can be conceived as an optimization process. Xin-She Yang (2010) introduced the firefly algorithm. This algorithm has been designed from the inspiration of attraction models produced by fireflies when they interact in groups.

The firefly method considers as a simplified behavior the following rules:

1. All the firefly insects maintain the same behavior regardless of their gender (male or female).

2. On the relationship between two fireflies, the firefly that emits a lower intensity of light will be attracted by the firefly with greater intensity. The attraction is proportional to the difference of the light emitted.

In the firefly algorithm, there are two important elements: the light intensity difference and the attraction model. For simplicity, it is assumed that the attraction of a firefly is determined by the intensity of the light emitted. From the point of view of metaheuristic computation, such intensity is associated with the quality (fitness) of the candidate solution who symbolizes a firefly. In the case of maximization, the light intensity I emitted by a firefly in a particular position x can be modeled as $I(x) \approx f(x)$. The intensity of light is appreciated in relationship for other fireflies which observe in other positions. Therefore, the intensity will vary with regard to the distance r_{ij} which represents the distance of the Firefly i regarding to Firefly j. This process can be modeled by the following formulation:

$$I(r) = I_0 \cdot e^{-\gamma r^2}, \tag{9.8}$$

where I_0 represents the original light intensity and γ is a factor that adjusts the magnitude under which the light loses intensity as the distance becomes larger. Since the attraction β between the fireflies is proportional to the light intensity perceived by other fireflies, Eq. 9.8 can be redefined by the following model:

$$\beta = \beta_0 \cdot e^{-\gamma r_{ij}^2}, \tag{9.9}$$

where β_0 represents the attraction at $r = 0$. r_{ij} is the distance between two fireflies i and j at positions $\mathbf{x}_i$ and $\mathbf{x}_j$, respectively. Under such conditions, r_{ij} is calculated by the Euclidean distance:

$$r_{ij} = \left\| \mathbf{x}_i - \mathbf{x}_j \right\| = \sqrt{\sum_{k=1}^{d} \left(x_k^i - x_k^j \right)^2}, \tag{9.10}$$

where x_k^i is the decision variable k of Firefly i. In the context of metaheuristic methods, the light intensity refers to the quality of an individual in terms of the objective function, while an individual represents a firefly.

Therefore, the attraction of Firefly $\mathbf{x}_i$ (candidate solution) to another Firefly $\mathbf{x}_j$ will take place when the quality of $\mathbf{x}_j$ is greater than $\mathbf{x}_i$ in terms of the function objective $\left(f(\mathbf{x}_j) \triangleright f(\mathbf{x}_i) \right)$. The operator $\triangleright$ will be used in this section to indicate that $\mathbf{x}_j$ has a superior quality than $\mathbf{x}_i$. The attraction movement is determined by the following model:

$$\mathbf{x}_i = \mathbf{x}_i + \beta_0 \cdot e^{-\gamma r_{ij}^2} \left(\mathbf{x}_j - \mathbf{x}_i \right) + \alpha R, \tag{9.11}$$

where the second term $\beta_0 \cdot e^{-\gamma r_{ij}^2} \left(\mathbf{x}_j - \mathbf{x}_i \right)$ represents the attraction movement of attraction while the third element αR corresponds to a random perturbation produced by a constant factor α and a uniformly distributed random number $\mathbf{U}\,[0,1]$. The simplest way to implement a random movement in MATLAB is to use the following sentence `alfa*(rand-(1/2))`. The model of attraction (Eq. 9.11) is applied on Firefly $\mathbf{x}_i$ if it has a quality lower than $\mathbf{x}_j$. If this condition is not fulfilled the position $\mathbf{x}_i$ remains unchanged. Figure 9.6 illustrates of the process of attraction.

The value of γ has a great importance in the performance of the algorithm. Since this factor regulates the attraction process, its magnitude determines the speed of convergence and the ability of the algorithm to identify as many local optima as possible. If its value is small, the attraction between individuals will be stronger, and if its value is large, the attraction will be lower.

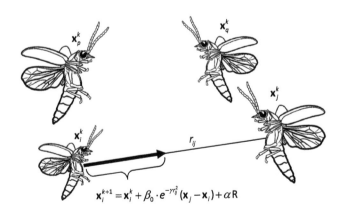

FIGURE 9.6   Attraction process in the firefly algorithm.

From a metaheuristic perspective, the firefly algorithm maintains a population $\mathbf{P}^k\left(\mathbf{x}_1^k, \mathbf{x}_2^k, \ldots, \mathbf{x}_N^k\right)$ of N candidate solutions which evolve (change) during a maximum number of iterations (*niter*), from an initial state to final one. In the initial state, the algorithm configures a set of candidate solution with a random value within the limits of the search space $\mathbf{X}$. In each generation, the quality of each firefly is compared with the rest. If a Firefly $\mathbf{x}_i^k$ has a quality less than $\mathbf{x}_j^k\left(f\left(\mathbf{x}_j^k\right) \triangleright f\left(\mathbf{x}_i^k\right)\right)$, $\mathbf{x}_i^k$ will exert an attraction movement of attraction on $\mathbf{x}_j^k$. Otherwise, $\mathbf{x}_i^k$ will remain without changes. Once the fireflies have changed their position as a result of the attraction process, the new positions will represent the new population $\mathbf{P}^{k+1}$. This process will be repeated until the number of iterations *niter* has been reached. The implementation steps of the firefly algorithm are exposed in Algorithm 9.1 in the form of a pseudocode. Under this scheme, the attraction movement from $\mathbf{x}_i^k$ to $\mathbf{x}_i^k$ could provoke that the new value $\mathbf{x}_i^{k+1}$ would be located outside the search space $\mathbf{X}$. In those locations, the objective function is not defined. To avoid this problem, the algorithm must protect the adjustment of candidate solutions so that it remains inside the search space $\mathbf{X}$.

Algorithm 9.1 Firefly Method

1. Configure β, γ y N.
2. Initialize $\mathbf{P}^k\left(\mathbf{x}_1^k, \mathbf{x}_2^k, \ldots, \mathbf{x}_N^k\right)$ with random values within the search space
3. **while** ($k < Niter$) {
4. **for** $i = 1$ **to** N{
5. **for** $j = 1$ **to** N{
6. **if** $\left(f\left(\mathbf{x}_j^k\right) \triangleright f\left(\mathbf{x}_i^k\right)\right)$
7. $\left\{r_{ij} = \left\|\mathbf{x}_i - \mathbf{x}_j\right\|\right.$
8. $\mathbf{x}_i^{k+1} = \mathbf{x}_i^k + \beta_0 \cdot e^{-\gamma r_{ij}^2}\left(\mathbf{x}_j - \mathbf{x}_i\right) + \alpha \mathbf{R}\Big\}$
9. **else**
10. $\left\{\mathbf{x}_i^{k+1} = \mathbf{x}_i^k\right\}\}\}$
11. $k \leftarrow k + 1$}

9.6.1 Computational Example in MATLAB

To illustrate the operation of the firefly algorithm and its practical implementation in MATLAB, solving the following maximization problem is considered:

$$\text{Maximize} \quad f(x_1, x_2) = \frac{\text{sen}^2(x_1 - x_2) \cdot \text{sen}^2(x_1 + x_2)}{\sqrt{x_1^2 + x_2^2}}$$

$$0 \leq x_1 \leq 10 \tag{9.12}$$

$$\text{Subject to:}$$

$$0 \leq x_2 \leq 10$$

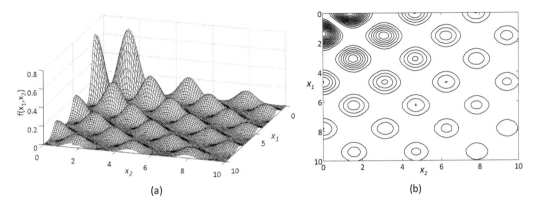

(a) (b)

FIGURE 9.7 Graphical representation of (a) $f(x_1,x_2)=\dfrac{\operatorname{sen}^2(x_1-x_2)\cdot\operatorname{sen}^2(x_1+x_2)}{\sqrt{x_1^2+x_2^2}}$ and (b) its contours.

This formulation considers a function $f(x_1,x_2)$ of two dimensions with a search space defined on the interval [0,10] for each decision variable x_1 and x_2. Figure 9.7 shows a representation of the objective function $f(x_1,x_2)$.

In order to assist the reader in the implementation of Algorithm 9.1, Program 9.10 shows its MATLAB code. The program includes three different functions in its structure: the random initialization of the population (Program 9.11), the attraction process (Program 9.12), and the limitation of the search space (Program 9.13).

Program 9.10 Main Structure of the Firefly Algorithm

```
%%%%%%%%%%%%%%%%%%%%%%%%%%%%%%%%%%%%%%%%%%%%%%%%%%%%%%%%%%%%%%%
% Firefly algorithm
% Erik Cuevas, Alma Rodríguez
%%%%%%%%%%%%%%%%%%%%%%%%%%%%%%%%%%%%%%%%%%%%%%%%%%%%%%%%%%%%%%%
% Clear memory
clear all
% Number of iterations
n=250; MaxGeneration=100;
rand('state' ,0);
% Objective Function definition
funstr='(((sin(x-y))^2)*((sin(x+y))^2))/(sqrt(x^2+y^2))';
f=vectorize(inline(funstr));
% Search space Definition
range=[0 10 0 10];
% Parameter configuration
alpha=0.01;
gamma=4.0;
% Draw the objective Function
Ndiv=100;
```

```matlab
dx=(range(2)-range(1))/Ndiv; dy=(range(4)-range(3))/Ndiv;
[x,y]=meshgrid(range(1):dx:range(2),range(3):dy:range(4));
z=f(x,y);
figure(1);  surfc(x,y,z); figure(2);
% Initialize population
[xn,yn,Lightn]=init_ffa(n,range);
% Begin the Optimization process
for i=1:MaxGeneration
        % Draw the contour of the objective function
        contour(x,y,z,15); hold on;
        % Solution evaluation
        zn=f(xn,yn);
        % Light calculation
        Lightn=zn;
        xo=xn; yo=yn;  Lighto=Lightn;
        % Draw the candidate solution
        plot(xn,yn,'.','markersize',10,'markerfacecolor','g');
        % Attraction computation Eq. 9.11
        [xn,yn]=ffa_move(xn,yn,Lightn,xo,yo,Lighto,alpha,gamma,range);
        drawnow;
        hold off;
end
```

Program 9.11 Function That Initializes the Population

```matlab
%%%%%%%%%%%%%%%%%%%%%%%%%%%%%%%%%%%%%%%%%%%%%%%%%%%%%%%%%%%%%%%%%%%
% Function that initializes the population
% Erik Cuevas, Alma Rodríguez
%%%%%%%%%%%%%%%%%%%%%%%%%%%%%%%%%%%%%%%%%%%%%%%%%%%%%%%%%%%%%%%%%%%
function [xn,yn,Lightn]=init_ffa(n,range)
        % Random initialization of the individuals
        xrange=range(2)-range(1);
        yrange=range(4)-range(3);
        xn=rand(1,n)*xrange+range(1);
        yn=rand(1,n)*yrange+range(3);
        Lightn=zeros(size(yn));
end
```

Program 9.12 Function for the Attraction Process

```matlab
%%%%%%%%%%%%%%%%%%%%%%%%%%%%%%%%%%%%%%%%%%%%%%%%%%%%%%%%%%%%%%%%%%%
% Function for the attraction process
% Erik Cuevas, Alma Rodríguez
%%%%%%%%%%%%%%%%%%%%%%%%%%%%%%%%%%%%%%%%%%%%%%%%%%%%%%%%%%%%%%%%%%%
function [xn,yn]=ffa_move(xn,yn,Lightn,xo,yo,Lighto,alpha,gamma,
range)
        % Population size
        ni=size(yn,2);
        for i=1:ni
```

```
        for j=1:ni
                % Distance computation between i j
                r=sqrt((xn(i)-xo(j))^2+(yn(i)-yo(j))^2);
                if Lightn(i)<Lighto(j) % Quality test
                        beta0=1;
                        beta=beta0*exp(-gamma*r.^2);
                        xn(i)=xn(i).*(1-beta)+xo(j).*beta+alpha.*
                        (rand-0.5);
                        yn(i)=yn(i).*(1-beta)+yo(j).*beta+alpha.*
                        (rand-0.5);
                end
        end % End for j
    end % End for i
    % If the solution is outside the search space
    [xn,yn]=findrange(xn,yn,range);
end
```

Program 9.13 Function to Limit the Position Within the Search Space

```
%%%%%%%%%%%%%%%%%%%%%%%%%%%%%%%%%%%%%%%%%%%%%%%%%%%%%%%%%%%%%%%%%%%
% Function to limit the position within the search space
% Erik Cuevas, Alma Rodríguez
%%%%%%%%%%%%%%%%%%%%%%%%%%%%%%%%%%%%%%%%%%%%%%%%%%%%%%%%%%%%%%%%%%%
function [xn,yn]=findrange(xn,yn,range)
        % Limit the position within the search space
        for i=1:length(yn)
                if xn(i)<=range(1)
                        xn(i)=range(1);
                end
                if xn(i)>=range(2)
                        xn(i)=range(2);
                end
                if yn(i)<=range(3)
                        yn(i)=range(3);
                end
                if yn(i)>=range(4)
                        yn(i)=range(4);
                end
        end
end
```

According to Program 9.7, the firefly algorithm is configured such that $\beta_0 = 1$, $\alpha = 0.01$, $N = 100$, $\gamma = 4$, and $niter = 100$. In the operation of Program 9.7, first, the objective function is plotted in order to visualize its characteristics. Then, iteratively, the set of solutions generated from its initial population $\mathbf{P}^1$ is shown until most of the local optima have been detected. Figure 9.8 shows the solution distribution during the evolution process in different generations: (a) $k = 1$, (b) $k = 10$, (c) $k = 50$, and (d) $k = 100$.

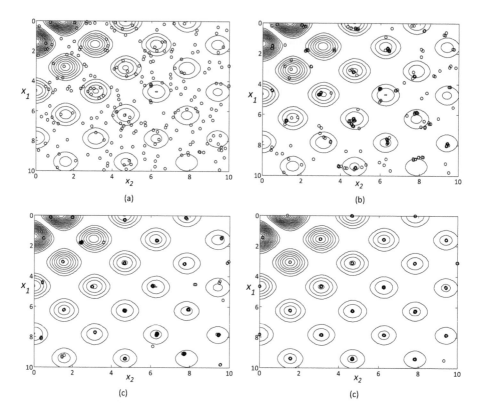

FIGURE 9.8   Evolution process of the firefly algorithm for formulation Eq. 9.12. (a) $k = 1$, (b) $k = 10$, (c) $k = 50$, and (d) $k = 100$.

EXERCISES

9.1   A populzation **P** of five individuals $(x_A, x_B, x_C, x_D, x_E)$ is assumed, whose position x and quality $f(x)$ are defined in Table 9.2. Considering the parameters as $\sigma_s = 0.4$ and $\alpha = 1$,

   a.   Determine the fitness degradation $f'(x_C)$ over the individual x_C.

   b.   Compute also the fitness degradation $f'(x_E)$ over the element x_E.

Figure 9.9 shows the solution distribution.

TABLE 9.2

Solution	Position	$f(x)$
x_A	0.63	1.51
x_B	0.68	1.69
x_C	0.77	1.75
x_D	0.80	1.72
x_E	1.53	1.48

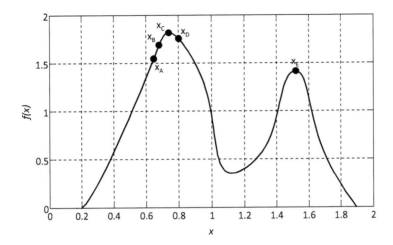

FIGURE 9.9   Solution distribution considering data from Table 9.2.

9.2   From the data of Exercise 1.1, determine which of the two individuals x_C or x_E would have more probabilities to be selected according to their degraded qualities $f'(x_C)$ and $f'(x_E)$.

9.3   Recalculate the fitness degradations $f'(x_C)$ and $f'(x_E)$ from Exercise 1.1 considering that instead of the use of the sharing function model $Co(d_{ij})$ defined in Eq. 9.3, the model $Co(d_{ij}) = e^{(-10 \cdot d_{ij})}$ is assumed.

9.4   Modify Program 9.7 so that it can solve the following multimodal optimization problem:

$$\text{Maximize} \quad f_1(x) = e^{(-x \cdot 0.1)} \cdot \text{sen}(2 \cdot x) + 1$$
$$\text{Subject to:} \quad 0 \le x \le 10$$

Then, analyze the performance when the parameter σ_s assumes the following values: 0.1, 1, 2, 5, and 10.

9.5   Rewrite Program 9.7 so that it can solve the following multimodal optimization task:

$$\text{Maximize} \quad f_2(x) = \left(\frac{x}{10}\right) \cdot \text{sen}(2 \cdot x)$$
$$\text{Subject to:} \quad 0 \le x \le 10$$

a.   Considering the parameter σ_s, analyze the performance of the algorithm assuming the following values: 0.1, 0.5, 1, 2, and 5.

b.   Compare the obtained results with those generated from Exercise 9.4.

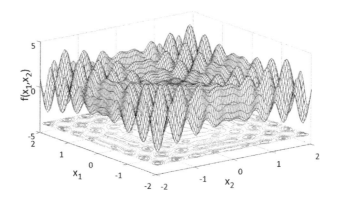

FIGURE 9.10 Multimodal function used in Exercise 9.6.

9.6 Modify Program 9.10 so that it can resolve the following multimodal optimization problem:

$$\text{Minimize} \quad f_3(x_1,x_2)=x_1\cdot\text{sen}(4\cdot\pi\cdot x_1)-x_2\cdot\text{sen}(4\cdot\pi\cdot x_2+\pi)+1$$

$$-2\leq x_1\leq 2$$

Subject to:

$$-2\leq x_2\leq 2$$

Figure 9.10 shows the objective function considered in this exercise.

a. Find the parameter values of α and γ that allow to detect more local optima.

b. Analyze the performance of the firefly method when the parameter α assumes the following values: 0.01, 0.1, and 0.3.

9.7 Rewrite Program 9.10 so that it can resolve the following multimodal optimization problem:

$$\text{Minimize} \quad f_4(x_1,x_2)=\frac{1}{1+|x_1+j\cdot x_2+1|}$$

$$-2\leq x_1\leq 2$$

Subject to:

$$-2\leq x_2\leq 2$$

a. Configure the parameters α and γ so that they allow to detect more local optima.

b. Analyze the performance of the firefly scheme when the parameter γ assumes the following values: 0.5, 2, and 4.

c. Compare the obtained results with those produced in Exercise 9.6.

Figure 9.11 shows a graphical representation of the objective function.

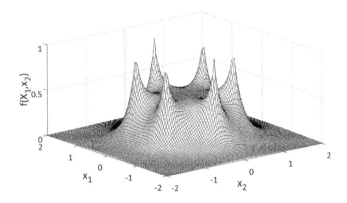

FIGURE 9.11   Multimodal function used in Exercise 9.7.

REFERENCES

Cavicchio, D. J. (1970). *Adaptive search using simulated evolution* (PhD thesis). University of Michigan, Ann Arbor.

Deb, K. (2001). *Multi-objective optimization using evolutionary algorithms*. New York, NY: John Wiley & Sons, Inc.

DeJong, K. A. (1975). *An analysis of the behavior of a class of genetic adaptive systems* (PhD thesis). University of Michigan, Ann Arbor.

Goldberg, D. E., & Deb, K. A comparison of selection schemes used in genetic algorithms. In *Foundations of genetic algorithms (FOGA-1)* (pp. 69–93).

Goldberg, D. E., & Richardson, J. (1987). Genetic algorithms with sharing for multimodal function optimization. In *Proceedings of the First International Conference on Genetic Algorithms and their Applications* (pp. 41–49). Massachusetts: Cambridge. ISBN: 0805801588.

Yang, X.-S. (2010). *Engineering optimization*. New York, NY: John Wiley & Sons, Inc.

Index